4th Workshop on Computational Approaches to Subjectivity, Sentiment and Social Media Analysis

(WASSA 2013)

Atlanta, Georgia, USA
14 June 2013

ISBN: 978-1-62993-009-1

Printed from e-media with permission by:

Curran Associates, Inc.
57 Morehouse Lane
Red Hook, NY 12571

Some format issues inherent in the e-media version may also appear in this print version.

Printed by Curran Associates, Inc. (2013)

For permission requests, please contact the Association for Computational Linguistics
at the address below.

Association for Computational Linguistics
209 N. Eighth Street
Stroudsburg, Pennsylvania 18360

Phone: 1-570-476-8006
Fax: 1-570-476-0860

acl@aclweb.org

Additional copies of this publication are available from:

Curran Associates, Inc.
57 Morehouse Lane
Red Hook, NY 12571 USA
Phone: 845-758-0400
Fax: 845-758-2634
Email: curran@proceedings.com
Web: www.proceedings.com

WASSA 2013

4th Workshop on Computational Approaches to Subjectivity, Sentiment and Social Media Analysis

Proceedings of the Workshop

14 June 2013
Atlanta, Georgia, U.S.A.

Introduction

Research in automatic Subjectivity and Sentiment Analysis, as subtasks in Affective Computing within the Artificial Intelligence field of Natural Language Processing (NLP), has flourished in the past years. The growth in interest in these tasks was motivated by the birth and rapid expansion of the Social Web that made it possible for people all over the world to share, comment or consult content on any given topic. In this context, opinions, sentiments and emotions expressed in Social Media texts have been shown to have a high influence on the social and economic behaviour worldwide.

The aim of the 4th Workshop on Computational Approaches to Subjectivity, Sentiment and Social Media Analysis (WASSA 2013) was to continue the line of the previous three editions, bringing together researchers in Computational Linguistics working on Subjectivity and Sentiment Analysis and researchers working on interdisciplinary aspects of affect computation from text. Additionally, this year, we extended the focus to Social Media phenomena and the impact of affect-related phenomena in this context. WASSA 2013 was organized in conjunction to the 2013 Conference of the North American Chapter of the Association for Computational Linguistics: Human Language Technologies, on June 14, 2013, in Atlanta, Georgia, United States of America.

At this fourth edition of the workshop, we received a total of 29 submissions, from a wide range of countries, of which 8 were accepted as long and another 8 as short papers. Each paper has been thoroughly reviewed by 2 members of the Program Committee. The accepted papers were all highly assessed by the reviewers, the best paper receiving an average punctuation (computed as an average of all criteria used to assess the papers) of 4.75 out of 5.

The main topics of the accepted papers are related to affect in Social Media - the creation and evaluation of resources for subjectivity, sentiment and emotion in social media, cross-lingual and multilingual resource creation and use, the detection of sarcasm and spam and the detection of illegal activities in digital social settings.

The invited talks reflected the multimodal and interdisciplinary nature of the research in affect-related phenomena, from topics related to multimodal methods for emotion detection, theories of emotion and applications of emotion detection in Social Media.

This year's edition has shown again that the topics addressed by WASSA are of high interest to the research community and that the contributions presented in this forum bring an important development both to the theoretical, as well as to the application-oriented scenarios.

We would like to thank the NAACL-HLT 2013 Organizers for the help and support at the different stages of the workshop organization process. We are also especially grateful to the Program Committee members and the external reviewers for the time and effort spent assessing the papers. We would like to extend our thanks to our invited speakers – Prof. Rosalind Picard, Prof. Jonathan Gratch and Dr. Theresa Wilson, for accepting to deliver the keynote talks.

Secondly, we would like to express our gratitude for the official endorsement we received from SIGNLL (the ACL Special Interest Group on Natural Language Learning) and SIGANN, the ACL Special Interest Group for Annotation.

Further on, we would like to thank the Editors of the "Information Processing and Management", published by Elsevier, for accepting to organize a Special Issue of this journal containing the extended versions of the best full papers accepted at WASSA 2013.

We would like to express our gratitude to Yaniv Steiner, who created the WASSA logo and to the entire OPTIMA action team at the European Commission Joint Research Centre, for the technical support they provided.

Last, but not least, we are grateful for the financial support given by the Academic Institute for Research in Computer Science of the University of Alicante (Instituto Universitario para la Investigación en Informática, Universidad de Alicante).

Alexandra Balahur, Erik van der Goot and Andrés Montoyo
WASSA 2013 Chairs

Organizers:

Alexandra Balahur
European Commission Joint Research Centre
Institute for the Protection and Security of the Citizen

Erik van der Goot
European Commission Joint Research Centre
Institute for the Protection and Security of the Citizen

Andrés Montoyo
University of Alicante
Department of Software and Computing Systems

Program Committee:

Nicoletta Calzolari, CNR Pisa (Italy)
Erik Cambria, University of Stirling (U.K.)
José Carlos Cortizo, European University Madrid (Spain)
Fermin Cruz Mata, University of Seville (Spain)
Michael Gamon, Microsoft (U.S.A.)
Jesús M. Hermida, European Commission Joint Research Centre (Italy)
Veronique Hoste, University of Ghent (Belgium)
Zornitsa Kozareva, Information Sciences Institute California (U.S.A.)
Isa Maks, University of Amsterdam (The Netherlands)
Diana Maynard, University of Sheffield (U.K.)
Saif Mohammad, National Research Council (Canada)
Karo Moilanen, University of Oxford (U.K.)
Günter Neumann, DFKI (Germany)
Constantin Orasan, University of Wolverhampton (U.K.)
Viktor Pekar, University of Wolverhampton (U.K.)
Veronica Perez Rosas, University of North Texas (U.S.A.)
Paolo Rosso, Technical University of Valencia (Spain)
Josef Steinberger, Charles University Prague (The Czech Republic)
Hristo Tanev, European Commission Joint Research Centre (Italy)
Maite Taboada, Simon Fraser University (Canada)
Mike Thelwall, University of Wolverhampton (U.K.)
Dan Tufis, RACAI (Romania)
Alfonso Ureña, University of Jaén (Spain)

Marilyn Walker, University of California Santa Cruz (U.S.A.)
Michael Wiegand, Saarland University (Germany)
Theresa Wilson, John Hopkins University (U.S.A.)
Taras Zagibalov, Brantwatch (U.K.)

Invited Speakers:

Prof. Dr. Jonathan Gratch, University of South California (U.S.A.)
Prof. Dr. Rosalind Picard, MIT Media Laboratory (U.S.A.)
Dr. Theresa Wilson, John Hopkins University (U.S.A.)

Table of Contents

Workshop Program

Friday, June 14, 2013

8:30–8:40 Opening Remarks

8:40–9:20 Invited talk: Prof. Dr. Rosalind Picard

Recent adventures with emotion-reading technology
Rosalind Picard

Session 1:Affect Recognition in Text (I)

9:20–9:45 *Bootstrapped Learning of Emotion Hashtags #hashtags4you*
Ashequl Qadir and Ellen Riloff

9:45–10:10 *Fine-Grained Emotion Recognition in Olympic Tweets Based on Human Computation*
Valentina Sintsova, Claudiu Musat and Pearl Pu

10:10–10:30 *Spanish DAL: A Spanish Dictionary of Affect in Language*
Matías Dell' Amerlina Ríos and Agustin Gravano

10:30–11:00 Break

11:00–11:40 Invited talk: Prof. Dr. Jonathan Gratch

Session 2: Affect Recognition in Text (II)

11:40–12:05 *The perfect solution for detecting sarcasm in tweets #not*
Christine Liebrecht, Florian Kunneman and Antal Van den Bosch

12:05–12:30 *Using PU-Learning to Detect Deceptive Opinion Spam*
Donato Hernández, Rafael Guzmán, Manuel Móntes y Gomez and Paolo Rosso

12:30–12:55 *Sexual predator detection in chats with chained classifiers*
Hugo Jair Escalante, Esaú Villatoro-Tello, Antonio Juárez, Manuel Montes-y-Gómez and Luis Villaseñor

12:55–14:00 Lunch Break

Friday, June 14, 2013 (continued)

14:00–14:40 Invited talk: Dr. Theresa Wilson

Session 3: Multilinguality in Social Media

14:40–15:05 *Subjectivity and Sentiment Analysis of Modern Standard Arabic and Arabic Microblogs*
Ahmed Mourad and Kareem Darwish

15:05–15:30 *Sentiment Analysis in Czech Social Media Using Supervised Machine Learning*
Ivan Habernal, Tomáš Ptáček and Josef Steinberger

15:30–16:00 Break

Session 4: Subjectity, Sentiment and Social Media Analysis (I)

16:00–16:15 *Tagging Opinion Phrases and their Targets in User Generated Textual Reviews*
Narendra Gupta

16:15–16:30 *From newspaper to microblogging: What does it take to find opinions?*
Wladimir Sidorenko, Jonathan Sonntag, Nina Krüger, Stefan Stieglitz and Manfred Stede

16:30–16:45 *Bilingual Experiments on an Opinion Comparable Corpus*
Eugenio Martínez-Cámara, M. Teresa Martín-Valdivia, M. Dolores Molina-González and L. Alfonso Ureña-López

16:45–17:00 *RA-SR: Using a ranking algorithm to automatically building resources for subjectivity analysis over annotated corpora*
Yoan Gutiérrez, Andy González, Antonio Fernández, Andrés Montoyo and Rafael Muñoz

17:00–17:15 Break

Friday, June 14, 2013 (continued)

Session 5: Subjectivity, Sentiment and Social Media Analysis (II)

17:15–17:30 *Sentiment analysis on Italian tweets*
Valerio Basile and malvina nissim

17:30–17:45 *Sentence-Level Subjectivity Detection Using Neuro-Fuzzy Models*
Samir Rustamov, Elshan Mustafayev and Mark Clements

17:45–18:00 *Sentiment Classification using Rough Set based Hybrid Feature Selection*
Basant Agarwal and Namita Mittal

18:00–18:15 *Sentiment Analysis in Social Media Texts*
Alexandra Balahur

18:15–18:30 Closing remarks

Recent adventures with emotion-reading technology

Rosalind W. Picard
MIT Media Lab, E14-374G
75 Amherst St; Cambridge, MA 02139
picard@media.mit.edu

1 Abstract of the talk

This talk will share stories from recent investigations at the MIT Media Lab in creating technology to recognize and better communicate emotion. Examples include automating facial affect recognition online for sharing media experiences, gathering the worlds largest sets of natural expressions (instead of lab-elicited data) and training machine learning models to predict liking of the experience based on expression dynamics throughout the experience. We also have found that most people have difficulty discriminating peak smiles of frustration from peak smiles of delight in static images. With machine learning and dynamic features, we were able to teach the computer to be highly accurate at discriminating these. These kinds of tools can potentially help many people with nonverbal learning disabilities, limited vision, social phobia, or autism who find it challenging to read the faces of those around them. I will also share recent findings from people wearing physiological sensors 24/7, and how weve been learning about connections between the emotion system, sleep and seizures. Finally, I will share some of our newest work related to crowd sourcing cognitive-behavioral therapy and computational empathy, where sentiment analysis could be of huge benefit.

Bootstrapped Learning of Emotion Hashtags #hashtags4you

Ashequl Qadir
School of Computing
University of Utah
Salt Lake City, UT 84112, USA
asheq@cs.utah.edu

Ellen Riloff
School of Computing
University of Utah
Salt Lake City, UT 84112, USA
riloff@cs.utah.edu

Abstract

We present a bootstrapping algorithm to automatically learn hashtags that convey emotion. Using the bootstrapping framework, we learn lists of emotion hashtags from unlabeled tweets. Our approach starts with a small number of seed hashtags for each emotion, which we use to automatically label tweets as initial training data. We then train emotion classifiers and use them to identify and score candidate emotion hashtags. We select the hashtags with the highest scores, use them to automatically harvest new tweets from Twitter, and repeat the bootstrapping process. We show that the learned hashtag lists help to improve emotion classification performance compared to an N-gram classifier, obtaining 8% micro-average and 9% macro-average improvements in F-measure.

1 Introduction

The increasing popularity of social media has given birth to new genres of text that have been the focus of NLP research for applications such as event discovery (Benson et al., 2011), election outcome prediction (Tumasjan et al., 2011; Bermingham and Smeaton, 2011), user profile classification (De Choudhury et al., 2012), conversation modeling (Ritter et al., 2010), consumer insight discovery (Chamlertwat et al., 2012), etc. A hallmark of social media is that people tend to share their personal feelings, often in publicly visible forums. As a result, social media has also been the focus of NLP research on sentiment analysis (Kouloumpis et al., 2011), emotion classification and lexicon generation (Mohammad, 2012), and sarcasm detection (Davidov et al., 2010). Identifying emotion in social media text could be beneficial for many application areas, for example to help companies understand how people feel about their products, to assist governments in recognizing growing anger or fear associated with an event, and to help media outlets understand the public's emotional response toward controversial issues or international affairs.

Twitter, a micro-blogging platform, is particularly well-known for its use by people who like to instantly express thoughts within a limited length of 140 characters. These status updates, known as tweets, are often emotional. Hashtags are a distinctive characteristic of tweets, which are a community-created convention for providing meta-information about a tweet. Hashtags are created by adding the '#' symbol as a prefix to a word or a multi-word phrase that consists of concatenated words without whitespace (e.g., *#welovehashtags*). People use hashtags in many ways, for example to represent the topic of a tweet (e.g., *#graduation*), to convey additional information (e.g., *#mybirthdaytoday*), or to express an emotion (e.g., *#pissedoff*).

The usage of hashtags in tweets is common, as reflected in the study of a sample of 0.6 million tweets by Wang et al. (2011) which found that 14.6% of tweets in their sample had at least one hashtag. In tweets that express emotion, it is common to find hashtags representing the emotion felt by the tweeter, such as *"the new iphone is a waste of money! nothing new! #angry"* denoting anger or *"buying a new sweater for my mom for her birthday! #loveyoumom"* denoting affection.

Identifying the emotion conveyed by a hashtag has not yet been studied by the natural language processing community. The goal of our research is to automatically identify hashtags that express one of five emotions: *affection*, *anger/rage*, *fear/anxiety*, *joy*, or *sadness/disappointment*. The learned hashtags are then used to recognize tweets that express one of these emotions. We use a bootstrapping approach that begins with 5 seed hashtags for each emotion class and iteratively learns more hashtags from unlabeled tweets. We show that the learned hashtags can accurately identify tweets that convey emotion and yield additional coverage beyond the recall of an N-gram classifier.

The rest of the paper is divided into the following sections. In Section 2, we present a brief overview of previous research related to emotion classification in social media and the use of hashtags. In Section 3, we describe our bootstrapping approach for learning lists of emotion hashtags. In Section 4 we discuss the data collection process and our experimental design. In Section 5, we present the results of our experiments. Finally, we conclude by summarizing our findings and presenting directions for future work.

2 Related Work

Recognizing emotions in social media texts has grown popular among researchers in recent years. Roberts et al. (2012) investigated feature sets to classify emotions in Twitter and presented an analysis of different linguistic styles people use to express emotions. The research of Kim et al. (2012a) is focused on discovering emotion influencing patterns to classify emotions in social network conversations. Esmin et al. (2012) presented a 3-level hierarchical emotion classification approach by differentiating between emotion vs. non-emotion text, positive vs. negative emotion, and then classified different emotions. Yang et al. (2007b) investigated sentence contexts to classify emotions in blogs at the document level. Some researchers have also worked on analyzing the correlation of emotions with topics and trends. Kim et al. (2012b) analyzed correlations between topics and emotions in Twitter using topic modeling. Gilbert and Karahalios (2010) analyzed correlation of anxiety, worry and fear with downward trends in the stock market. Bollen et al. (2011) modeled public mood and emotion by creating six-dimensional mood vectors to correlate with popular events that happened in the timeframe of the dataset.

On the other hand, researchers have recently started to pay attention to the hashtags of tweets, but mostly to use them to collect labeled data. Davidov et al. (2010) used *#sarcasm* to collect sarcastic tweets from twitter. Choudhury et al. (2012) used hashtags of 172 mood words to collect training data to find associations between mood and human affective states, and trained classifiers with unigram and bigram features to classify these states. Purver and Battersby (2012) used emotion class name hashtags and emoticons as distant supervision in emotion classification. Mohammad (2012) also used emotion class names as hashtags to collect labeled data from Twitter, and used these tweets to generate emotion lexicons. Wang et al. (2012) used a selection of emotion hashtags as the means to acquire labeled data from twitter, and found that a combination of unigrams, bigrams, sentiment/emotion-bearing words, and parts-of-speech information to be the most effective in classifying emotions. A study by Wang et al. (2012) also shows that hashtags can be used to create a high quality emotion dataset. They found about 93.16% of the tweets having emotion hashtags were relevant to the corresponding emotion.

However, none of this work investigated the use of emotion hashtag lists to help classify emotions in tweets. In cases where hashtags were used to collect training data, the hashtags were manually selected for each emotion class. In many cases, only the name of the emotion classes were used for this purpose. The work most closely related to our research focus is the work of Wang et al. (2011) where they investigated several graph based algorithms to collectively classify hashtag sentiments. However, their work is focused on classifying hashtags of positive and negative sentiment polarities, and they made use of sentiment polarity of the individual tweets to classify hashtag sentiments. On the contrary, we learn emotion hashtags and use the learned hashtag lists to classify emotion tweets. To the best of our knowledge, we are the first to present a bootstrapped learning framework to automatically learn emotion hashtags from unlabeled data.

3 Learning Emotion Hashtags via Bootstrapping

3.1 Motivation

The hashtags that people use in tweets are often very creative. While it is common to use just single word hashtags (e.g., *#angry)*, many hashtags are multi-word phrases (e.g., *#LoveHimSoMuch*). People also use elongated[1] forms of words (e.g., *#yaaaaay*, *#goawaaay*) to put emphasis on their emotional state. In addition, words are often spelled creatively by replacing a word with a number or replacing some characters with phonetically similar characters (e.g., *#only4you*, *#YoureDaBest*). While many of these hashtags convey emotions, these stylistic variations in the use of hashtags make it very difficult to create a repository of emotion hashtags manually. While emotion word lexicons exist (Yang et al., 2007a; Mohammad, 2012), and adding a '#' symbol as a prefix to these lexicon entries could potentially give us lists of emotion hashtags, it would be unlikely to find multi-word phrases or stylistic variations frequently used in tweets. This drives our motivation to automatically learn hashtags that are commonly used to express emotion in tweets.

3.2 Emotion Classes

For this research, we selected 5 prominent emotion classes that are frequent in tweets: *Affection*, *Anger/Rage*, *Fear/Anxiety*, *Joy* and *Sadness/Disappointment*. We started by analyzing Parrott's (Parrott, 2001) emotion taxonomy and how these emotions are expressed in tweets. We also wanted to ensure that the selected emotion classes would have minimal overlap with each other. We took Parrott's primary emotion *Joy* and *Fear*[2] directly. We merged Parrott's secondary emotion *Affection* and *Lust* into our *Affection* class and merged Parrott's secondary emotion *Sadness* and *Disappointment* into our *Sadness/Disappointment* class, since these emotions are often difficult to distinguish from each other. Lastly, we mapped Parrott's secondary emotion *Rage* to our *Anger/Rage* class directly. There were other emotions in Parrott's taxonomy such as *Surprise*, *Neglect*, etc. that we did not use for this research. In addition to the five emotion classes, we used a *None of the Above* class for tweets that do not carry any emotion or that carry an emotion other than one of our five emotion classes.

[1]This feature has also been found to have a strong association with sentiment polarities (Brody and Diakopoulos, 2011)

[2]we renamed the *Fear* class as *Fear/Anxiety*

3.3 Overview of Bootstrapping Framework

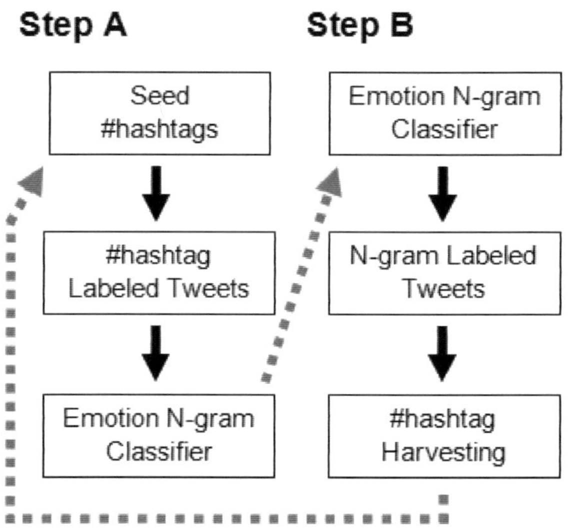

Figure 1: Bootstrapping Architecture

Figure 1 presents the framework of our bootstrapping algorithm for learning emotion hashtags. The algorithm runs in two steps. In the first step, the bootstrapping process begins with five manually defined "seed" hashtags for each emotion class. For each seed hashtag, we search Twitter for tweets that contain the hashtag and label these tweets with the emotion class associated with the hashtag. We use these labeled tweets to train a supervised N-gram classifier for every emotion $e \in E$, where E is the set of emotion classes we are classifying.

In the next step, the emotion classifiers are applied to a large pool of unlabeled tweets and we collect the tweets that are labeled by the classifiers. From these labeled tweets, we extract the hashtags found in these tweets to create a candidate pool of emotion hashtags. The hashtags in the candidate pool are then scored and ranked and we select the most highly ranked hashtags to add to a hashtag repository for each emotion class.

Finally, we then search for tweets that contain the learned hashtags in a pool of unlabeled tweets and label each of these with the appropriate emotion class. These newly labeled tweets are added to the set of training instances. The emotion classifiers are retrained using the larger set of training instances, and the bootstrapping process continues.

3.4 Seeding

For each of the 5 emotion classes, we manually selected 5 seed hashtags that we determined to be strongly representative of the emotion. Before collecting the initial training tweets containing the seed hashtags, we manually searched in Twitter to ensure that these seed hashtags are frequently used by tweeters. Table 1 presents our seed hashtags.

Emotion Classes	Seed Hashtags
AFFECTION	*#loveyou, #sweetheart, #bff #romantic, #soulmate*
ANGER & RAGE	*#angry, #mad, #hateyou #pissedoff, #furious*
FEAR & ANXIETY	*#afraid, #petrified, #scared #anxious, #worried*
JOY	*#happy, #excited, #yay #blessed, #thrilled*
SADNESS & DISAPPOINTMENT	*#sad, #depressed #disappointed, #unhappy #foreveralone*

Table 1: Seed Emotion Hashtags

3.5 N-gram Tweet Classifier

The tweets acquired using the seed hashtags are used as training instances to create emotion classifiers with supervised learning. We first pre-process the training instances by tokenizing the tweets with a freely available tokenizer for Twitter (Owoputi et al., 2013). Although it is not uncommon to express emotion states in tweets with capitalized characters inside words, the unique writing styles of the tweeters often create many variations of the same words and hashtags. We, therefore, normalized case to ensure generalization.

We trained one logistic regression classifier for each emotion class. We chose logistic regression as the classification algorithm because it produces probabilities along with each prediction that we later use to assign scores to candidate emotion hashtags. As features, we used unigrams to represent all of the words and hashtags in a tweet, but we removed the seed hashtags that were used to select the tweets (or the classifier would simply learn to recognize the seed hashtags). Our hypothesis is that the seed hashtag will not be the only emotion indicator in a tweet, most of the time. The goal is for the classifier to learn to recognize words and/or additional hashtags that are also indicative of the emotion. Additionally, we removed from the feature set any user mentions (by looking for words with '@' prefix). We also removed any word or hashtag from the feature set that appeared only once in the training data.

For emotion e, we used the tweets containing seed hashtags for e as the positive training instances and the tweets containing hashtags for the other emotions as negative instances. However, we also needed to provide negative training instances that do not belong to any of the 5 emotion classes. For this purpose, we added 100,000 randomly collected tweets to the training data. While it is possible that some of these tweets are actually positive instances for e, our hope is that the vast majority of them will not belong to emotion e.

We experimented with feature options such as bigrams, unigrams with the '#' symbol stripped off from hashtags, etc., but the combination of unigrams and hashtags as features worked the best. We used the freely available java version of the LIBLINEAR (Fan et al., 2008) package with its default parameter settings for logistic regression.

3.6 Learning Emotion Hashtags

The next step is to learn emotion hashtags. We apply the emotion classifiers to a pool of unlabeled tweets and collect all of the tweets that the classifier can label. For each emotion $e \in E$, we first create a candidate pool of emotion hashtags H_e, by collecting all of the hashtags in the labeled tweets for emotion e. To limit the size of the candidate pool, we discarded hashtags with just one character or more than 20 characters, and imposed a frequency threshold of 10. We then score these hashtags to select the top N emotion hashtags we feel most confident about.

To score each candidate hashtag $h \in H_e$, we compute the average of the probabilities assigned by the logistic regression classifier to all the tweets containing hashtag h. We expect the classifier to assign higher probabilities only to tweets it feels confident about. Therefore, if h conveys e, we expect that the average probability of all the tweets containing h will also be high. We select the top 10 emotion hashtags for each emotion class e, and add them to our list of learned hashtags for e.

3.7 Adding New Training Instances for Bootstrapping

To facilitate the next stage of bootstrapping, we collect all tweets from the unlabeled data that contain hashtag h and label them with the emotion associated with h. By adding more training instances, we expect to provide the classifiers with new tweets that will contain a potentially more diverse set of words that the classifiers can consider in the next stage of the bootstrapping.

When the new tweets are added to the training set, we remove the hashtags from them that we used for labelling to avoid bias, and the bootstrapping process continues. We ran the bootstrapped learning for 100 iterations. Since we learned 10 hashtags during each iteration, we ended up with emotion hashtag lists consisting of 1000 hashtags for each emotion.

4 Experimental Setup

4.1 Data Collection

To collect our initial training data, we searched Twitter for the seed hashtags mentioned in Section 3.4 using Twitter's Search API[3] over a period of time. To ensure that the collected tweets are written in English, we used a freely available language recognizer trained for tweets (Carter et al., 2013). We filtered out tweets that were marked as re-tweets using *#rt* or beginning with *"rt"*[4] because re-tweets are in many cases exactly the same or very similar to the original. We also filtered out any tweet containing a URL because if such a tweet contains emotion, it is possible that the emotion indicator may be present only on the linked website (e.g., a link to a comic strip followed by an emotion hashtag). After these filtering steps, we ended up with a seed labeled training dataset of 325,343 tweets.

In addition to the seed labeled data, we collected random tweets using Twitter's Streaming API[5] over a period of time to use as our pool of unlabeled tweets. Like the training data, we filtered out re-tweets and tweets containing a URL as well as tweets containing any of the seed hashtags. Since our research focus is on learning emotion hashtags, we also filtered out any tweet that did not have at least one hashtag. After filtering, we ended up with roughly 2.3 million unlabeled tweets.

4.2 Test Data

Since manual annotation is time consuming, to ensure that many tweets in our test data have at least one of our 5 emotions, we manually selected 25 topic keywords/phrases[6] that we considered to be strongly associated with emotions, but not necessarily any specific emotion. We then searched in Twitter for any of these topic phrases and their corresponding hashtags. These 25 topic phrases are: *Prom, Exam, Graduation, Marriage, Divorce, Husband, Wife, Boyfriend, Girlfriend, Job, Hire, Laid Off, Retirement, Win, Lose, Accident, Failure, Success, Spider, Loud Noise, Chest Pain, Storm, Home Alone, No Sleep* and *Interview*. Since the purpose of collecting these tweets is to evaluate the quality and coverage of the emotion hashtags that we learn, we filtered out any tweet that did not have at least one hashtag (other than the topic hashtag).

To annotate tweets with respect to emotion, two annotators were given definitions of the 5 emotion classes from Collins English Dictionary[7], Parrott's (Parrott, 2001) emotion taxonomy of these 5 emotions and additional annotation guidelines. The annotators were instructed to label each tweet with up to two emotions. The instructions specified that the emotion must be felt by the tweeter at the time the tweet was written. After several trials and discussions, the annotators reached a satisfactory agreement level of 0.79 Kappa (κ) (Carletta, 1996). The annotation disagreements in these 500 tweets were then adjudicated, and each annotator labeled an additional 2,500 tweets. Altogether this gave us an emotion annotated dataset of 5,500 tweets. We randomly separated out 1,000 tweets from this collection as a tuning set, and used the remaining 4,500 tweets as evaluation data.

In Table 2, we present the emotion distribution in

[3]https://dev.twitter.com/docs/api/1/get/search

[4]a typical convention to mark a tweet as a re-tweet

[5]https://dev.twitter.com/docs/streaming-apis

[6]This data collection process is similar to the emotion tweet dataset creation by Roberts et al. (2012)

[7]http://www.collinsdictionary.com/

tweets that were labeled using the seed hashtags in the second column. In the next column, we present the emotion distribution in the tweets that were annotated for evaluation by the human annotators.

Emotion	Tweets with Seed Hashtags	Evaluation Tweets
AFFECTION	14.38%	6.42%
ANGER/RAGE	14.01%	8.91%
FEAR/ANXIETY	11.42%	13.16%
JOY	37.47%	22.33%
SADNESS/ DISAPPOINTMENT	23.69%	12.45%
NONE OF THE ABOVE	-	42.38%

Table 2: Distribution of emotions in tweets with seed hashtags and evaluation tweets

4.3 Evaluating Emotion Hashtags

For comparison, we trained logistic regression classifiers with word unigrams and hashtags as features for each emotion class, and performed 10-fold cross-validation on the evaluation data. As a second baseline for comparison, we added bigrams to the feature set of the classifiers.

To decide on the optimum size of the lists for each emotion class, we performed list lookup on the tuning data that we had set aside before evaluation. For any hashtag in a tweet in the tuning dataset, we looked up that hashtag in our learned lists, and if found, assigned the corresponding emotion as the label for that tweet. We did this experiment starting with only seeds in our lists, and incrementally increased the sizes of the lists by 50 hashtags at each experiment. We decided on the optimum size based on the best F-measure obtained for each emotion class. In Table 3, we show the list sizes we found to achieve the best F-measure for each emotion class in the tuning dataset.

Emotion	List Sizes
AFFECTION	500
ANGER/RAGE	1000
FEAR/ANXIETY	850
JOY	1000
SADNESS/DISAPPOINTMENT	400

Table 3: Optimum list sizes decided from tuning dataset

To use the learned lists of emotion hashtags for classifying emotions in tweets, we first used them as features for the logistic regression classifiers. We created 5 list features with binary values, one for each emotion class. Whenever a tweet in the evaluation data contained a hashtag from one of the learned emotion hashtags lists, we set the value of that list feature to be 1, and 0 otherwise. We used these 5 new features in addition to the word unigrams and hashtag features, and evaluated the classification performance of the logistic regression classifiers in a 10-fold cross-validation setup by calculating precision, recall and F-measure.

Since the more confident hashtags are added to the lists at the beginning stages of bootstrapping, we also tried creating subsets from each list by grouping hashtags together that were learned after each 5 iterations of bootstrapping (50 hashtags in each subset). We then created 20 list subset features for each emotion with binary values, yielding 100 additional features in total. We also evaluated this feature representation of the hashtag lists in a 10-fold cross-validation setup.

As a different approach, we also used the lists independently from the logistic regression classifiers. For any hashtag in the evaluation tweets, we looked up the hashtag in our learned lists. If the hashtag was found, we assigned the corresponding emotion class label to the tweet containing the hashtag. Lastly, we combined the list lookup decisions with the decisions of the baseline logistic regression classifiers by taking a union of the decisions, i.e., if either assigned an emotion to a tweet, we assigned that emotion as the label for the tweet. We present the results of these different approaches in Section 5.

5 Results and Analysis

Table 4 shows the precision, recall and F-measure of the N-gram classifier as well as several different utilizations of the learned hashtag lists. The first and the second row in Table 4 correspond to the results for the baseline unigram classifier (UC) alone and when bigrams are added to the feature set. These baseline classifiers had low recall for most emotion classes, suggesting that the N-grams and hashtags are not adequate as features to recognize the emotion classes.

Results of using the hashtag lists as 5 additional features for the classifier are shown in the third row

Evaluation	Affection			Anger Rage			Fear Anxiety			Joy			Sadness Disappointment		
	P	R	F	P	R	F	P	R	F	P	R	F	P	R	F
Baseline Classifiers															
Unigram Classifier (UC)	67	43	52	51	19	28	63	33	43	65	48	55	57	29	39
UC + Bigram Features	70	38	50	52	15	23	64	29	40	65	45	53	57	25	34
Baseline Classifier with List Features															
UC + List Features	71	49	58	56	28	37	67	41	51	66	50	57	61	34	44
UC + List Subset Features	73	45	56	58	23	33	69	38	49	66	48	55	61	32	42
List Lookup															
Seed Lookup	**94**	06	11	**75**	01	03	**100**	06	11	**93**	04	08	**81**	02	05
List Lookup	73	40	52	59	25	35	61	36	45	70	16	26	80	17	28
Baseline Classifier with List Lookup															
UC ∪ Seed Lookup	68	45	54	52	21	30	63	33	44	66	49	56	58	31	40
UC ∪ List Lookup	63	**60**	**61**	52	**38**	**44**	56	**53**	**54**	64	**54**	**59**	59	**38**	**46**

Table 4: Emotion classification result (P = Precision, R = Recall, F = F-measure)

of Table 4. The hashtag lists consistently improve precision and recall across all five emotions. Compared to the unigram classifier, F-measure improved by 6% for AFFECTION, by 9% for ANGER/RAGE, by 8% for FEAR/ANXIETY, by 2% for JOY, and by 5% for SADNESS/DISAPPOINTMENT. The next row presents the results when the list subset features were used. Using this feature representation as opposed to using each list as a whole shows precision recall tradeoff as the classifier learns to rely on the subsets of hashtags that are good, resulting in improved precision for several emotion classes, but recognizes emotions in fewer tweets, which resulted in less recall.

The fifth and the sixth rows of Table 4 show results of list lookup only. As expected, seed lookup recognizes emotions in tweets with high precision, but does not recognize the emotions in many tweets because the seed lists have only 5 hashtags per emotion class. Comparatively, using learned hashtag lists shows substantial improvement in recall as the learned lists contain a lot more emotion hashtags than the initial seeds.

Finally, the last two rows of Table 4 show classification performance of taking the union of the decisions made by the unigram classifier and the decisions made by matching against just the seed hashtags or the lists of learned hashtags. The union with the seed hashtags lookup shows consistent improvement across all emotion classes compared to the unigram baseline but the improvements are small. The union with the lookup in the learned lists of emotion hashtags shows substantial recall gains. This approach improves recall over the unigram baseline by 17% for AFFECTION, 19% for ANGER/RAGE, 20% for FEAR/ANXIETY, 6% for JOY, and 9% for SADNESS/DISAPPOINTMENT. At the same time, we observe that despite this large recall gain, precision is about the same or just a little lower. As a result, we observe an overall F-measure improvement of 9% for AFFECTION, 16% for ANGER/RAGE, 11% for FEAR/ANXIETY, 4% for JOY, and 7% for SADNESS/DISAPPOINTMENT.

Evaluation	Micro Average			Macro Average		
	P	R	F	P	R	F
Baseline Classifiers						
Unigram Classifier (UC)	62	37	46	61	34	44
UC + Bigram Features	63	33	43	62	30	41
Baseline Classifier with List Features						
UC + List Features	65	42	51	64	40	49
UC + List Subset Features	66	39	49	65	37	48
List Lookup						
Seed Lookup	**93**	04	08	**89**	04	08
List Lookup	67	24	35	68	27	38
Baseline Classifier with List Lookup						
UC ∪ Seed Lookup	63	38	47	61	36	45
UC ∪ List Lookup	60	**49**	**54**	59	**49**	**53**

Table 5: Micro and Macro averages

Table 5 shows the overall performance improvement of the classifiers, averaged across all five emotion classes, measured as micro and macro aver-

AFFECTION	ANGER RAGE	FEAR ANXIETY	JOY	SADNESS DISAPPOINT-MENT
#youthebest	#godie	#hatespiders	#thankinggod	#catlady
#yourthebest	#donttalktome	#freakedout	#thankyoulord	#buttrue
#hyc	#fuckyourself	#creepedout	#thankful	#singleprobs
#yourethebest	#getoutofmylife	#sinister	#superexcited	#singleproblems
#alwaysandforever	#irritated	#wimp	#tripleblessed	#lonelytweet
#missyou	#pieceofshit	#shittingmyself	#24hours	#lonely
#loveyoumore	#ruinedmyday	#frightened	#ecstatic	#crushed
#loveyoulots	#notfriends	#paranoid	#happyme	#lonerproblems
#thanksforeverything	#yourgross	#haunted	#lifesgood	#unloved
#flyhigh	#madtweet	#phobia	#can'twait	#friendless
#comehomesoon	#stupidbitch	#shittingbricks	#grateful	#singlepringle
#yougotthis	#sofuckingannoying	#hateneedles	#goodmood	#brokenheart
#missyoutoo	#annoyed	#biggestfear	#superhappy	#singleforever
#youdabest	#fuming	#worstfear	#missedthem	#nosociallife
#otherhalf	#wankers	#concerned	#greatmood	#teamnofriends
#youramazing	#asshole	#waitinggame	#studio	#foreverugly
#cutiepie	#dontbothermewhen	#mama	#tgfl	#nofriends
#bestfriendforever	#fu	#prayforme	#exicted	#leftout
#alwayshereforyou	#fuckyou	#nightmares	#smiles	#singleforlife
#howimetmybestfriend	#yousuck	#baddriver	#liein	#:'(

Table 6: Top 20 hashtags learned for each emotion class

age precision, recall and F-measure scores. We see both types of feature representations of the hashtag lists improve precision and recall across all emotion classes over the N-gram classifier baselines. Using the union of the classifier and list lookup, we see a 12% recall gain with only 2% precision drop in micro-average over the unigram baseline, and 15% recall gain with only 2% precision drop in macro-average. As a result, we see an overall 8% micro-average F-measure improvement and 9% macro-average F-measure improvement.

In Table 6, we show the top 20 hashtags learned in each emotion class by our bootstrapped learning. While many of these hashtags express emotion, we also notice a few hashtags representing reasons (e.g., *#baddriver* in FEAR/ANXIETY) that are strongly associated with the corresponding emotion, as well as common misspellings (e.g., *#exicted* in JOY).

6 Conclusions

In this research we have presented a bootstrapped learning framework to automatically learn emotion hashtags. Our approach makes use of supervision from seed hashtag labeled tweets, and through a bootstrapping process, iteratively learns emotion hashtags. We have experimented with several approaches to use the lists of emotion hashtags for emotion classification and have found that the hashtag lists consistently improve emotion classification performance in tweets. In future research, since our bootstrapped learning approach does not rely on any language specific techniques, we plan to learn emotion hashtags in other prominent languages such as Spanish, Portuguese, etc.

7 Acknowledgments

This work was supported by the Intelligence Advanced Research Projects Activity (IARPA) via Department of Interior National Business Center (DoI / NBC) contract number D12PC00285. The U.S. Government is authorized to reproduce and distribute reprints for Governmental purposes notwithstanding any copyright annotation thereon. The views and conclusions contained herein are those of the authors and should not be interpreted as necessarily representing the official policies or endorsements, either expressed or implied, of IARPA, DoI/NBE, or the U.S. Government.

References

Edward Benson, Aria Haghighi, and Regina Barzilay. 2011. Event discovery in social media feeds. In *Proceedings of the 49th Annual Meeting of the Association for Computational Linguistics: Human Language Technologies - Volume 1*, HLT '11, pages 389–398.

Adam Bermingham and Alan Smeaton. 2011. On using twitter to monitor political sentiment and predict election results. In *Proceedings of the Workshop on Sentiment Analysis where AI meets Psychology (SAAIP 2011)*, pages 2–10.

Johan Bollen, Huina Mao, and Alberto Pepe. 2011. Modeling public mood and emotion: Twitter sentiment and socio-economic phenomena. In *Proceedings of the Fifth International Conference on Weblogs and Social Media*.

Samuel Brody and Nicholas Diakopoulos. 2011. Cooooooooooooooollllllllllllll!!!!!!!!!!!!!!: using word lengthening to detect sentiment in microblogs. In *Proceedings of the Conference on Empirical Methods in Natural Language Processing*, EMNLP '11, pages 562–570.

Jean Carletta. 1996. Assessing agreement on classification tasks: the kappa statistic. *Comput. Linguist.*, 22:249–254, June.

S. Carter, W. Weerkamp, and E. Tsagkias. 2013. Microblog language identification: Overcoming the limitations of short, unedited and idiomatic text. *Language Resources and Evaluation Journal*, 47(1).

Wilas Chamlertwat, Pattarasinee Bhattarakosol, Tippakorn Rungkasiri, and Choochart Haruechaiyasak. 2012. Discovering consumer insight from twitter via sentiment analysis. *Journal of Universal Computer Science*, 18(8):973–992, apr.

Munmun De Choudhury, Michael Gamon, and Scott Counts. 2012. Happy, nervous or surprised? classification of human affective states in social media. In *Proceedings of the Sixth International Conference on Weblogs and Social Media*.

Dmitry Davidov, Oren Tsur, and Ari Rappoport. 2010. Semi-supervised recognition of sarcastic sentences in twitter and amazon. In *Proceedings of the Fourteenth Conference on Computational Natural Language Learning*, CoNLL '10, pages 107–116.

Munmun De Choudhury, Nicholas Diakopoulos, and Mor Naaman. 2012. Unfolding the event landscape on twitter: classification and exploration of user categories. In *Proceedings of the ACM 2012 conference on Computer Supported Cooperative Work*, CSCW '12, pages 241–244.

Ahmed Ali Abdalla Esmin, Roberto L. De Oliveira Jr., and Stan Matwin. 2012. Hierarchical classification approach to emotion recognition in twitter. In *Proceedings of the 11th International Conference on Machine Learning and Applications, ICMLA, Boca Raton, FL, USA, December 12-15, 2012. Volume 2*, pages 381–385. IEEE.

Rong-En Fan, Kai-Wei Chang, Cho-Jui Hsieh, Xiang-Rui Wang, and Chih-Jen Lin. 2008. Liblinear: A library for large linear classification. *J. Mach. Learn. Res.*, 9:1871–1874, June.

Eric Gilbert and Karrie Karahalios. 2010. Widespread worry and the stock market. In *Proceedings of the International AAAI Conference on Weblogs and Social Media*.

Suin Kim, JinYeong Bak, and Alice Oh. 2012a. Discovering emotion influence patterns in online social network conversations. *SIGWEB Newsl.*, (Autumn):3:1–3:6, September.

Suin Kim, JinYeong Bak, and Alice Oh. 2012b. Do you feel what i feel? social aspects of emotions in twitter conversations. In *International AAAI Conference on Weblogs and Social Media*.

Efthymios Kouloumpis, Theresa Wilson, and Johanna Moore. 2011. Twitter sentiment analysis: The good the bad and the omg! In *Proceedings of the Fifth International Conference on Weblogs and Social Media*.

Saif Mohammad. 2012. #emotional tweets. In **SEM 2012: The First Joint Conference on Lexical and Computational Semantics*, pages 246–255.

Olutobi Owoputi, Brendan OConnor, Chris Dyer, Kevin Gimpel, Nathan Schneider, and Noah A. Smith. 2013. Improved part-of-speech tagging for online conversational text with word clusters. In *Proceedings of the North American Chapter of the Association for Computational Linguistics (NAACL-2013)*.

W. Gerrod Parrott, editor. 2001. *Emotions in Social Psychology*. Psychology Press.

Matthew Purver and Stuart Battersby. 2012. Experimenting with distant supervision for emotion classification. In *Proceedings of the 13th Conference of the European Chapter of the Association for Computational Linguistics*, EACL '12, pages 482–491.

Alan Ritter, Colin Cherry, and Bill Dolan. 2010. Unsupervised modeling of twitter conversations. In *Human Language Technologies: The 2010 Annual Conference of the North American Chapter of the Association for Computational Linguistics*, HLT '10, pages 172–180.

Kirk Roberts, Michael A. Roach, Joseph Johnson, Josh Guthrie, and Sanda M. Harabagiu. 2012. Empatweet: Annotating and detecting emotions on twitter. In *Proceedings of the Eighth International Conference on Language Resources and Evaluation (LREC-2012)*, pages 3806–3813. ACL Anthology Identifier: L12-1059.

Andranik Tumasjan, Timm O. Sprenger, Philipp G. Sandner, and Isabell M. Welpe. 2011. Election forecasts with twitter: How 140 characters reflect the political landscape. *Social Science Computer Review*, 29(4):402–418, November.

Xiaolong Wang, Furu Wei, Xiaohua Liu, Ming Zhou, and Ming Zhang. 2011. Topic sentiment analysis in twitter: a graph-based hashtag sentiment classification approach. In *Proceedings of the 20th ACM international conference on Information and knowledge management*, CIKM '11, pages 1031–1040.

Wenbo Wang, Lu Chen, Krishnaprasad Thirunarayan, and Amit P. Sheth. 2012. Harnessing twitter "big data" for automatic emotion identification. In *Proceedings of the 2012 ASE/IEEE International Conference on Social Computing and 2012 ASE/IEEE International Conference on Privacy, Security, Risk and Trust*, SOCIALCOM-PASSAT '12, pages 587–592.

Changhua Yang, Kevin Hsin-Yih Lin, and Hsin-Hsi Chen. 2007a. Building emotion lexicon from weblog corpora. In *Proceedings of the 45th Annual Meeting of the ACL on Interactive Poster and Demonstration Sessions*, ACL '07, pages 133–136.

Changhua Yang, Kevin Hsin-Yih Lin, and Hsin-Hsi Chen. 2007b. Emotion classification using web blog corpora. In *Proceedings of the IEEE/WIC/ACM International Conference on Web Intelligence*, WI '07, pages 275–278.

Fine-Grained Emotion Recognition in Olympic Tweets Based on Human Computation

Valentina Sintsova[a, b] **Claudiu Musat**[a] **Pearl Pu**[b]
[a]Artificial Intelligence Laboratory [b]Human Computer Interaction Group
School of Computer and Communication Sciences
Swiss Federal Institute of Technology (EPFL)
CH-1015, Lausanne, Switzerland
{valentina.sintsova, claudiu-cristian.musat, pearl.pu}@epfl.ch

Abstract

In this paper, we detail a method for domain specific, multi-category emotion recognition, based on human computation. We create an Amazon Mechanical Turk[1] task that elicits emotion labels and phrase-emotion associations from the participants. Using the proposed method, we create an emotion lexicon, compatible with the 20 emotion categories of the Geneva Emotion Wheel. GEW is the first computational resource that can be used to assign emotion labels with such a high level of granularity. Our emotion annotation method also produced a corpus of emotion labeled sports tweets. We compared the cross-validated version of the lexicon with existing resources for both the positive/negative and multi-emotion classification problems. We show that the presented domain-targeted lexicon outperforms the existing general purpose ones in both settings. The performance gains are most pronounced for the fine-grained emotion classification, where we achieve an accuracy twice higher than the benchmark.[2]

1 Introduction

Social media platforms such as Twitter.com have become a common way for people to share opinions and emotions. Sports events are traditionally accompanied by strong emotions and the 2012 summer Olympic Games in London were not an exception. In this paper we describe methods to analyze and data mine the emotional content of tweets about this event using human computation. Our goal is to create an emotion recognition method, capable of classifying domain specific emotions with a high emotion granularity. In the stated case, domain specificity refers not only to the sport event, but also to the Twitter environment.

We focus on the categorical representation of emotions because it allows a more fine-grained analysis and it is more natural for humans. In daily life we use emotion names to describe specific feelings rather than give numerical evaluations or specify polarity. So far, the multi-item emotion classification problem has received much less attention.

One reason is that high quality training corpora are difficult to construct largely due to the cost of human annotators. Further, if emotion representation is not carefully designed, the annotator agreement can be very low. The higher the number of considered emotions is, the more difficult it is for humans to agree on a label for a given text. Low quality labeling leads to difficulties in extracting powerful classification features. This problem is further compounded in parsimonious environments, like Twitter, where the short text leads to a lack of emotional cues. All this presents challenges in developing a high-quality emotion recognition system operating with a fine-grained emotion category set within a chosen domain.

In this paper, we show how to tackle the above challenges through human computation, using an online labor market such as the Amazon Mechanical Turk or AMT (Snow et al., 2008). To overcome the possible difficulties in annotation we employ a well-designed emotion assessment tool, the Geneva

[1]www.mturk.com

[2]The corpus and the lexicon are available upon email request

Emotion Wheel (GEW) (Scherer, 2005). Having 20 separate emotion categories, it provides a desirable high level of emotion granularity. In a given task, we show the annotators the tweets, related to the aforementioned sports event, and ask them to classify the tweets' emotional content into one of the provided emotion categories. The action sequence requires them to both label the tweets and to specify the textual constructs that support their decision. We view the selected textual constructs as probable classification features. The proposed method thus simultaneously produces *an emotion annotated corpus* of tweets and creates an *emotion lexicon*. The resulting weighted emotion lexicon is a list of phrases indicative of emotion presence. It consists solely of ones selected by respondents, while their weights were learnt based on their occurrence in the constructed Sports-Related Emotion Corpus (SREC).

We show that the human-based lexicon is well suited for the particularities of the chosen environment, and also for an emotion model with a high number of categories. Firstly, we show that domain specificity matters, and that non-specialists, using their common sense, can extract features that are useful in classification. We use the resulting lexicon, $OlympLex$, in a binary polarity classification problem on the domain data and show that it outperforms several traditional lexicons.

In multi-emotion classification, we show that it is highly accurate in classifying tweets into 20 emotion categories of the Geneva Emotion Wheel (GEW) (Scherer, 2005). As a baseline for comparison we use the Geneva wheel compatible lexicon, the Geneva Affect Label Coder (GALC) (Scherer, 2005). The experiments show that $OlympLex$ significantly outperforms this baseline.

Such a detailed emotion representation allows us to create an accurate description of the sentiment the chosen event evokes in its viewers. For instance, we find that *Pride* is the dominant emotion, and that it is 2.3 times more prevalent than *Anger*.

2 Related Work

GEW Emotion Representation Model In our work we used the emotion categories from the Geneva Emotion Wheel (GEW, version 2.0). GEW was developed as a tool for obtaining self-reports of emotional experience with a goal to structure the exhaustive list of possible emotion names used in free-format self-reports with minimal loss in expressibility. It presents 20 (10 positive/10 negative) emotion categories frequently answered in free-format self-reports as main options. Each emotion category is represented by two common emotion names to emphasize its family nature (e.g. *Happiness/Joy*[3]). These categories are arranged on the circle following the underlying 2-dimensional space of valence (positive-negative) and control (high-low). Several levels of intensity for each emotion category are presented as answer options. Also, 2 other answers are possible: *No emotion* and *Other emotion* with free-format input in the latter case.

Compared to raw dimensional models where emotion states are described as points in space (e.g. Pleasure-Arousal-Dominance model, PAD (Mehrabian, 1996)) GEW has an advantage of categorical representation where emotion state is described in terms of discrete set of emotion names. It allows humans to measure their emotions in terms of emotion names they accustomed to instead of unnatural numerical measurements. Among commonly used emotion categories sets GEW categories are the most fine-grained, compared, for instance, to Ekman's (1992) or Plutchik's (1980) basic emotions. While these models have been popular in emotion recognition research, their main shortcoming is their limited items. In sports events, fans and spectators not only feel strong emotions, but also likely want to express them in multitudes of expressions. *Pride/Elation*, *Envy/Jealousy* are just two examples that are missed in those models with basic emotions.

Lexical Resources Emotion recognition is closely related to the positive/negative sentiment classification. In a traditional approach the units defining the polarity of the text are polarity-bearing terms. A list of such terms with corresponding polarity label or score forms a polarity lexicon. Commonly used examples of polarity lexicons include GI (Stone et al., 1968), Bing Liu's lexicon (Hu and Liu, 2004), and OpinionFinder (Wilson et al., 2009).

Similarly, emotion lexicons can be defined as lists of terms bearing emotions with their corre-

[3]In the paper text we often use one name per category for brevity reasons

sponding emotion information. Depending on the construction methods, they can be separated into those that constructed manually (GALC (Scherer, 2005)), semi-automatically (WordNet-Affect (Strapparava and Valitutti, 2004)) or via human computation (ANEW (Bradley and Lang, 1999), NRC (Mohammad and Turney, 2010; Mohammad and Turney, 2012)). Our work is most closely related to the NRC lexicon which was also extracted via human computation on AMT. The authors developed a task where, for a given term, the annotators rated to what extent the term is associated to each emotion of Plutchik's set. In contrast, in our work, we harvest emotional labels and features in context. The terms are associated with emotions in the context of the tweet they appear in. We use the approach suggested by (Aman and Szpakowicz, 2007) where humans are asked to select an excerpt of the text expressing emotion. Moreover, we ask the annotators for additional interchangeable, emotional expressions for the same situation. Lexicons obtained from unsupervised learning methods using automatically annotated Twitter data (Mohammad, 2012) have also been proposed, but their performance has been shown to be inferior to benchmarks such as NRC.

The underlying emotion representation model differs from one emotion lexicon to another. For instance, ANEW uses the PAD dimensions, Plutchik's basic categories are used by NRC and Ekman's categories in WordNet-Affect. However, such representations do not provide a sufficient emotion granularity level. There is only one lexicon which incorporates GEW emotion model: the GALC (Scherer, 2005) lexicon. It contains 279 unigram stems (e.g. *happ**) explicitly expressing one of 36 emotion categories (covering all GEW categories). We use therefore this lexicon for benchmarking.

The main differences of our lexicon compared to its predecessors lie in the usage of new fine-grained emotion set, new methods of human computation employed in its construction and specificity to the context of Twitter posts and sport-related emotions.

3 Emotional Labeling and Emotion Feature Elicitation

We created a Human Computation method, using the online labor market (Amazon Mechanical Turk or AMT) to simultaneously accomplish two goals. The first is to have a reliable, human annotation of the emotions within a text corpus. The second is to enable the respondents to provide us with the features needed to construct an emotion lexicon. In this section we describe the processes of data selection, annotation, and refinement, as well as provide the statistical description of the obtained data.

3.1 Data Collection

Our goal is to analyze the emotions of the spectators of Olympic games. We consider the tweets about the Olympics posted during the 2012 Olympic games as a data source for this analysis. We assume that the same emotions are expressed in the same way for all the sports. We thus narrow the scope of our analysis to a single sport – gymnastics.

Traditionally, the gymnastics teams from the USA have strong bid for victory. Thus, we assume that a large group of English-speaking nation may be interested in it. Then, gymnastics is a dynamic type of sport where each moment of performance can play a crucial role in final results, enhancing the emotional experience in audience. Also, it is less common than, for instance, running or swimming, thus the occurrence of this term in tweets, at the time of the Olympics, will more likely signal a reference to the Olympic gymnasts.

We used the hashtag *#gymnastics* (hashtags represent topics in tweets) to obtain the tweets related to the gymnastic competitions during the Olympics time resulting in $199,730$ such tweets. An emotional example is *"Well done #gymnastics we have a SILVER yeayyyyyyyyy!!!! Wohoooo"*.

3.2 Annotation Process

We developed a Human-Intelligence Task (HIT) on the AMT for annotation of a subset of the collected tweets with emotion-related information.

3.2.1 Task description

One HIT consisted of the annotation of one presented tweet. A worker was asked to read a tweet text and to fulfill the following subtasks:

Subtask 1 Decide on the dominant emotion the author of the tweet felt in the moment of its writing (***emotion label***) and how strong it was (***emotion strength***). Even though an emotion mixture could

Iteration		1	2 (B_{en})	2 (B_{all})	3	4	5	4+5
Polarity agreement		78.5	68	33.3	66.7	73.9	75.9	75.7
Emotion agreement		38.5	24.7	13.34	29.3	25.84	29.7	29.3
Average number of emotion	tweet	1.6	1.26	0.64	1.28	1.2	1.72	1.67
indicators per answer[a]	additional	-	0.25	0.36	1.41	1.3	2.05	1.99

Table 1: Basic statistics on the data collected over the annotation iterations.

[a]only among answers where non-neutral emotion label is assigned

be felt, a worker had to choose one emotion that prevailed all others. This kept him focused on one main emotion in the subtasks 2 and 3. To elicit this information we employed the Geneva Emotion Wheel (GEW) described in the Related Work with minor changes: we used 3 strength labels (low, medium and high) instead of 5 in initial version. The set of emotion categories remained unchanged: 20 GEW emotion categories plus 2 additional answer options: *No emotion* and *Other emotion*. We required workers to type the emotion name in latter case.

Subtask 2 In case an emotion was present, a worker was then asked to choose the excerpts of the tweet indicating its presence, the (***tweet emotion indicators***). She was asked to find all the expressions of the chosen emotion present in the tweet text. It could be one word, emoticon, or subsequence of the tweet words. We asked her to also include the words modifying the strength of emotion (e.g. to choose *so excited* instead of *excited*).

Subtask 3 Input ***additional emotion indicators*** of chosen emotion. Similarly to the previous subtask, a worker was asked to input the textual expressions of the chosen emotion. However, in this case the expressions had to be not from the tweet text, but generated based on personal experience. E.g. she could state that she uses *poor thing* to express *Pity*.

3.2.2 HIT Iterations

The design of annotation schema and corresponding instructions as well as search for the optimal HIT parameters took several iterations. Table 1 contains the statistics on inter-annotator agreements and on the number of provided emotion indicators for each iteration. Beside emotion agreement, we also consider polarity agreement. The ***polarity label*** of an answer is defined as the polarity of its emotion label. *No emotion* implies a *Neutral* polarity. For answers with *Other emotion* we manually detected their polarity based on provided emotion name if applicable, or set *Neutral* polarity otherwise.

Iteration 1 Firstly, we annotated 200 tweets (set $\mathcal{S}_1$), using respondents within our laboratory, into a set of 12 emotion categories ($SportEm$) which we considered first to be representative for the emotions incited by sport events: *Love, Pride, Excitement, Positive Surprise, Joy, Like, Other Positive, Anger/Hate, Shame, Anxiety, Shock, Sadness, Dislike, Other Negative*. For each tweet an annotator gave the *emotion label* and chose corresponding *tweet emotion indicators*. The tweets of $\mathcal{S}_1$ included both tweets with predefined emotional words and without. The details of selection process are omitted due to space limitations.

Iteration 2 We launched two batches of HITs on AMT: B_{all} and B_{en}. A HIT batch is defined by a set of tweets to label, with some parameters specific for AMT, such as the number of different workers for each tweet (we used 4 in all our experiments), the payment for one HIT, or specific worker requirements, (e.g. for B_{en} we also required that workers should be from the U.S.). We grouped 25 tweets from $\mathcal{S}_1$ with HIT payment of \$0.05 in B_{en}, whereas for B_{all} we included only 10 tweets with payment of \$0.03. The annotation schema used the emotions of $SportEm$. For each tweet an annotator gave the *emotion label* and provided *tweet* emotion indicators. The field for *additional* emotion indicators input was presented as optional.

We discovered that the answers in B_{all} had an unacceptable quality, with a low agreement and many impossible labels. This can be explained either by lower understanding of English or less reliability of workers from all around the world compared to the U.S. workers. Consequently, all our next iterations had the requirement on workers to be from the U.S.

Iteration 3 We launched a new HIT batch to annotate the full $\mathcal{S}_1$ with emotions from $SportEm$. Starting with this iteration, the payment was set to $\$0.04$. The *additional emotion indicators* field was shown as compulsory. The experiment showed that AMT workers generally followed the instructions achieving emotion agreement only slightly worse than ours.

Iteration 4 We decided to use the more fine-grained and well researched GEW emotion categories. Thus, we launched another HIT batch to annotate $\mathcal{S}_1$ again, in terms of GEW emotion categories (with a schema given in Task Description). Even though a new task contained more answer options emotion agreement stayed in the same range between 0.25 and 0.3.

Iteration 5 We launched a final batch with the described GEW schema to annotate more tweets. We selected Olympics related tweets that had a high likelihood of being emotional. We first selected tweets using the emotion indicators obtained during the previous iterations and found more than 5 times in the collected corpus (418 terms). For each keyword in this list we extracted up to 3 tweets containing this term (1244 tweets). In addition, we added the tweets without keywords from the list, but posted by the users who used these emotional keywords in their other tweets, supposing that these users are more likely to express their emotions. Overall, 1800 tweets were selected, but 13 were excluded because they were not written in English.

The resulting corpus contains the data gathered during the iterations 4 and 5. It consists of 1987 tweets annotated each by 4 workers with emotion label, emotion strength, and related emotion indicators. The Fleiss Kappa (Fleiss, 1971) for emotion labels is 0.24 which is considered to be fair by Landis and Koch (1977), but quite low compared to usual kappa values in other tasks (e.g. polarity annotation usually has Kappa in a range of 0.7–0.8). We conclude that the annotation in terms of multi-category emotions is highly subjective and ambiguous task, confirming our assumptions on existence of emotion mixtures.

3.3 Quality Control

The results of crowdsourcing usually require additional refinement. The workers who give malicious answers intentionally or due to lack of understanding worsen the data quality. We detect such workers automatically using the following 2 criteria:

Average Polarity Conformity A worker's answer has a *polarity conformity* of 1 if at least one worker indicated the same polarity for the same tweet (0 otherwise). A worker's average polarity conformity is computed from all his answers. This criterion aims to detect the workers who repeatedly disagree with other workers.

Dominant Emotion Frequency The dominant emotion of a worker is the one which appears most frequently in his answers. The dominant emotion frequency, among the worker's answers, is the criterion value. This criterion aims to detect workers biased towards specific emotion.

A worker who has the average polarity conformity below a predefined threshold or the dominant emotion frequency above a threshold is considered to have an insufficient quality and all his answers are excluded from the corpus. The threshold for each criterion is computed as a percentile of an approximated normal distribution of workers criterion values for probability limit of 0.01.

To increase the confidence in the computed criteria values, we establish a minimum number of tweets T_{min} any worker should annotate to be subjected to the criteria. To establish this number for each criterion, we use the following algorithm:

Let $X_n(w)$ be the criterion value computed using only first n answers of worker w in order of their submission. For each worker we detect $N_{min}(w)$ – the minimum number of answers after which the criterion value stops varying greatly:

$$|X_n(w) - X_{n-1}(w)| \leq 0.05, \ \forall n \geq N_{min}(w) \quad (1)$$

We then compute T_{min} as the ceiling of the average value of of $N_{min}(w)$ among workers who annotated at least 20 tweets.

The described procedure on detection of bad workers allowed the analysis of 83% of the answers. Using it, we excluded 8 workers, with their corresponding 260 answers.

In addition to removing these workers, we also excluded malicious answers: 736 answers that had a polarity conformity of 0. This additional filter was applied to all the remaining answers from the previous method. We also excluded the 121 answers with

Other emotion and the answers for 12 tweets, that were left with only 1 answer by this stage.

As a result of quality control, there were excluded 14.2% of initial answers. Overall, 1957 tweets with corresponding 6819 annotations remained (3.48 answers per tweet in average). These answers compose the final Sport-Related Emotion Corpus (SREC).

3.4 Emotion distribution in SREC

To provide a glimpse of the data we present the distribution of emotion categories among all answers in the figure 1. The most frequently answered emotion category was *Pride*, followed by *Involvement*. These emotions are natural in the context of sport events, however course-grained emotion models could not distinguish them. It highlights the advantage of fine-grained GEW emotion set to express the subtleties of the domain.

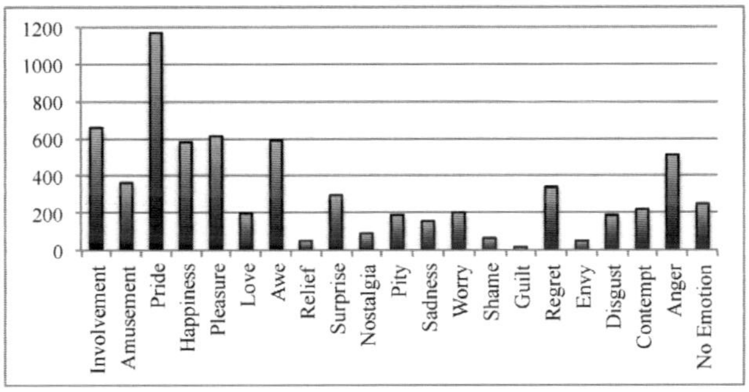

Figure 1: Distribution of emotion labels in worker's answers (after application of quality control)

4 Emotion Recognition Model

The output of our emotion recognition method is the distribution of emotions within a text, in terms of GEW emotion categories. It is represented as a tuple in the probability space

$$\mathbb{P} = \left\{ \bar{p} = (p_1, \ldots, p_{21}),\ \sum_{i=1}^{21} p_i = 1 \right\} \quad (2)$$

where p_i represents the percentage of ith emotion in felt emotion mixture. The emotion set contains 20 GEW categories and *No Emotion* as 21st category.

We use a lexicon of **emotion indicators**, which are words or word sequences indicative of emotion presence. Each indicator $term_t$ has attached emotion distribution tuple $\bar{p}_t \in \mathbb{P}$. To compute the result tuple $\bar{p}$ for a text d we sum up all the tuples of emotion indicators found within this text with the number of times they were found:

$$\bar{p}(d) = \sum_{term_t \in d} n_t(d)\ \bar{p}_t \quad (3)$$

If no indicators are present in the text, a full weight is given to *No emotion* category ($p_{21} = 1$). We also neglect all negated indicators occurrences detected by the negation words (*no, not, *n't, never*) placed ahead of an indicator.

Lexicon Construction We construct the lexicon by selecting the emotion indicators and computing their emotion distributions. We use a training corpus that has a format described in the previous section. The training process consists of the following steps:

Among all *tweet* and *additional* emotion indicators provided by workers, we select those that were suggested more than once.

For each tweet we have several emotion labels from the data. We determine the emotion distribution of the tweet by computing the frequency of each emotion label over all the answers corresponding to that tweet.

For each answer we construct a link between each term suggested in the *additional* emotion indicators field and the answer's emotion label. This link is represented as a tuple $\bar{p} \in \mathbb{P}$ with weight 1 for linked emotion category. Then, for each detected emotion indicator we compute its emotion distribution by averaging all the emotion distributions it appeared in. This includes the emotion distributions of the tweets where this indicator occurred without a negation and the emotion distributions of the corresponding indicator-emotion links.

We define an indicator to be ambiguous if its dominant polarity (polarity having the highest sum of the weights for corresponding emotions) has summary weight smaller than 0.75. All such terms are removed from the result lexicon.

Result Lexicon Description Following the specified process over the full SREC data, we computed an emotion lexicon, *OlympLex*, that contains 3193 terms. The ratio of positive terms to negative ones is 7:3 (term polarity is defined as dominant polarity of term emotion distribution). Unigrams compose 37.5% of the lexicon, bigrams – 30.5%, all other terms are ngrams of a higher order (up to 5).

5 Experimental Evaluation

We evaluated our lexicon on the SREC corpus as a classifier, using ten-fold cross-validation to avoid possible overfitting. The precompiled universal lexicons were used for benchmarking. As no training is required, we tested them over the full data.

5.1 Polarity Classification

We considered the basic polarity classification task with 3 classes (*Positive*, *Negative* and *Neutral*). We used only 1826 tweets that have one dominant polarity based on workers' answers. This dominant polarity was taken as a true polarity label of a tweet.

The output polarity label of our classifier is dominant polarity of found emotion distribution: a polarity having the highest sum of the weights for corresponding emotions. The output of prior sentiment lexicons is computed analogously: we sum up the number of found lexicon terms in the tweet text for each emotion or polarity category (depending on which categorization is provided by the lexicon) and output the polarity having the highest sum value. If two polarities have the same sum weight, the output polarity is *Neutral*.

We used standard classification evaluation measures: accuracy, precision, recall and F1-score. We considered only non-neutral classes (*Positive* and *Negative*) for precision and recall. Table 2 shows the results of our classifier, compared with other known sentiment lexicons. The proposed lexicon outperforms every other one, both in terms of accuracy and F1-score. As it was the only lexicon fitted to the Olympic gymnastics data, its superiority reveals the advantage of domain-targeted lexicon construction.

Lexicon	P	R	F1	A
*OlympLex**	**81.7**	**73.2**	**77.2**	**72.5**
BingLiu	80.4	52.9	63.8	53.6
OpinionFinder	66.0	46.6	54.6	46.6
GeneralInquirer	69.8	44.4	54.3	44.5
NRC*	60.6	39.7	48.0	40.4
WnAffect*	78.6	28.1	41.4	30.1
GALC*	81.6	25.6	39.0	27.9

Table 2: The results of polarity classification evaluation. P=precision, R=recall, F1 = F1-score, A=accuracy
*A lexicon employing several emotion categories

5.2 Emotion Classification

We evaluated emotion recognition results in the setting of a multi-label classification problem. The output is a set of labels instead of a standard single label answer. In this case, the output of the classifier (O_C) was defined as a set of dominant emotions in the found emotion distribution $\bar{p}$. This set contained the emotions having the highest weights p_i. The set of emotion labels given for this tweet by workers formed a true output – a set of true labels (O_T) of emotion classification. As a baseline for multi-category emotion classification we considered the GALC lexicon (Scherer, 2005).

Multi-label Evaluation We used the standard evaluation metrics adapted for multi-label output (Tsoumakas and Katakis, 2007). For each tweet, we first computed the precision $P = \frac{|O_C \cap O_T|}{|O_C|}$, which shows how many of emotions outputted by the classifier were correct. Then the recall $R = \frac{|O_C \cap O_T|}{|O_T|}$, which shows how many of true labels were found by classifier, and the accuracy $A = \frac{|O_C \cap O_T|}{|O_C \cup O_T|}$, which shows how close the sets of classifier and true labels were. These values were averaged among all applicable tweets. For precision and recall we used only the tweets with non-neutral answers in O_C and O_T correspondingly (meaning that *No emotion* label was not present in a set).

Table 3 shows the comparative results of our and GALC lexicons. Compared to the GALC baseline, our classifier has both higher precision and recall. Higher recall is explained by the fact that our lexicon is larger and contains also ngram terms. In addition, it includes not only explicit emotion expressions (e.g. *sad* or *proud*), but also implicit ones (e.g. *yes* or *mistakes*).

Per-Category Evaluation Another way to evaluate the output of multi-label classifier is to evaluate it for each emotion category separately. For each category we computed precision, recall and F1-score.

Lexicon	P	R	F1	A
GALC	49.0	10.2	16.8	12.5
OlympLex	**53.5**	**24.9**	**34.0**	**25.4**

Table 3: Results of multi-label evaluation. P=precision, R=recall, F1 = F1-score, A=accuracy

	GALC			*OlympLex*				GALC			*OlympLex*		
Negative	P	R	F1	P	R	F1	Positive	P	R	F1	P	R	F1
Anger	48.4	10.8	17.7	53.3	26	**35**	Involvement	52.4	2.4	4.6	49.4	17.6	**26**
Contempt	-	0	-	42.1	4.7	**8.5**	Amusement	51	11.6	18.9	55	24.6	**34**
Disgust	50	1.4	2.8	39.4	9.4	**15.2**	Pride	89.6	6.7	12.5	60.8	59.4	**60.1**
Envy	100	11.1	20	55.6	13.9	**22.2**	Happiness	46.3	8.8	14.8	45.1	9.8	**16.1**
Regret	53.3	3.4	6.4	36.3	12.4	**18.5**	Pleasure	44.8	5.9	10.4	48.8	17.9	**26.2**
Guilt	25	5.6	**9.1**	0	0	-	Love	38.1	27.4	**31.9**	48.0	8.2	14
Shame	18.5	9.8	**12.8**	25	3.9	6.8	Awe	42.9	6.7	11.5	54.2	23.7	**33**
Worry	54.8	21.5	**30.9**	43.2	15	22.2	Relief	100	17.1	**29.2**	50	4.9	8.9
Sadness	52.5	19.6	**28.6**	41.7	9.3	15.3	Surprise	38.3	9	**14.6**	33.3	6	10.2
Pity	75	2.5	4.9	57.8	31.4	**40.7**	Nostalgia	20.5	14.5	**17**	28.6	3.2	5.8

Table 4: Evaluation results at per-category level. P=precision, R=recall, F1 = F1-score

The results of this evaluation in comparison with benchmark GALC lexicon are presented in the table 4. Overall, our lexicon performs better on most of the categories (12 out of 20) in terms of F1-score. The highest F1-score is achieved for such Olympic related emotion as *Pride*.

5.3 Discussion

The fact that the terms from the GALC lexicon are found in 31% of tweets indicates that people do express their emotions explicitly with emotional terms. However, a list of currently available explicit emotional terms is not extensive. For instance, it does not cover slang terms. Moreover, people do not limit themselves to only explicit emotional terms. Our lexicon constructed based on the answers provided by non-expert humans achieves a significantly higher recall. This highlights the importance of employing the human common knowledge in the process of extraction of emotion bearing features.

6 Conclusion

We presented a context-aware human computation method for emotion labeling and feature extraction. We showed that inexpert annotators, using their common sense, can successfully attach emotion labels to tweets, and also extract relevant emotional features. Using their answers, we carefully constructed a linguistic resource for emotion classification. The suggested method can be reused to construct additional lexicons for different domains.

An important aspect that differentiates our work is the emotion granularity. To the best of our knowledge, this was the first attempt to create lexical resources for emotion classification based on the Geneva Emotion Wheel (GEW), which has as many as 20 emotion categories. This level of granularity enabled us to capture the subtleties of the emotional responses in the target domain, tweets regarding the 2012 summer Olympics in London. In this dataset, we found that the prevalent emotion is *Pride*, a detail which is unattainable using previous methods.

Another differentiator is that, unlike most previous approaches, we relied on human computation for both labeling and feature extraction tasks. We showed that human generated features can be successfully used in emotional classification, outperforming various existing methods. A further difference from prior lexicons is the fact that ours was built with a context-sensitive method. This led to a higher accuracy on the target domain, compared to the general purpose lexicon.

We benchmarked the cross-validated version of created *OlympLex* lexicon with the existing universal-domain lexicons for both polarity and multi-emotion problems. In suggested settings we showed that it can outperform general purpose lexicons in the binary classification due to its domain specificity. We also obtained significant improvements over the baseline GALC lexicon, which was the only preexisting one compatible with the GEW.

However, high domain specificity of the created lexicon and restricted variety of data used in its construction implies possible limitations of its usage for other types of data. Its porting and generalization to other domains is one of the future directions.

References

Cecilia Ovesdotter Alm, Dan Roth, and Richard Sproat. 2005. Emotions from text: machine learning for text-based emotion prediction. In *Proceedings of the conference on Human Language Technology and Empirical Methods in Natural Language Processing*, pages 579–586. Association for Computational Linguistics.

Saima Aman and Stan Szpakowicz. 2007. Identifying expressions of emotion in text. In *Text, Speech and Dialogue*, pages 196–205. Springer.

Margaret M Bradley and Peter J Lang. 1999. Affective norms for english words (anew): Instruction manual and affective ratings. Technical report, Technical Report C-1, The Center for Research in Psychophysiology, University of Florida.

Taner Danisman and Adil Alpkocak. 2008. Feeler: Emotion classification of text using vector space model. In *AISB 2008 Convention Communication, Interaction and Social Intelligence*, volume 1, page 53.

Paul Ekman. 1992. An argument for basic emotions. *Cognition & Emotion*, 6(3-4):169–200.

Joseph L Fleiss. 1971. Measuring nominal scale agreement among many raters. *Psychological bulletin*, 76(5):378.

Minqing Hu and Bing Liu. 2004. Mining and summarizing customer reviews. In *Proceedings of the tenth ACM SIGKDD international conference on Knowledge discovery and data mining*, pages 168–177. ACM.

Sunghwan Mac Kim, Alessandro Valitutti, and Rafael A Calvo. 2010. Evaluation of unsupervised emotion models to textual affect recognition. In *Proceedings of the NAACL HLT 2010 Workshop on Computational Approaches to Analysis and Generation of Emotion in Text*, pages 62–70. Association for Computational Linguistics.

J Richard Landis and Gary G Koch. 1977. The measurement of observer agreement for categorical data. *Biometrics*, pages 159–174.

Hugo Liu, Henry Lieberman, and Ted Selker. 2003. A model of textual affect sensing using real-world knowledge. In *Proceedings of the 8th international conference on Intelligent user interfaces*, pages 125–132. ACM.

Albert Mehrabian. 1996. Pleasure-arousal-dominance: A general framework for describing and measuring individual differences in temperament. *Current Psychology*, 14(4):261–292.

Saif M Mohammad and Peter D Turney. 2010. Emotions evoked by common words and phrases: Using mechanical turk to create an emotion lexicon. In *Proceedings of the NAACL HLT 2010 Workshop on Computational Approaches to Analysis and Generation of Emotion in Text*, pages 26–34.

Saif M Mohammad and Peter D Turney. 2012. Crowdsourcing a word–emotion association lexicon. *Computational Intelligence*.

Saif M Mohammad. 2012. # emotional tweets. In *Proceedings of the First Joint Conference on Lexical and Computational Semantics-Volume 1: Proceedings of the main conference and the shared task, and Volume 2: Proceedings of the Sixth International Workshop on Semantic Evaluation*, pages 246–255. Association for Computational Linguistics.

Alena Neviarouskaya, Helmut Prendinger, and Mitsuru Ishizuka. 2011. Affect analysis model: Novel rule-based approach to affect sensing from text. *Natural Language Engineering*, 17(1):95.

Robert Plutchik. 1980. A general psychoevolutionary theory of emotion. *Emotion: Theory, research, and experience*, 1(3):3–33.

Klaus R Scherer. 2005. What are emotions? and how can they be measured? *Social science information*, 44(4):695–729.

Rion Snow, Brendan O'Connor, Daniel Jurafsky, and Andrew Y Ng. 2008. Cheap and fast—but is it good?: evaluating non-expert annotations for natural language tasks. In *Proceedings of the Conference on Empirical Methods in Natural Language Processing*, pages 254–263. Association for Computational Linguistics.

Phil J Stone, Dexter C Dunphy, Marshall S Smith, and DM Ogilvie. 1968. The general inquirer: A computer approach to content analysis. *Journal of Regional Science*, 8(1).

Carlo Strapparava and Alessandro Valitutti. 2004. Wordnet-affect: an affective extension of wordnet. In *Proceedings of LREC*, volume 4, pages 1083–1086.

Grigorios Tsoumakas and Ioannis Katakis. 2007. Multi-label classification: An overview. *International Journal of Data Warehousing and Mining (IJDWM)*, 3(3):1–13.

Theresa Wilson, Janyce Wiebe, and Paul Hoffmann. 2009. Recognizing contextual polarity: An exploration of features for phrase-level sentiment analysis. *Computational linguistics*, 35(3):399–433.

Spanish DAL: A Spanish Dictionary of Affect in Language

Matías G. Dell' Amerlina Ríos and **Agustín Gravano**
Departamento de Computación, FCEyN
Universidad de Buenos Aires, Argentina
{mamerlin,gravano}@dc.uba.ar

Abstract

The topic of sentiment analysis in text has been extensively studied in English for the past 30 years. An early, influential work by Cynthia Whissell, the Dictionary of Affect in Language (DAL), allows rating words along three dimensions: pleasantness, activation and imagery. Given the lack of such tools in Spanish, we decided to replicate Whissell's work in that language. This paper describes the Spanish DAL, a knowledge base formed by more than 2500 words manually rated by humans along the same three dimensions. We evaluated its usefulness on two sentiment analysis tasks, which showed that the knowledge base managed to capture relevant information regarding the three affective dimensions.

1 Introduction

In an attempt to quantify emotional meaning in written language, Whissell developed the Dictionary of Affect in Language (DAL), a tool for rating words and texts in English along three dimensions – pleasantness, activation and imagery (Whissell et al., 1986; Whissell, 1989, inter alia). DAL works by looking up individual words in a knowledge base containing 8742 words. All words in this lexicon were originally rated by 200 naïve volunteers along the same three dimensions.

Whissell's DAL has subsequently been used in diverse research fields, for example as a keystone for sentiment analysis in written text (Yi et al., 2003, e.g.) and emotion recognition in spoken language (Cowie et al., 2001). DAL has also been used to aid the selection of emotionally balanced word stimuli for Neuroscience and Psycholinguistics experiments (Gray et al., 2002). Given the widespread impact of DAL for the English language, it would be desirable to create similar lexicons for other languages.

In recent years, there have been efforts to build cross-lingual resources, such as using sentiment analysis tools in English to score Spanish texts after performing machine translation (Brooke et al., 2009) or to automatically derive sentiment lexicons in Spanish (Pérez-Rosas et al., 2012). The purpose of the present work is to create a manually annotated lexicon for the Spanish language, replicating Whissell's DAL, aiming at alleviating the scarcity of resources for the Spanish language, and at determining if the lexicon-based approach would work in Spanish as well as it does in English. We leave for future work the comparison of the different approaches mentioned here. This paper describes the three steps performed to accomplish that goal: i) creating a knowledge base which is likely to have a good word coverage on arbitrary texts from any topic and genre (Section 2); ii) having a number of volunteers annotate each word for the three affective dimensions under study (Section 3); and iii) evaluating the usefulness of our knowledge base on simple tasks (Section 4).

2 Word selection

The first step in building a Spanish DAL consists in selecting a list of content words that is representative of the Spanish language, in the sense that it will have a good coverage of the words in arbitrary input texts from potentially any topic or genre. To accomplish this we decided to use texts downloaded from *Wikipedia* in Spanish[1] and from an online collection of short stories called *Los Cuentos*.[2] Articles from *Wikipedia* cover a wide range of topics and are gen-

[1] http://es.wikipedia.org

[2] http://www.loscuentos.net

erally written in encyclopedia style. We downloaded the complete set of articles in March, 2012, consisting of 834,460 articles in total. Short stories from *Los Cuentos* were written by hundreds of different authors, both popular and amateur, on various genres, including tales, essays and poems. We downloaded the complete collection from *Los Cuentos* in April, 2012, consisting of 216,060 short stories.

2.1 Filtering and lemmatizing words

We extracted all words from these texts, sorted them by frequency, and filtered out several word classes that we considered convey no affect by themselves (and thus it would be unnecessary to have them rated by the volunteers). Prepositions, determinants, possessives, interjections, conjunctions, numbers, dates and hours were tagged and removed automatically using the morphological analysis function included in the *Freeling* toolkit (Padró et al., 2010).[3] We also excluded the following adverb subclasses for the same reason: place, time, mode, doubt (e.g., *quizás*, maybe), negation, affirmation and amount.

Nouns and verbs were lemmatized using *Freeling* as well, except for augmentative and diminutive terminations, which were left intact due to their potential effect on a word's meaning and/or affect (e.g., *burrito* is either a small donkey, *burro*, or a type of Mexican food). Additionally, proper nouns were excluded. Names of cities, regions, countries and nationalities were marked and removed using *GeoWorldMap*,[4] a freely-available list of location names from around the world. Names of people were also filtered out. Proper names were manually inspected to avoid removing those with a lexical meaning, a common phenomenon in Spanish (e.g., *Victoria*). Other manually removed words include words in foreign languages (mainly in English), roman numbers (e.g., *XIX*) and numbers in textual form, such as *seis* (six), *sexto* (sixth), etc. Words with one or two characters were removed automatically, since we noticed that they practically always corresponded to noise in the downloaded texts.

2.2 Counting ⟨word, word-class⟩ pairs

We implemented a small refinement over Whissell's work, which consisted in considering ⟨word, word-class⟩ pairs, rather than single words, since in Spanish the same lexical form may have different senses. Thus, to each word (in its lemmatized form) we attached one of four possible word classes – noun, verb, adjective or adverb. For example, *bajo*$_{\text{prep}}$ (under) or *bajo*$_{\text{noun}}$ (bass guitar).

For each input word w, *Freeling*'s morphological analysis returns a sequence of tuples ⟨*lemma*, *POS-tag*, *probability*⟩, which correspond to the possible lemmas and part-of-speech tags for w, together with their prior probability. For example, the analysis for the word *bajo* returns four tuples: ⟨*bajo*, SPS00 (i.e, preposition), 0.879⟩, ⟨*bajo*, AQ0MS0 (adjective), 0.077⟩, ⟨*bajo*, NCMS000 (noun), 0.040⟩, and ⟨*bajar*, VMIP1S0 (verb), 0.004⟩. This means that *bajo*, considered without context, has 87.9% chances of being a noun, or 0.04% of being a verb.

Using this information, we computed the counts of all ⟨word, word-class⟩ pairs, taking into account their prior probabilities. For example, assuming the word *bajo* appeared 1000 times in the texts, it would contribute with $1000 * 0.879 = 879$ to the frequency of *bajo*$_{\text{prep}}$ (i.e., *bajo* as a preposition), 77 to *bajo*$_{\text{adj}}$, 40 to *bajo*$_{\text{noun}}$, and 4 to *bajar*$_{\text{verb}}$.

2.3 Merging *Wikipedia* and *Los Cuentos*

This process yielded 163,071 ⟨word, word-class⟩ pairs from the *Wikipedia* texts, and 30,544 from *Los Cuentos*. To improve readability, hereafter we will refer to ⟨word, word-class⟩ pairs simply as *words*. Figure 1 shows the frequency of each word count in our two corpora. We note that both graphics are practically identical, with a majority of low-count words and a long tail with few high-count words.

To create our final word list to be rated by volunteers, we needed to merge our two corpora from *Wikipedia* and *Los Cuentos*. To accomplish this, we

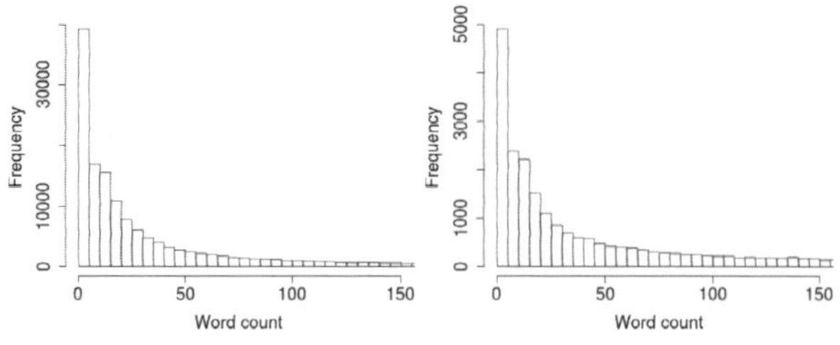

Figure 1: Frequency of word counts in texts taken from *Wikipedia* and *Los Cuentos*.

[3]http://nlp.lsi.upc.edu/freeling/

[4]http://www.geobytes.com/FreeServices.htm

normalized all word counts for corpus size (*normalized_count*(w) = *count*(w) / *corpus_size*), combined both lists and sorted the resulting list by the normalized word count (for the words that appeared in both lists, we used its average count instead). The resulting list contained 175,413 words in total.

The top 10 words from *Wikipedia* were *más*$_{\text{adv}}$, *año*$_{\text{noun}}$, *ciudad*$_{\text{noun}}$, *población*$_{\text{noun}}$, *estado*$_{\text{noun}}$, *nombre*$_{\text{noun}}$, *vez*$_{\text{noun}}$, *municipio*$_{\text{noun}}$, *grupo*$_{\text{noun}}$ and *historia*$_{\text{noun}}$ (*more, year, city, population, state, name, time*, as in 'first time', *municipality, group* and *history*, respectively). The 10 words most common from *Los Cuentos* were *más*$_{\text{adv}}$, *vez*$_{\text{noun}}$, *vida*$_{\text{noun}}$, *día*$_{\text{noun}}$, *tan*$_{\text{adv}}$, *tiempo*$_{\text{noun}}$, *ojo*$_{\text{noun}}$, *mano*$_{\text{noun}}$, *amor*$_{\text{noun}}$ and *noche*$_{\text{noun}}$ (*more, time, life, day, so, time, eye, hand, love* and *night*).

2.4 Assessing word coverage

Next we studied the coverage of the top k words from our list on texts from a third corpus formed by 3603 news stories downloaded from *Wikinews* in Spanish in April, 2012.[5] We chose news stories for this task because we wanted a different genre for studying the evolution of coverage.

Formally, let L be a word list, T any text, and $W(T)$ the set of words occurring at least once in T. We define the *coverage* of L on T as the percentage of words in $W(T)$ that appear in L. Figure 2 shows the evolution of the mean coverage on *Wikinews* articles of the top k words from our word list. In this figure we can observe that the mean coverage grows rapidly, until it reaches a plateau at around 80%. This suggests that even a low number of words may achieve a relatively high coverage on new texts. The 20% that remains uncovered, independently of the size of the word list, may be explained by the function words and proper names that were removed from our word list. Note that news articles normally contain many proper names, days, places and other words that we intentionally discarded.

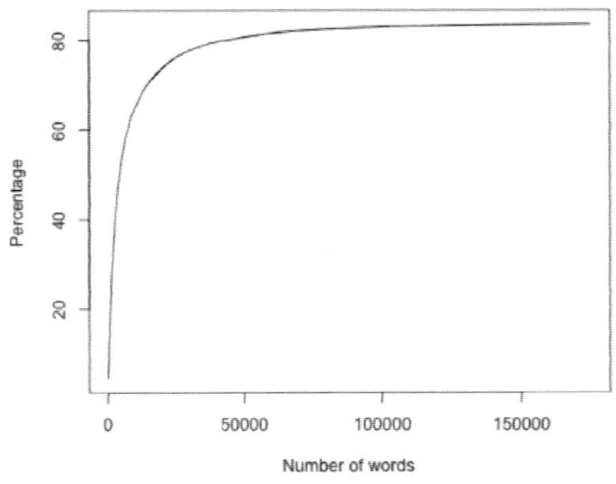

Figure 2: Mean coverage of the top k words from our list on *Wikinews* articles.

[5]http://es.wikinews.org

3 Word rating

After selecting the words, the next step consisted in having them rated by a group of volunteers. For this purpose we created a web interface, so that volunteers could complete this task remotely.

3.1 Web interface

On the first page of the web interface, volunteers were asked to enter their month and year of birth, their education level and their native language, and was asked to complete a reCAPTCHA[6] to avoid bots. Subsequently, volunteers were taken to a page with instructions for the rating task. They were asked to rate each word along the three dimensions shown in Table 1. These are the same three dimensions used in Whissell's work. Importantly, these concepts were not defined, to avoid biasing the judgments. Volunteers were also encouraged to follow their first impression, and told that there were no 'correct' answers. Appendix A shows the actual login and instructions pages used in the study.

	Pleasantness	**Activation**	**Imagery**
1	*Desagradable* (Unpleasant)	*Pasivo* (Passive)	*Difícil de imaginar* (Hard to imagine)
2	*Ni agradable ni desagradable* (In between)	*Ni activo ni pasivo* (In between)	*Ni difícil ni fácil de imaginar* (In between)
3	*Agradable* (Pleasant)	*Activo* (Active)	*Fácil de imaginar* (Easy to imagine)

Table 1: Possible values for each of the three dimensions.

After reading the instructions, volunteers proceeded to judge two practice words, intended to help them get used to the task and the interface, followed by 20 target words. Words were presented one per page. Figure 3 shows a screenshot of the page for rating the word *navegar*$_{\text{verb}}$. Note that the word class

[6]http://www.recaptcha.net

Figure 3: Screenshot of the web page for rating a word.

(verb in this example) is indicated right below the word. After completing the first batch of 20 words, volunteers were asked if they wanted to finish the study or do a second batch, and then a third, a fourth, and so on. This way, they were given the chance to do as many words as they felt comfortable with. If a volunteer left before completing a batch, his/her ratings so far were also recorded.

3.2 Volunteers

662 volunteers participated in the study, with a mean age of 33.3 (SD = 11.2). As to their level of education, 76% had completed a university degree, 23% had finished only secondary school, and 1% had completed only primary school. Only volunteers whose native language was Spanish were allowed to participate in the study. Each volunteer was assigned 20 words following this procedure: (1) The 175,413 words in the corpus were sorted by word count. (2) Words that had already received 5 or more ratings were excluded. (3) Words that had already been rated by a volunteer with the same month and year of birth were excluded, to prevent the same volunteer from rating twice the same word. (4) The top 20 words were selected.

Each volunteer rated 52.3 words on average (SD = 34.0). Roughly 30% completed 20 words or fewer; 24% completed 21-40 words; 18%, 41-60 words; and the remaining 28%, more than 60 words.

3.3 Descriptive statistics

A total of 2566 words were rated by at least 5 volunteers. Words with fewer annotations were excluded from the study. We assigned each rating a numeric value from 1 to 3, as shown in Table 1. Table 2 shows some basic statistics for each of the three dimensions.

	Mean	SD	Skewness	Kurtosis
Pleasantness	2.23	0.47	−0.47	−0.06
Activation	2.33	0.48	−0.28	−0.84
Imagery	2.55	0.42	−0.90	0.18

Table 2: Descriptive statistics for the three dimensions.

The five **most pleasant** words, according to the volunteers, were *jugar*$_{\text{verb}}$, *beso*$_{\text{noun}}$, *sonrisa*$_{\text{noun}}$, *compañía*$_{\text{noun}}$ and *reir*$_{\text{verb}}$ (*play, kiss, smile, company* and *laugh*, respectively). The **least pleasant** ones were *asesinato*$_{\text{noun}}$, *caro*$_{\text{adj}}$, *ahogar*$_{\text{verb}}$, *herida*$_{\text{noun}}$ and *cigarro*$_{\text{noun}}$ (*murder, expensive, drown, wound* and *cigar*).

Among the **most active** words appear *idea*$_{\text{noun}}$, *publicar*$_{\text{verb}}$, *violento*$_{\text{adj}}$, *sexual*$_{\text{adj}}$ and *talento*$_{\text{noun}}$ (*idea, publish, violent, sexual* and *talent*). Among the **least active**, we found *yacer*$_{\text{verb}}$, *espiritual*$_{\text{adj}}$, *quieto*$_{\text{adj}}$, *esperar*$_{\text{verb}}$ and *cadáver*$_{\text{adj}}$ (*lay, spiritual, still, wait* and *corpse*).

The **easiest to imagine** include *sucio*$_{\text{adj}}$, *silencio*$_{\text{noun}}$, *dar*$_{\text{verb}}$, *pez*$_{\text{noun}}$ and *pensar*$_{\text{verb}}$ (*dirty, silence, give, fish* and *think*). Finally, the **hardest to imagine** include *consistir*$_{\text{verb}}$, *constar*$_{\text{verb}}$, *morfología*$_{\text{noun}}$, *piedad*$_{\text{noun}}$ and *tendencia*$_{\text{noun}}$ (*consist, consist, morphology, compassion* and *tendency*).

We conducted Pearson's correlation tests between the different dimensions. Table 3 shows the correlation matrix. Correlations among rating dimensions were very weak, which supports the assumption that pleasantness, activation and imagery are three independent affective dimensions. These numbers are very similar to the ones reported in Whissell's work.

	Pleasantness	Activation	Imagery
Pleasantness	1.00	0.14	0.10
Activation	0.14	1.00	0.11
Imagery	0.10	0.11	1.00

Table 3: Correlation between the different dimensions

Next, we computed Cohen's κ to measure the degree of agreement above chance between volunteers (Cohen, 1968).[7] Given that we used a three-point scale for rating each affective dimension, we used

[7] This measure of agreement above chance is interpreted as follows: 0 = None, 0 - 0.2 = Small, 0.2 - 0.4 = Fair, 0.4 - 0.6 = Moderate, 0.6 - 0.8 = Substantial, 0.8 - 1 = Almost perfect.

a weighted version of κ, thus taking into account the distance on that scale between disagreements. For example, the distance between *pleasant* and *unpleasant* was 2, and the distance between *pleasant* and *in-between* was 1. We obtained a weighted κ measure of 0.42 for pleasantness, 0.30 for activation, and 0.14 for imagery. Considering that these were highly subjective rating tasks, the agreement levels for pleasantness and activation were quite high. The imagery task seemed somewhat more difficult, although we still observed some agreement above chance. These results indicate that our knowledge base managed to, at least partially, capture information regarding the three affective dimensions.

4 Evaluation

Next we proceeded to evaluate the usefulness of our knowledge base. For this purpose, we developed a simple system for estimating affect along our three affective dimensions, and evaluated it on two different sentiment-analysis tasks. The first task consisted in a set of texts labeled by humans, and served to compare the judgments of human labelers with the predictions of our system. The second task consisted in classifying a set of user product reviews into 'positive' or 'negative' opinions, a common application for online stores.

4.1 Simple system for estimating affect

We created a simple computer program for automatically estimating the degree of pleasantness, activation and imagery of an input text, based on the knowledge base described in the previous sections.

For each word in the knowledge base, we calculated its mean rating for each dimension. Subsequently, for an input text T we used *Freeling* to generate a full syntactic parsing, from which we extracted all $\langle$word, word-class$\rangle$ pairs in T. The system calculates the value for affective dimension d using the following procedure:

$score \leftarrow 0$
$count \leftarrow 0$
for each word w in T (counting repetitions):
  if w is included in KB:
    $score \leftarrow score + KB_d(w)$
    $count \leftarrow count + 1$
return $score/count$

where KB is our knowledge base, and $KB_d(w)$ is the value for w in KB for dimension d.

For example, given the sentence *"Mi amiga esperaba terminar las pruebas a tiempo"* (*"My female-friend was hoping to finish the tests on time"*), and assuming our knowledge base contains the numbers shown in Table 4, the three values are computed as follows. First, all words are lemmatized (i.e., *mi amigo esperar terminar el prueba a tiempo*). Second, the mean of each dimension is calculated with the described procedure, yielding a pleasantness of 2.17, activation of 2.27 and imagery of 2.53.

word	word-class	mean P	mean A	mean I
amigo	noun	3.0	2.4	3
esperar	verb	1.2	1	2.8
poder	verb	2.8	2.8	2.2
terminar	verb	2.2	3	2.8
prueba	noun	1.8	2.4	2.2
tiempo	noun	2	2	2.2
	mean:	2.17	2.27	2.53

Table 4: Knowledge base for the example text (P = pleasantness; A = activation; I = imagery).

It is important to mention that this system is just a proof of concept, motivated by the need to evaluate the effectiveness of our knowledge base. It could be used as a baseline system against which to compare more complex affect estimation systems. Also, if results are good enough with such a simple system, this would indicate that the information contained in the knowledge base is useful, and in the future it could help create more complex systems.

4.2 Evaluation #1: Emotion estimation

The first evaluation task consisted in comparing predictions made by our simple system against ratings assigned by humans (our gold standard), on a number of sentences and paragraphs extracted from *Wikipedia* and *Los Cuentos*.

4.2.1 Gold standard

From each corpus we randomly selected 15 sentences with 10 or more words, and 5 paragraphs with at least 50 words and two sentences – i.e. 30 sentences and 10 paragraphs in total. These texts were subsequently rated by 5 volunteers (2 male, 3 female), who were instructed to rate each entire text (sentence or paragraph) for pleasantness, activation and imagery using the same three-point scale shown in Table 1. The weighted κ measure for these ratings was 0.17 for pleasantness, 0.17 for activation and 0.22 for imagery. Consistent with the subjectivity of these tasks, the degree of inter-labeler agreement was rather low, yet still above chance level. Note also that for pleasantness and activation the agreement level was lower for texts than for individual words, while the opposite was true for imagery.

4.2.2 Results

To evaluate the performance of our system, we conducted Pearson's correlation test for each affective dimension, in order to find the degree of correlation between the system's predictions for the 40 texts and their corresponding mean human ratings. Table 5 shows the resulting ρ coefficients.

System \ GS	Pleasantness	Activation	Imagery
Pleasantness	0.59 *	0.15 *	−0.18 *
Activation	0.13 *	0.40 *	0.14 *
Imagery	0.16	0.19	0.07

Table 5: Correlations between gold standard and system's predictions. Statistically significant results are marked with '*' (t-tests, $p < 0.05$).

The coefficient for pleasantness presented a high value at 0.59, which indicates that the system's estimation of pleasantness was rather similar to the ratings given by humans. For activation the correlation was weaker, although still significant. On the other hand, for imagery this simple system did not seem able to successfully emulate human judgments.

These results suggest that, at least for pleasantness and activation, our knowledge base successfully captured useful information regarding how humans perceive those affective dimensions. For imagery, it is not clear whether the information base did not capture useful information, or the estimation system was too simplistic.

4.2.3 Effect of word count on performance

Next we studied the evolution of performance as a function of the knowledge base size, aiming at assessing the potential impact of increasing the number of words annotated by humans. Figure 4 summarizes the results of a simulation, in which successive systems were built and evaluated using the top 250, 350, 450, ..., 2350, 2450 and 2566 words in our knowledge base.

The green line (triangles) represents the mean coverage of the system's knowledge base on the gold standard texts; the corresponding scale is shown on the right axis. Similarly to Figure 2, the coverage grew rapidly, starting at 18% when using 250 words to 44% when using all 2566 words.

The blue (circles), red (squares) and purple (diamonds) lines correspond to the correlations of the system's predictions and the gold standard ratings for pleasantness, activation and imagery, respectively; the corresponding scale is shown on the left axis. The black lines are a logarithmic function fit to each of the three curves ($\rho^2 = 0.90$, 0.72 and 0.68, respectively).

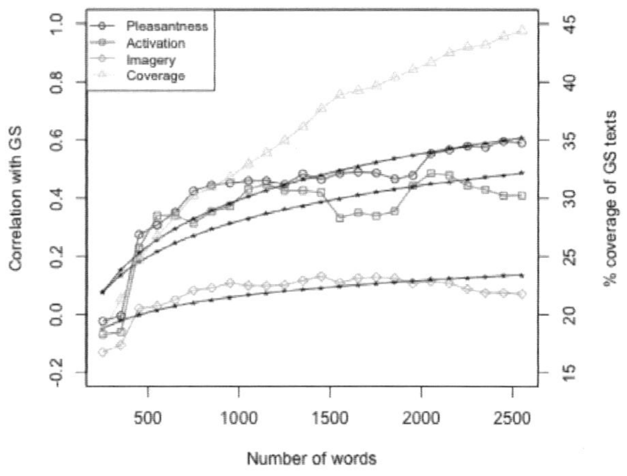

Figure 4: Evolution of the correlation between system predictions and Gold Standard, with respect to the knowledge base size.

These results indicate that the system performance (measured as the correlation with human judgments) grew logarithmically with the number of words in the knowledge base. Interestingly, the performance grew at a slower pace than word coverage. In other words, an increase in the proportion of words in a text that were known by the system did not lead to a similar increase in the accuracy of the predictions. An explanation may be that, once an emotion had been established based on a percentage of words in the text, the addition of a few extra words did not significantly change the outcome.

In consequence, if we wanted to do a substantial improvement to our baseline system, it would probably not be a good idea to simply annotate more words. Instead, it may be more effective to work on *how* the system uses the information contained in the knowledge base.

4.3 Evaluation #2: Classification of reviews

The second evaluation task consisted in using our baseline system for classifying user product reviews into positive or negative opinions.

4.3.1 Corpus

For this task we used a corpus of 400 user reviews of products such as cars, hotels, dishwashers, books, cellphones, music, computers and movies, extracted from the Spanish website *Ciao.es*.[8] This is the same corpus used by Brooke (2009), who employed sentiment analysis tools in English to score Spanish texts after performing machine translation.

On *Ciao.es*, users may enter their written reviews and associate a numeric score to them, ranging from 1 to 5 stars. For this evaluation task, we made the assumption that there was a strong relation between the written reviews and their corresponding numeric scores. Following this assumption, we tagged reviews with 1 or 2 stars as 'negative' opinions, and reviews with 4 or 5 stars as 'positive'. Reviews with 3 stars were considered neutral, and ignored.

4.3.2 Results

We used our system in a very simple way for predicting the polarity of opinions. First we computed M, the mean pleasantness score on 80% of the reviews. Subsequently, for each review in the remaining 20%, if its pleasantness score was greater than M, then it was classified as 'positive'; otherwise, it was classified as 'negative'.

After repeating this procedure five times using 5-fold cross validation, the overall accuracy was 62.33%. Figure 5 shows the evolution of the system's accuracy with respect to the number of words in the knowledge base. The green line (triangles) represents the mean coverage of the system's knowledge base on user review texts; the corresponding scale is shown on the right axis. The blue line (circles) corresponds to the classification accuracy; the corresponding scale is shown on the left axis. The black line is a logarithmic function fit to this curve ($\rho^2 = 0.80$).

[8] http://ciao.es

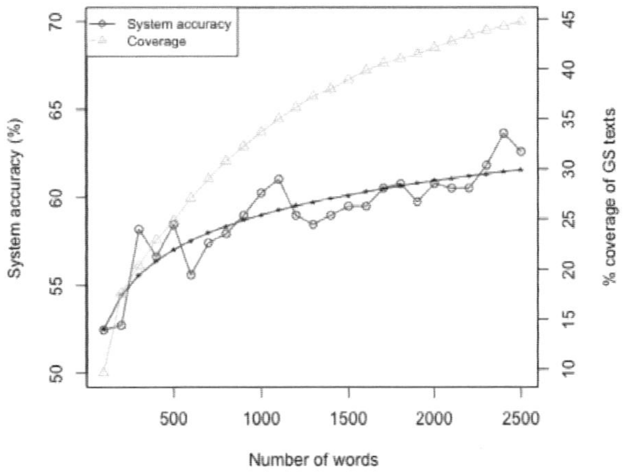

Figure 5: Evolution of the classification accuracy with respect to the size of the knowledge base.

Notably, with as few as 500 words the accuracy is already significantly above chance level, which is 50% for this task. This indicates that our knowledge base managed to capture information on pleasantness that may aid the automatic classification of positive and negative user reviews.

Also, similarly to our first evaluation task, we observe that the accuracy increased as more words were added to the knowledge base. However, it did so at a logarithmic pace slower than the growth of the word coverage on the user reviews. This suggests that adding more words labeled by humans to the knowledge base would only have a limited impact on the performance of this simple system.

5 Conclusion

In this work we presented a knowledge base of Spanish words labeled by human volunteers for three affective dimensions – pleasantness, activation and imagery, inspired by the English DAL created by Whissell (1986; 1989). The annotations of these three dimensions were weakly intercorrelated, indicating a high level of independence of each other. Additionally, the agreement between volunteers was quite high, especially for pleasantness and activation, given the subjectivity of the labeling task.

To evaluate the usefulness of our lexicon, we built a simple emotion prediction system. When used for predicting the same three dimensions on new texts, its output significantly correlated with human judgments for pleasantness and activation, but the results for imagery were not satisfactory. Also, when used for classifying the opinion polarity of user product reviews, the system managed to achieve an accuracy better than random. These results suggest that our knowledge base successfully captured useful information of human perception of, at least, pleasantness and activation. For imagery, either it failed to capture any significant information, or the system we created was too simple to exploit it accordingly.

Regarding the evolution of the system's performance as a function of the size of the lexicon, the results were clear. When more words were included, the system performance increased only at a logarithmic pace. Thus, working on more complex systems seems to be more promising than adding more human-annotated words.

In summary, this work presented a knowledge base that may come handy to researchers and developers of sentiment analysis tools in Spanish. Additionally, it may be useful for disciplines that need to select emotionally balanced word stimuli, such as Neuroscience or Psycholinguistics. In future work we will compare the usefulness of our manually annotated lexicon and cross-linguistic approaches (Brooke et al., 2009; Pérez-Rosas et al., 2012).

Acknowledgments

This work was funded in part by ANPCYT PICT-2009-0026 and CONICET. The authors thank Carlos 'Greg' Diuk and Esteban Mocskos for valuable suggestions and comments, and Julian Brooke, Milan Tofiloski and Maite Taboada for kindly sharing the Ciao corpus.

References

J. Brooke, M. Tofiloski, and M. Taboada. 2009. Cross-linguistic sentiment analysis: From English to Spanish. In *International Conference on Recent Advances in NLP, Borovets, Bulgaria*, pages 50–54.

J. Cohen. 1968. Weighted kappa: Nominal scale agreement provision for scaled disagreement or partial credit. *Psychological bulletin*, 70(4):213.

R. Cowie, E. Douglas-Cowie, N. Tsapatsoulis, G. Votsis, S. Kollias, W. Fellenz, and J.G. Taylor. 2001. Emotion recognition in human-computer interaction. *Signal Processing Magazine, IEEE*, 18(1):32–80.

J.R. Gray, T.S. Braver, and M.E. Raichle. 2002. Integration of emotion and cognition in the lateral prefrontal cortex. *Proceedings of the National Academy of Sciences*, 99(6):4115.

L. Padró, M. Collado, S. Reese, M. Lloberes, and I. Castellón. 2010. Freeling 2.1: Five years of open-source language processing tools. In *International Conf. on Language Resources and Evaluation (LREC)*.

V. Pérez-Rosas, C. Banea, and R. Mihalcea. 2012. Learning sentiment lexicons in spanish. In *Int. Conf. on Language Resources and Evaluation (LREC)*.

C. Whissell, M. Fournier, R. Pelland, D. Weir, and K. Makarec. 1986. A dictionary of affect in language: Iv. reliability, validity, and applications. *Perceptual and Motor Skills*, 62(3):875–888.

Cynthia Whissell. 1989. The dictionary of affect in language. *Emotion: Theory, research, and experience*, 4:113–131.

J. Yi, T. Nasukawa, R. Bunescu, and W. Niblack. 2003. Sentiment analyzer: Extracting sentiments about a given topic using NLP techniques. In *3rd IEEE Int. Conf. on Data Mining*, pages 427–434. IEEE.

A Login and instructions pages

Figures 6 and 7 show the screenshots of the login and instructions pages of our web interface for rating words.

Figure 6: Screenshot of the login page.

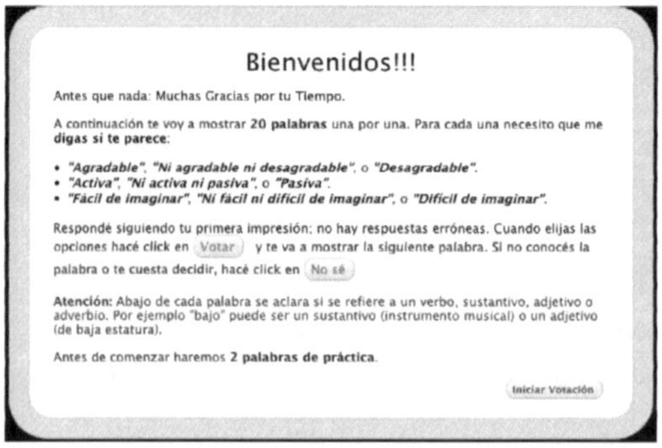

Figure 7: Screenshot of the instructions page.

The perfect solution for detecting sarcasm in tweets #not

Christine Liebrecht
Centre for Language Studies
Radboud University Nijmegen
P.O. Box 9103
NL-6500 HD Nijmegen
c.liebrecht@let.ru.nl

Florian Kunneman
Centre for Language Studies
Radboud University Nijmegen
P.O. Box 9103
NL-6500 HD Nijmegen
f.kunneman@let.ru.nl

Antal van den Bosch
Centre for Language Studies
Radboud University Nijmegen
P.O. Box 9103
NL-6500 HD Nijmegen
a.vandenbosch@let.ru.nl

Abstract

To avoid a sarcastic message being understood in its unintended literal meaning, in microtexts such as messages on Twitter.com sarcasm is often explicitly marked with the hashtag '#sarcasm'. We collected a training corpus of about 78 thousand Dutch tweets with this hashtag. Assuming that the human labeling is correct (annotation of a sample indicates that about 85% of these tweets are indeed sarcastic), we train a machine learning classifier on the harvested examples, and apply it to a test set of a day's stream of 3.3 million Dutch tweets. Of the 135 explicitly marked tweets on this day, we detect 101 (75%) when we remove the hashtag. We annotate the top of the ranked list of tweets most likely to be sarcastic that do not have the explicit hashtag. 30% of the top-250 ranked tweets are indeed sarcastic. Analysis shows that sarcasm is often signalled by hyperbole, using intensifiers and exclamations; in contrast, non-hyperbolic sarcastic messages often receive an explicit marker. We hypothesize that explicit markers such as hashtags are the digital extralinguistic equivalent of nonverbal expressions that people employ in live interaction when conveying sarcasm.

1 Introduction

In the general area of sentiment analysis, sarcasm plays a role as an interfering factor that can flip the polarity of a message. Unlike a simple negation, a sarcastic message typically conveys a negative opinion using only positive words – or even intensified positive words. The detection of sarcasm is therefore important, if not crucial, for the development and refinement of sentiment analysis systems, but is at the same time a serious conceptual and technical challenge. In this paper we introduce a sarcasm detection system for tweets, messages on the microblogging service offered by Twitter.[1]

In doing this we are helped by the fact that sarcasm appears to be a well-understood concept by Twitter users, as seen by the relatively accurate use of an explicit marker of sarcasm, the hashtag '#sarcasm'. Hashtags in messages on Twitter (tweets) are explicitly marked keywords, and often act as categorical labels or metadata in addition to the body text of the tweet. By using the explicit hashtag any remaining doubt a reader may have is taken away: the message is intended as sarcastic.

In communication studies, sarcasm has been widely studied, often in relation with, or encompassed by concepts such as irony as a broader category term, and in particular in relation with (or synonymous to) verbal irony. A brief overview of definitions, hypotheses and findings from communication studies regarding sarcasm and verbal irony may help clarify what the hashtag '#sarcasm' conveys.

1.1 Definitions

Many researchers treat irony and sarcasm as strongly related (Attardo, 2007; Brown, 1980; Gibbs and O'Brien, 1991; Kreuz and Roberts, 1993; Muecke, 1969; Mizzau, 1984), and sometimes even equate the terms in their studies in order to work with an usable definition (Grice, 1978; Tsur et al., 2010). We are interested in sarcasm as a linguistic phenomenon, and how we can detect it in social me-

[1] http://www.twitter.com

dia messages. Yet, Brown (1980) warns that sarcasm 'is not a discrete logical or linguistic phenomenon' (p. 111), while verbal irony is; we take the liberty of using the term sarcasm while verbal irony would be the more appropriate term. Even then, according to Gibbs and Colston (2007) the definition of verbal irony is still a 'problem that surfaces in the irony literature' (p. 584).

There are many different theoretical approaches to verbal irony. Burgers (2010), who provides an overview of approaches, distinguishes a number of features in ironic utterances that need to be included in an operational definition of irony: (1) irony is always implicit (Giora, 1995; Grice, 1978), (2) irony is evaluative (Attardo, 2000; Kotthoff, 2003; Sperber and Wilson, 1995), it is possible to (3) distinguish between a non-ironic and an ironic reading of the same utterance (Grice, 1975; Grice, 1978), (4) between which a certain type of opposition may be observed (see also Kawakami, 1984, 1988, summarized in (Hamamoto, 1998; Partington, 2007; Seto, 1998). Burgers' own definition of verbal irony is 'an evaluative utterance, the valence of which is implicitly reversed between the literal and intended evaluation' (Burgers, 2010, p. 19).

Thus, a sarcastic utterance involves a shift in evaluative valence, which can go two ways: it could be a shift from a literally positive to an intended negative meaning, or a shift from a literally negative to an intended positive evaluation. Since Reyes et al. (2012b) also argue that users of social media often use irony in utterances that involve a shift in evaluative valence, we use Burgers' (2010) definition of verbal irony in this study on sarcasm, and we use both terms synonymously. The definition of irony as saying the opposite of what is meant is commonly used in previous corpus-analytic studies, and is reported to be reliable (Kreuz et al., 1996; Leigh, 1994; Srinarawat, 2005).

Irony is used relatively often in dialogic interaction. Around 8% of conversational turns between American college friends contains irony (Gibbs, 2007). According to Gibbs (2007), group members use irony to 'affirm their solidarity by directing comments at individuals who are not group members and not deemed worthy of group membership' (p. 341). When an individual sees a group's normative standards violated, he uses sarcasm to vent frustration. Sarcasm is also used when someone finds a situation or object offensive (Gibbs, 2007). Sarcasm or irony is always directed at someone or something; its target. A target is the person or object against whom or which the ironic utterance is directed (Livnat, 2004). Targets can be the sender himself, the addressee or a third party (or a combination of the three). Burgers (2010) showed that in Dutch written communication, the target of the ironic utterance is often a third party. These findings may be interesting for our research, in which we study microtexts of up to 140 characters from Twitter.

Sarcasm in written and spoken interaction may work differently (Jahandarie, 1999). In spoken interaction, sarcasm is often marked with a special intonation (Attardo et al., 2003; Bryant and Tree, 2005; Rockwell, 2007) or an incongruent facial expression (Muecke, 1978; Rockwell, 2003; Attardo et al., 2003). Burgers (2010) argues that in written communication, authors do not have clues like 'a special intonation' or 'an incongruent facial expression' at their disposal. Since sarcasm is more difficult to comprehend than a literal utterance (Gibbs, 1986; Giora, 2003; Burgers, 2010), it is likely that addressees do not pick up on the sarcasm and interpret the utterances literally. Acoording to Gibbs and Izett (2005), sarcasm divides its addressees into two groups; a group of people who understand sarcasm (the so-called group of *wolves*) and a group of people who do not understand sarcasm (the so-called group of *sheep*). In order to ensure that the addressees detect the sarcasm in the utterance, senders use linguistic markers in their utterances. According to Attardo (2000) those markers are clues a writer can give that 'alert a reader to the fact that a sentence is ironical' (p. 7). On Twitter, the hashtag '#sarcasm' is a popular marker.

1.2 Intensifiers

There are sarcastic utterances which would still be qualified as sarcastic when all markers were removed from it (Attardo et al., 2003), for example the use of a hyperbole (Kreuz and Roberts, 1995). It may be that a sarcastic utterance with a hyperbole ('fantastic weather' when it rains) is identified as sarcastic with more ease than a sarcastic utterance without a hyperbole ('the weather is good' when it rains). While both utterances convey a literally positive attitude towards the weather, the utterance with the hyperbolic 'fantastic' may be easier to interpret as sarcastic than the utterance with the non-hyperbolic 'good'. Such hyperbolic words which strengthen the evaluative utterance are called intensifiers. Bowers (1964) defines language intensity as 'the quality of language which indicates the degree to which the speaker's attitude toward a concept deviates from neutrality' (p. 416). According to Van Mulken and Schellens (2012), an intensifier is a linguistic element that can be removed or replaced while respecting the linguistic correctness of the sentence and context, but resulting in a weaker evaluation. A commonly used way to intensify utterances is by using word classes such as adverbs ('very') or adjectives ('fantastic' instead of 'good'). It may be that senders use such intensifiers in their tweets to make the utterance hyperbolic and thereby sarcastic, without using a linguistic marker such as '#sarcasm'.

1.3 Outline

In this paper we describe the design and implementation of a sarcasm detector that marks unseen tweets as being sarcastic or not. We analyse the predictive performance of the classifier by testing its capacity on test tweets that are explicitly marked with the hashtag #sarcasme (Dutch for 'sarcasm'), left out during testing, and its capacity to rank likely sarcastic tweets that do not have the #sarcasme mark. We also provide a qualitative linguistic analysis of the features that the classifier thinks are the most discriminative. In a further qualitative analysis of sarcastic tweets in the test set we find that the use of an explicit hashtag marking sarcasm occurs relatively often without other indicators of sarcasm such as intensifiers or exclamations.

2 Related Research

The automatic classification of communicative constructs in short texts has become a widely researched subject in recent years. Large amounts of opinions, status updates and personal expressions are posted on social media platforms such as Twitter. The automatic labeling of their polarity (to what extent a text is positive or negative) can reveal, when aggregated or tracked over time, how the public in general thinks about certain things. See Montoyo et al. (2012) for an overview of recent research in sentiment analyis and opinion mining.

A major obstacle for automatically determining the polarity of a (short) text are constructs in which the literal meaning of the text is not the intended meaning of the sender, as many systems for the detection of polarity primarily lean on positive and negative words as markers. The task to identify such constructs can improve polarity classification, and provide new insights into the relatively new genre of short messages and microtexts on social media. Previous works describe the classification of irony (Reyes et al., 2012b), sarcasm (Tsur et al., 2010), satire (Burfoot and Baldwin, 2009), and humor (Reyes et al., 2012a).

Most common to our research are the works by Reyes et al. (2012b) and Tsur et al. (2010). Reyes et al. (2012b) collect a training corpus of irony based on tweets that consist of the hashtag #irony in order to train classifiers on different types of features (signatures, unexpectedness, style and emotional scenarios) and try to distinguish #irony-tweets from tweets containing the hashtags #education, #humour, or #politics, achieving F1-scores of around 70. Tsur et al. (2010) focus on product reviews on the World Wide Web, and try to identify sarcastic sentences from these in a semi-supervised fashion. Training data is collected by manually annotating sarcastic sentences, and retrieving additional training data based on the annotated sentences as queries. Sarcasm is annotated on a scale from 1 to 5. As features, Tsur et al. look at the patterns in these sentences, consisting of high-frequency words and content words. Their system achieves an F1-score of 79 on a testset of product reviews, after extracting and annotating a sample of 90 sentences classified as sarcastic and 90 sentences classified as not sarcastic.

In the two works described above, a system is tested in a controlled setting: Reyes et al. (2012b) compare irony to a restricted set of other topics, while Tsur et al. (2010) took from the unlabeled test set a sample of product reviews with 50% of the sentences classified as sarcastic. In contrast, we apply a trained sarcasm detector to a real-world test set representing a realistically large sample of tweets posted on a specific day of which the vast majority is not sarcastic. Detecting sarcasm in social media is, arguably, a needle-in-a-haystack problem (of the 3.3 million tweets we gathered on a single day, 135 are explicitly marked with the hashtag #sarcasm), and it is only reasonable to test a system in the context of a typical distribution of sarcasm in tweets. Like in the research of (Reyes et al., 2012b), we train a classifier based on tweets with a specific hashtag.

3 Experimental Setup

3.1 Data

For the collection of tweets for this study we make use of a database provided by the Netherlands e-Science Centre, consisting of a substantial portion of all Dutch tweets posted from December 2010 onwards.[2] From this database, we collected all tweets that contained the marker '#sarcasme', the Dutch word for sarcasm with the hashtag prefix. This resulted in a set of 77,948 tweets. We also collected all tweets posted on a single day, namely February 1, 2013.[3] This set of tweets contains approximately 3,3 million tweets, of which 135 carry the hashtag #sarcasme.

3.2 Winnow classification

Both the collected tweets with a #sarcasme hashtag and the tweets that were posted on a single day were tokenized and stripped of punctuation. Capitals were not removed, as they might be used to signal sarcasm (Burgers, 2010). We made use of word uni-, bi- and trigrams as features. Terms that occurred three times or less or in two tweets or less in the whole set were removed, as well as the hashtag #sarcasme. Features were weighted by the χ^2 metric.

As classification algorithm we made use of Balanced Winnow (Littlestone, 1988) as implemented in the Linguistic Classification System.[4] This algorithm is known to offer state-of-the-art results in text classification, and produces interpretable per-class weights that can be used to, for example, inspect the highest-ranking features for one class label. The α and β parameters were set to 1,05 and 0,95 respectively. The major threshold ($\theta+$) and the minor threshold ($\theta-$) were set to 2,5 and 0,5. The number of iterations was bounded to a maximum of three.

[2] http://twiqs.nl/

[3] All tweets from February 1, 2013 onwards were removed from the set of sarcasm tweets.

[4] http://www.phasar.cs.ru.nl/LCS/

3.3 Experiment

In order to train the classifier on distinctive features of sarcasm in tweets, we combined the set of 78 thousand sarcasm tweets with a random sample of other tweets posted on February 1, 2013 as background corpus. We made sure the background corpus did not contain any of the 135 explicitly marked sarcasm tweets posted that day. As the size of a background corpus can influence the performance of the classifier (in doubt, a classifier will be biased by the skew of the distribution of classes in the training-data), we performed a comparitive experiment with two distributions between sarcasm-labeled tweets and background tweets: in the first variant, the division between the two is 50%–50%, in the second, 25% of the tweets are sarcasm-labeled, and 75% are background.

4 Results

To evaluate the outcome of our machine learning experiment, we ran two evaluations. The first evaluation focuses on the 135 tweets with explicit #sarcasme hastags posted on February 1, 2013. We measured how well these tweets were identified using the true positive rate (TPR), false positive rate (FPR, also known as recall), and their joint score, the area under the curve (AUC). AUC is a common evaluation metric that is argued to be more resistant to skew than F-score, due to using TPR rather than precision (Fawcett, 2004). Results are displayed in Table 1. The first evaluation, on the variant with a balanced distribution of the two classes, leads to a retrieval of 101 of the 135 sarcasm-tweets (75%), while nearly 500 thousand tweets outside of these were also classified as being sarcastic. When a quarter of the training tweets has a sarcasm label, a smaller amount of 76 sarcasm tweets are retrieved. The AUC scores for the two ratios indicates that the 50%–50% balance leads to the highest AUC score (0.79) for sarcasm. Our subsequent analyses are based on the outcomes when using this distribution in training.

Besides generating an absolute winner-take-all classification, our Balanced Winnow classifier also assigns scores to each label that can be seen as its

Pos/Neg Ratio Training Examples	Label	# Training tweets	# Test tweets	TPR	FPR	AUC	Classified	Correct
50/50	sarcasm	77,948	135	0,75	0,16	0,79	487,955	101
	background	77,499	3,246,806	0,79	0,25	0,77	2,575,206	2,575,173
25/75	sarcasm	77,948	135	0,56	0,05	0,75	162,400	76
	background	233,834	3,090,472	0,92	0,43	0,74	2,830,103	2,830,045

Table 1: Scores on the test set with two relative sizes of background tweets (TPR = True Positive Rate, FPR = False Positive Rate, AUC = Area Under the Curve

confidence in that label. We can rank its predictions by the classifier's confidence on the 'sarcasm' label and inspect manually which of the top-ranking tweets is indeed sarcastic. We generated a list of the 250 most confident 'sarcasm'-labeled tweets. Three annotators (the authors of this paper) made a judgement for these tweets as being either sarcastic or not. In order to test for intercoder reliability, Cohen's Kappa was used. In line with Siegel and Castellan (1988), we calculated a mean Kappa based on pairwise comparisons of all possible coder pairs. The mean intercoder reliability between the three possible coder pairs is substantial ($\kappa = .79$).

When taking the majority vote of the three annotators as the golden label, a curve of the precision at all points in the ranking can be plotted. This curve is displayed in Figure 1. As can be seen, the overall performance is poor (the average precision is 0.30). After peaking at 0.50 after 22 tweets, precision slowly decreases when descending to lower rankings. During the first five tweets, the curve is at 0.0; these tweets, receiving the highest overall confidence scores, are relatively short and contain one strong sarcasm feature in the classifier without any negative feature.

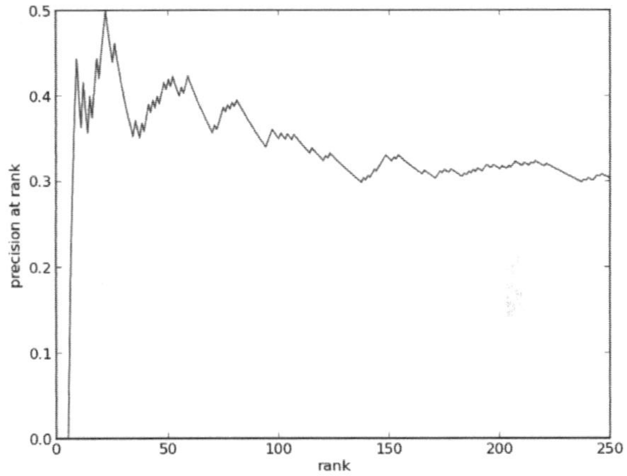

Figure 1: Precision at $\{1 \ldots 250\}$ on the sarcasm class

5 Analysis

Our first closer analysis of our results concerns the reliability of the user-generated hastag #sarcasme as a golden label, as Twitter users cannot all be assumed to be experts in sarcasm or understand what sarcasm is. The three annotators who annotated the ranked classifier output also coded a random sample of 250 tweets with the #sarcasme hashtag from the training set. The average score of agreement between the three possible coder pairs turned out to be moderate ($\kappa = .54$). Taking the majority vote over the three annotations as the reference labeling, 85% (212) of the 250 annotated #sarcasme tweets were found to be sarcastic.

While the classifier performance gives an impression of its ability to distinguish sarcastic tweets, the strong indicators of sarcasm as discovered by the classifier may provide additional insight into the usage of sarcasm by Twitter users: in particular, the typical targets of sarcasm, and the different linguistic markers that are used. We thus set out to analyze the feature weights assigned by the Balanced Winnow classifier ranked by the strength of their connection to the sarcasm label, taking into account the 500 words and n-grams with the highest positive weight towards the sarcasm class. These words and n-grams provide insight into the topics Twitter users are talking about: their targets. People often talk about school and related subjects such as homework, books, exams, classes (French, chemistry, physics), teachers, the school picture, sports day, and (returning from) vacation. Another popular target of sarcasm is the weather: the temperature, rain, snow, and sunshine. Apart from these two common topics, people tend to be sarcastic about social media itself, holidays, public transport, soccer, television programs (The Voice of Holland), celebrities (Justin Bieber), the church, the dentist and vacuum cleaning. Many of these topics are indicative of the young age, on average, of Twitter users.

The strongest linguistic markers of sarcastic utterances are markers that can be seen as synonyms for *#sarcasme*, such as *sarcasme* (without #), *#ironie* and *ironie* (irony), *#cynisme* and *cynisme* (cynicism), or words that are strongly related to those concepts by marking the opposite of the expressed utterance: *#humor*, *#LOL*, *#joke* (grapje), and *#NOT*.

Second, the utterances contain much positive exclamations that make the utterance hyperbolic and thereby sarcastic. Examples of those markers in Dutch are (with and without # and/or capitals): *jippie, yes, goh, joepie, jeej, jeuj, yay, woehoe*, and *wow*.

We suspected that the sarcastic utterances contained intensifiers to make the tweets hyperbolic. The list of strongest predictors show that some intensifiers are indeed strong predictors of sarcasm, such as *geweldig* (awesome), *heerlijk* (lovely), *prachtig* (wonderful), *natuurlijk* (of course), *gelukkig* (fortunately), *zoooo* (soooo), *allerleukste* (most fun), *fantastisch* (fantastic), and *heeel* (veeery). Besides these intensifiers many unmarked positive words occur in the list of strongest predictors as well, such as *fijn* (nice), *gezellig* (cozy), *leuk* (fun), *origineel* (original), *slim* (smart), *favoriet* (favorite), *nuttig* (useful), and chill. Considerably less negative words occur as strong predictors. This supports our hypothesis that the utterances are mostly positive, while the opposite meaning is meant. This finding corresponds with the results of Burgers (2010), who show that 77% of the ironic utterances in Dutch communication are literally positive.

To inspect whether sarcastic tweets are always intensified to be hyperbolic, we need to further analyse the sarcastic tweets our classifier correctly identifies. Analyzing the 76 tweets that our classifier correctly identifies in the top-250 tweets the classifier rates as sarcastic, we see that intensifiers do not dominate in occurrence; supporting numbers are listed in Table 2. About one in three sarcastic tweets, 34.2%, are not hyperbolic at all: they are only explicitly marked, most of the times with a hashtag. A majority of 59.2% of the tweets does contain hyperbole-inducing elements, such as an intensifier or an exclamation, or combinations of these elements. A full combination of explicit markers, intensifiers, and exclamations only rarely occurs, however (2.6%). The three categories of predictive word types do cover 93.4% of the tweets.

Type	Relative occurrence (%)
Marker only	34.2
Intensifier only	9.2
Exclamation only	17.1
Marker + Intensifier	10.5
Marker + Exclamation	9.2
Intensifier + Exclamation	10.5
Marker + Intensifier + Exclamation	2.6
Other	6.6
Total	*100*

Table 2: Relative occurrence (%) of word types and their combinations in the tweets annotated as sarcastic by a majority vote.

6 Conclusion

In this study we developed and tested a system that detects sarcastic tweets in a realistic sample of 3.3 million Dutch tweets posted on a single day, trained on a set of nearly 78 thousand tweets, harvested over time, marked by the hashmark #sarcasme by the senders. The classifier is able to correctly detect 101 of the 135 tweets among the 3.3 million that were explicitly marked with the hashtag, with the hashtag removed. Testing the classifier on the top 250 of the tweets it ranked as most likely to be sarcastic, it attains only a 30% average precision. We can conclude that it is fairly hard to distinguish sarcastic tweets from literal tweets in an open setting, though the top of the classifier's ranking does identify many sarcastic tweets which were not explicitly marked with a hashtag.

An additional linguistic analysis provides some insights into the characteristics of sarcasm on Twitter. We found that most tweets contain a literally positive message, take common teenager topics as target (school, homework, family life) and further contain three types of words: explicit markers (the word *sarcasme* and pseudo-synonyms, with or without the hashmark #), intensifiers, and exclamations. The latter two categories of words induce hyperbole, but together they only occur in about 60% of sarcastic tweets; in 34% of the cases, sarcastic tweets are not hyperbolic, but only have an explicit marker, most of which hashtags. This indicates that the hashtag can and does replace linguistic markers that otherwise would be needed to mark sarcasm. Arguably, extralinguistic elements such as hashtags can be seen as the social media equivalent of nonverbal expressions that people employ in live interaction when conveying sarcasm. As Burgers (2010) show, the more explicit markers an ironic utterance contains, the better the utterance is understood, the less its perceived complexity is, and the better it is rated. Many Twitter users already seem to apply this knowledge.

Although in this research we focused on the Dutch language, our findings may also apply to languages similar to Dutch, such as English and German. Future research would be needed to chart the prediction of sarcasm in languages that are more distant to Dutch. Sarcasm may be used differently in other cultures (Goddard, 2006). Languages may use the same type of marker in different ways, such as a different intonation in spoken sarcasm by English and Cantonese speakers (Cheang and Pell, 2009). Such a difference between languages in the use of the same marker may also apply to written sarcastic utterances.

Another strand of future research would be to expand our scope from sarcasm to other more subtle variants of irony, such as understatements, euphemisms, and litotes. Based on Giora et al. (2005), there seems to be a spectrum of degrees of irony from the sarcastic 'Max is exceptionally bright' via the ironic 'Max is not exceptionally bright', the understatement 'Max is not bright' to the literal 'Max is stupid'. In those utterances, there is a gap between what is literally said and the intended meaning of the sender. The greater the gap or contrast, the easier it is to perceive the irony. But the negated *not bright* is still perceived as ironic; more ironic than the literal utterance (Giora et al., 2005). We may need to combine the sarcasm detection task with the problem of the detection of negation and hedging markers and their scope (Morante et al., 2008; Morante and Daelemans, 2009) in order to arrive at a comprehensive account of polarity-reversing mechanisms, which in sentiment analysis is still highly desirable.

References

S. Attardo, J. Eisterhold, J. Hay, and I. Poggi. 2003. Visual markers of irony and sarcasm. *Humor*, 16(2):243–260.

S. Attardo. 2000. Irony as relevant inappropriateness. *Journal of Pragmatics*, 32(6):793–826.

S. Attardo. 2007. Irony as relevant inappropriateness. In R. W. Gibbs, R. W. Gibbs Jr., and H. Colston, editors, *Irony in language and thought: A cognitive science reader*, pages 135–170. Lawrence Erlbaum, New York, NY.

J. W. Bowers. 1964. Some correlates of language intensity. *Quarterly Journal of Speech*, 50(4):415–420, December.

R. L. Brown. 1980. The pragmatics of verbal irony. In R. W. Shuy and A. Shnukal, editors, *Language use and the uses of language*, pages 111–127. Georgetown University Press, Washington, DC.

G. A. Bryant and J. E. Fox Tree. 2005. Is there an ironic tone of voice? *Language and Speech*, 48(3):257–277.

C. Burfoot and T. Baldwin. 2009. Automatic satire detection: Are you having a laugh? In *Proceedings of the ACL-IJCNLP 2009 Conference Short Papers*, pages 161–164. Association for Computational Linguistics.

C. F. Burgers. 2010. *Verbal irony: Use and effects in written discourse*. Ipskamp, Nijmegen, The Netherlands.

H. S. Cheang and M. D. Pell. 2009. Acoustic markers of sarcasm in Cantonese and English. *The Journal of the Acoustical Society of America*, 126:1394.

T. Fawcett. 2004. ROC graphs: Notes and practical considerations for researchers. Technical Report HPL-2003-4, Hewlett Packard Labs.

R. W. Gibbs and H. Colston. 2007. Irony as persuasive communication. In R. W. Gibbs, R. W. Gibbs Jr., and H. Colston, editors, *Irony in language and thougt: A cognitive science reader*, pages 581–595. Lawrence Erlbaum, New York, NY.

R. W. Gibbs and C. Izett. 2005. Irony as persuasive communication. In H. Colston and A. Katz, editors, *Figurative language comprehension: Social and cultural influences*, pages 131–151. Lawrence Erlbaum, New York, NY.

R. W. Gibbs and J. O'Brien. 1991. Psychological aspects of irony understanding. *Journal of pragmatics*, 16(6):523–530.

R. W. Gibbs. 1986. On the psycholinguistics of sarcasm. *Journal of Experimental Psychology: General*, 115(1):3.

R. W. Gibbs. 2007. On the psycholinguistics of sarcasm. In R. W. Gibbs, R. W. Gibbs Jr., and H. Colston, editors, *Irony in language and thougt: A cognitive science reader*, pages 173–200. Lawrence Erlbaum, New York, NY.

R. Giora, O. Fein, J. Ganzi, N. Levi, and H. Sabah. 2005. On negation as mitigation: the case of negative irony. *Discourse Processes*, 39(1):81–100.

R. Giora. 1995. On irony and negation. *Discourse processes*, 19(2):239–264.

R. Giora. 2003. *On our mind: Salience, context, and figurative language*. Oxford University Press.

C. Goddard. 2006. "lift your game Martina!": Deadpan jocular irony and the ethnopragmatics of Australian English. *APPLICATIONS OF COGNITIVE LINGUISTICS*, 3:65.

H. Grice. 1975. Logic and conversation. In P. Cole and J. Morgan, editors, *Speech acts: Syntax and semantics*, pages 41–58. Academic Press, New York, NY.

H. Grice. 1978. Further notes on logic and conversation. In P. Cole, editor, *Pragmatics: syntax and semantics*, pages 113–127. Academic Press, New York, NY.

H. Hamamoto. 1998. Irony from a cognitive perspective. In R. Carston and S. Uchida, editors, *Relevance theory: Applications and implications*, pages 257–270. John Benjamins, Amsterdam, The Netherlands.

K. Jahandarie. 1999. *Spoken and written discourse: A multi-disciplinary perspective*. Greenwood Publishing Group.

H. Kotthoff. 2003. Responding to irony in different contexts: On cognition in conversation. *Journal of Pragmatics*, 35(9):1387–1411.

R. J. Kreuz and R. M. Roberts. 1993. The empirical study of figurative language in literature. *Poetics*, 22(1):151–169.

R. J. Kreuz and R. M. Roberts. 1995. Two cues for verbal irony: Hyperbole and the ironic tone of voice. *Metaphor and symbol*, 10(1):21–31.

R. Kreuz, R. Roberts, B. Johnson, and E. Bertus. 1996. Figurative language occurrence and co-occurrence in contemporary literature. In R. Kreuz and M. MacNealy, editors, *Empirical approaches to literature and aesthetics*, pages 83–97. Ablex, Norwood, NJ.

J. H Leigh. 1994. The use of figures of speech in print ad headlines. *Journal of Advertising*, pages 17–33.

N. Littlestone. 1988. Learning quickly when irrelevant attributes abound: A new linear-threshold algorithm. *Machine Learning*, 2:285–318.

Z. Livnat. 2004. On verbal irony, meta-linguistic knowledge and echoic interpretation. *Pragmatics & Cognition*, 12(1):57–70.

M. Mizzau. 1984. *L'ironia: la contraddizione consentita*. Feltrinelli, Milan, Italy.

A. Montoyo, P. Martínez-Barco, and A. Balahur. 2012. Subjectivity and sentiment analysis: An overview of the current state of the area and envisaged developments. *Decision Support Systems*.

R. Morante and W. Daelemans. 2009. Learning the scope of hedge cues in biomedical texts. In *Proceedings of the Workshop on BioNLP*, pages 28–36. Association for Computational Linguistics.

R. Morante, A. Liekens, and W. Daelemans. 2008. Learning the scope of negation in biomedical texts. In *Proceedings of the 2008 Conference on Empirical Methods in Natural Language Processing*, pages 715–724.

D. C. Muecke. 1969. *The compass of irony*. Oxford Univ Press.

D. C. Muecke. 1978. Irony markers. *Poetics*, 7(4):363–375.

A. Partington. 2007. Irony and reversal of evaluation. *Journal of Pragmatics*, 39(9):1547–1569.

A. Reyes, P. Rosso, and D. Buscaldi. 2012a. From humor recognition to irony detection: The figurative language of social media. *Data & Knowledge Engineering*.

A. Reyes, P. Rosso, and T. Veale. 2012b. A multidimensional approach for detecting irony in twitter. *Language Resources and Evaluation*, pages 1–30.

P. Rockwell. 2003. Empathy and the expression and recognition of sarcasm by close relations or strangers. *Perceptual and motor skills*, 97(1):251–256.

P. Rockwell. 2007. Vocal features of conversational sarcasm: A comparison of methods. *Journal of psycholinguistic research*, 36(5):361–369.

K.-i. Seto. 1998. On non-echoic irony. In R. Carson and S. Uchida, editors, *Relevance theory: Applications and implications*, pages 239–255. John Benjamins, Amsterdam, The Netherlands.

S. Siegel and N. Castellan. 1988. *Nonparametric statistics for the behavioral sciences*. McGraw Hill, New York.

D. Sperber and D. Wilson. 1995. *Relevance: Communication and cognition*. Blackwell Publishers, Oxford, UK, 2nd edition.

D. Srinarawat. 2005. Indirectness as a politeness strategy of Thai speakers. In R. Lakoff and S. Ide, editors, *Broadening the horizon of linguistic politeness*, pages 175–193. John Benjamins, Amsterdam, The Netherlands.

O. Tsur, D. Davidov, and A. Rappoport. 2010. Icwsm–a great catchy name: Semi-supervised recognition of sarcastic sentences in online product reviews. In *Proceedings of the Fourth International AAAI Conference on Weblogs and Social Media*, pages 162–169.

M. Van Mulken and P. J. Schellens. 2012. Over loodzware bassen en wapperende broekspijpen. gebruik en perceptie van taalintensiverende stijlmiddelen. *Tijdschrift voor taalbeheersing*, 34(1):26–53.

Using PU-Learning to Detect Deceptive Opinion Spam

Donato Hernández Fusilier[1,2]
Rafael Guzmán Cabrera
División de Ingenierías
Campus Irapuato-Salamanca.
[1]Universidad de Guanajuato
Mexico.
{donato, guzmanc}@ugto.mx

Manuel Montes-y-Gómez
Laboratorio de Tecnologías
del Lenguaje.
Instituto Nacional de
Astrofísica, Óptica y Electrónica.
Mexico.
mmontesg@inaoep.mx

Paolo Rosso
Natural Language
Engineering Lab., ELiRF.
[2]Universitat Politècnica de
València
Spain.
prosso@dsic.upv.es

Abstract

Nowadays a large number of opinion reviews are posted on the Web. Such reviews are a very important source of information for customers and companies. The former rely more than ever on online reviews to make their purchase decisions and the latter to respond promptly to their clients' expectations. Due to the economic importance of these reviews there is a growing trend to incorporate spam on such sites, and, as a consequence, to develop methods for opinion spam detection. In this paper we focus on the detection of *deceptive opinion spam*, which consists of fictitious opinions that have been deliberately written to sound authentic, in order to deceive the consumers. In particular we propose a method based on the PU-learning approach which learns only from a few positive examples and a set of unlabeled data. Evaluation results in a corpus of hotel reviews demonstrate the appropriateness of the proposed method for real applications since it reached a f-measure of 0.84 in the detection of deceptive opinions using only 100 positive examples for training.

1 Introduction

The Web is the greatest repository of digital information and communication platform ever invented. People around the world widely use it to interact with each other as well as to express opinions and feelings on different issues and topics. With the increasing availability of online review sites and blogs, costumers rely more than ever on online reviews to make their purchase decisions and businesses to respond promptly to their clients' expectations. It is not surprising that opinion mining technologies have been witnessed a great interest in recent years (Zhou et al., 2008; Mihalcea and Strapparava, 2009). Research in this field has been mainly oriented to problems such as opinion extraction (Liu B., 2012) and polarity classification (Reyes and Rosso., 2012). However, because of the current trend about the growing number of online reviews that are fake or paid by companies to promote their products or damage the reputation of competitors, the automatic detection of opinion spam has emerged as a highly relevant research topic (Jindal et al., 2010; Jindal and Liu, 2008; Lau et al., 2011; Wu et al., 2010; Ott et al., 2011; Sihong et al., 2012).

Detecting opinion spam is a very challenging problem since opinions expressed in the Web are typically short texts, written by unknown people using different styles and for different purposes. Opinion spam has many forms, e.g., fake reviews, fake comments, fake blogs, fake social network postings and deceptive texts. Opinion spam reviews may be detected by methods that seek for duplicate reviews (Jindal and Liu, 2008), however, this kind of opinion spam only represents a small percentage of the opinions from review sites. In this paper we focus on a potentially more insidious type of opinion spam, namely, *deceptive opinion spam*, which consists of fictitious opinions that have been deliberately written to sound authentic, in order to deceive the consumers.

The detection of deceptive opinion spam has been traditionally solved by means of supervised text classification techniques (Ott et al., 2011). These techniques have demonstrated to be very robust if they are trained using large sets of labeled instances from both classes, deceptive opinions (positive instances) and truthful opinions (negative examples). Nevertheless, in real application scenarios it is very difficult to construct such large training sets and, moreover, it is almost impossible to determine the authenticity of the opinions (Mukherjee et al., 2011). In order to meet this restriction we propose a method that learns only from a few positive examples and a set of unlabeled data. In particular, we propose applying the PU-Learning approach (Liu et al., 2002; Liu et al., 2003) to detect deceptive opinion spam.

The evaluation of the proposed method was carried out using a corpus of hotel reviews under different training conditions. The results are encouraging; they show the appropriateness of the proposed method for being used in real opinion spam detection applications. It reached a f-measure of 0.84 in the detection of deceptive opinions using only 100 positive examples, greatly outperforming the effectiveness of the traditional supervised approach and the one-class SVM model.

The rest of the paper is organized as follows. Section 2 presents some related works in the field of opinion spam detection. Section 3 describes our adaptation of the PU-Learning approach to the task of opinion spam detection. Section 4 presents the experimental results and discusses its advantages and disadvantages. Finally, Section 5 indicates the contributions of the paper and provides some future work directions.

2 Related Work

The detection of spam in the Web has been mainly approached as a binary classification problem (spam vs. non-spam). It has been traditionally studied in the context of e-mail (Drucker et al., 2002), and web pages (Gyongyi et al., 2004; Ntoulas et al., 2006). The detection of opinion spam, i.e., the identification of fake reviews that try to deliberately mislead human readers, is just another face of the same problem (Lau et al., 2011). Nevertheless, the construction of automatic detection methods for this task is more complex than for the others since manually gathering labeled reviews –particularly truthful opinions– is very hard, if not impossible (Mukherjee et al., 2011).

One of the first works regarding the detection of opinion spam reviews was proposed by (Jindal and Liu, 2008). He proposed detecting opinion spam by identifying duplicate content. Although this method showed good precision in a review data set from Amazon[1], it has the disadvantage of under detecting original fake reviews. It is well known that spammers modify or paraphrase their own reviews to avoid being detected by automatic tools.

In (Wu et al., 2010), the authors present a method to detect hotels which are more likely to be involved in spamming. They proposed a number of criteria that might be indicative of suspicious reviews and evaluated alternative methods for integrating these criteria to produce a suspiciousness ranking. Their criteria mainly derive from characteristics of the network of reviewers and also from the impact and ratings of reviews. It is worth mentioning that they did not take advantage of reviews' content for their analysis.

Ott et al. (2011) constructed a classifier to distinguish between deceptive and truthful reviews. In order to train their classifier they considered certain types of near duplicates reviews as positive (deceptive) training data and *the rest* as the negative (truthful) training data. The review spam detection was done using different stylistic, syntactical and lexical features as well as using SVM as base classifier.

In a recent work, Sihong et al. (2012) demonstrated that a high correlation between the increase in the volume of (singleton) reviews and a sharp increase or decrease in the ratings is a clear signal that the rating is manipulated by possible spam reviews. Supported by this observation they proposed a spam detection method based on time series pattern discovery.

The method proposed in this paper is similar to Ott's et al. method in the sense that it also aims to automatically identify deceptive and truthful reviews. However, theirs shows a key problem: it depends on the availability of labeled negative instances which are difficult to obtain, and that causes traditional text classification techniques to be ineffective for real application scenarios. In contrast,

[1]http://www.Amazon.com

our method is specially suited for this application since it builds accurate two-class classifiers with only positive and unlabeled examples, but not negative examples. In particular we propose using the PU-Learning approach (Liu et al., 2002; Liu et al., 2003) for opinion spam detection. To the best of our knowledge this is the first time that this technique, or any one-class classification approach, has been applied to this task. In (Ferretti et al., 2012) PU-learning was successfully used in the task of Wikipedia flaw detection[2].

3 PU-Learning for opinion spam detection

PU-learning is a partially supervised classification technique. It is described as a two-step strategy which addresses the problem of building a two-class classifier with only positive and unlabeled examples (Liu et al., 2002; Liu et al., 2003; Zhang and Zuo, 2009). Broadly speaking this strategy consists of two main steps: i) to identify a set of reliable negative instances from the unlabeled set, and ii) to apply a learning algorithm on the refined training set to build a two-class classifier.

Figure 1 shows our adaptation of the PU-learning approach for the task of opinion spam detection. The proposed method is an iterative process with two steps. In the first step the whole unlabeled set is considered as the negative class. Then, we train a classifier using this set in conjunction with the set of positive examples. In the second step, this classifier is used to classify (automatically label) the unlabeled set. The instances from the unlabeled set classified as positive are eliminated; the rest of them are considered as the reliable negative instances for the next iteration. This iterative process is repeated until a stop criterion is reached. Finally, the latest built classifier is returned as the final classifier.

In order to clarify the construction of the opinion spam classifier, Algorithm 1 presents the formal description of the proposed method. In this algorithm P is the set of positive instances and U_i represents the unlabeled set at iteration i; U_1 is the original unlabeled set. C_i is used to represent the classifier that was built at iteration i, and W_i indicates the set of unlabeled instances classified as positive by the classifier C_i. These instances have to be removed from the training set for the next iteration. Therefore, the negative class for next iteration is defined as $U_i - W_i$. Line 4 of the algorithm shows the stop criterion that we used in our experiments, $|W_i| <= |W_{i-1}|$. The idea of this criterion is to allow a continue but gradual reduction of the negative instances.

1: $i \leftarrow 1$
2: $|W_0| \leftarrow |U_1|$
3: $|W_1| \leftarrow |U_1|$
4: **while** $|W_i| <= |W_{i-1}|$ **do**
5: $\quad C_i \leftarrow Generate\_Classifier(P, U_i)$
6: $\quad U_i^L \leftarrow C_i(U_i)$
7: $\quad W_i \leftarrow Extract\_Positives(U_i^L)$
8: $\quad U_{i+1} \leftarrow U_i - W_i$
9: $\quad i \leftarrow i + 1$
10: Return Classifier C_i

Algorithm 1: PU-Learning for opinion spam detection

4 Evaluation

4.1 Datasets

The evaluation of the proposed method was carried out using a dataset of reviews assembled by Ott et al. (2011). This corpus contains 800 opinions, 400 deceptive and 400 truthful opinions. These opinions are about the 20 most popular Chicago hotels; deceptive opinions were generated using the Amazon Mechanical Turk (AMT)[3], whereas –possible– truthful opinions were mined from a total of 6,977 reviews on TripAdvisor[4]. The following paragraphs show two opinions taken from (Ott et al., 2011). These examples are very interesting since they show the great complexity of the automatically –and even manually– detection of deceptive opinions. Both opinions are very similar and just minor details can help distinguishing one from the other. For example, in his research Ott et al. (2011) found that deceptive reviews used the words "experience", "my husband", "I", "feel", "business", and "vacation" more than genuine ones.

[2] http://www.webis.de/research/events/pan-12

[3] http://www.mturk.com

[4] http://www.tripadvisor.com

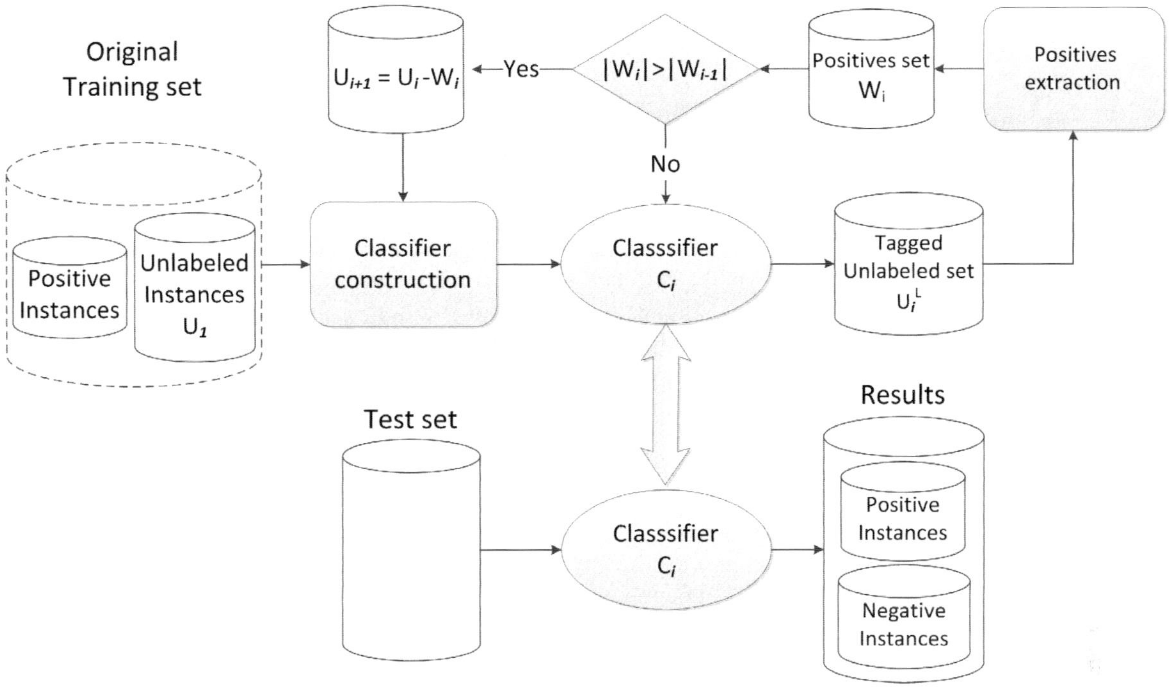

Figure 1: Classifier construction with PU-Learning approach.

Example of a truthful opinion

We stay at Hilton for 4 nights last march. It was a pleasant stay. We got a large room with 2 double beds and 2 bathrooms, The TV was Ok, a 27' CRT Flat Screen. The concierge was very friendly when we need. The room was very cleaned when we arrived, we ordered some pizzas from room service and the pizza was ok also. The main Hall is beautiful. The breakfast is charged, 20 dollars, kinda expensive. The internet access (WiFi) is charged, 13 dollars/day. Pros: Low rate price, huge rooms, close to attractions at Loop, close to metro station. Cons: Expensive breakfast, Internet access charged. Tip: When leaving the building, always use the Michigan Ave exit. It's a great view.

Example of a deceptive opinion

My husband and I stayed for two nights at the Hilton Chicago, and enjoyed every minute of it! The bedrooms are immaculate, and the linens are very soft. We also appreciated the free WiFi, as we could stay in touch with friends while staying in Chicago. The bathroom was quite spacious, and I loved the smell of the shampoo they provided-not like most hotel shampoos. Their service was amazing, and we absolutely loved the beautiful indoor pool. I would recommend staying here to anyone.

In order to simulated real scenarios to test our method we assembled several different sub-corpora from Ott's et al. (2011) dataset. First we randomly selected 80 deceptive opinions and 80 truthful opinions to build a fixed test set. The remaining 640 opinions were used to build six training sets of different sizes and distributions. They contain 20, 40, 60, 80, 100 and 120 positive instances (deceptive opinions) respectively. In all cases we used a set of 520 unlabeled instances containing a distribution of 320 truthful opinions and 200 deceptive opinions.

4.2 Evaluation Measure

The evaluation of the effectiveness of the proposed method was carried out by means of the f-measure. This measure is a linear combination of the precision and recall values. We computed this measure for both classes, deceptive and –possible– truthful opinions, nevertheless, the performance on the deceptive opinions is the only measure of real relevance. The f-measure for each opinion category O_i is defined as follows:

$$f - measure(O_i) = \frac{2 \times recall(O_i) \times precision(O_i)}{recall(O_i) + precision(O_i)} \quad (1)$$

$$recall(O_i) = \frac{number\ of\ correct\ predictions\ of\ O_i}{number\ of\ opinions\ of\ O_i} \quad (2)$$

$$precision(O_i) = \frac{number\ of\ correct\ predictions\ of\ O_i}{number\ of\ predictions\ as\ O_i} \quad (3)$$

4.3 Results

Tables 1 and 2 show the results from all the experiments we carried out. It is important to notice that we used Naïve Bayes and SVM classifiers as learning algorithms in our PU-learning method. These learning algorithms as well as the one-class implementation of SVM were also used to generated baseline results. In all the experiments we used the default implementations of these algorithms in the Weka experimental platform (Hall et al., 2009).

In order to make easy the analysis and discussion of the results we divided them in three groups: baseline results, one-class classification results, and PU-learning results. The following paragraphs describe these results.

Baseline results: The baseline results were obtained by training the NB and SVM classifiers using the unlabeled dataset as the negative class. This is a common approach to build binary classifiers in lack of negative instances. It also corresponds to the results of the first iteration of the proposed PU-learning based method. The rows named as "BASE NB" and "BASE SVM" show these results. They results clearly indicate the complexity of the task and the inadequacy of the traditional classification approach. The best f-measure in the deceptive opinion class (0.68) was obtained by the NB classifier when using 120 positive opinions for training. For the cases considering less number of training instances this approach generated very poor results. In addition we can also noticed that NB outperformed SVM in all cases.

One-class classification results: These results correspond to the application of the one-class SVM learning algorithm (Manevitz et al., 2002), which is a very robust approach for this kind of problems. This algorithm only uses the positive examples to build the classifier and does not take advantage of the available unlabeled instances. Its results are shown in the rows named as "ONE CLASS"; these results are very interesting since clearly show that this approach is very robust when there are only some examples of deceptive opinions (please refer to Table 1). On the contrary, it is also clear that this approach was outperformed by others, especially by our PU-learning based method, when more training data was available.

PU-Learning results: Rows labeled as "PU-LEA NB" and "PU-LEA SVM" show the results of the proposed method when the NB and SVM classifiers were used as base classifiers respectively. These results indicate that: i) the application of PU-learning improved baseline results in most of the cases, except when using 20 and 40 positive training instances; ii) PU-Learning results clearly outperformed the results from the one-class classifier when there were used more than 60 deceptive opinions for training; iii) results from "PU-LEA NB" were usually better than results from "PU-LEA SVM". It is also important to notice that both methods quickly converged, requiring less than seven iterations for all cases. In particular, "PU-LEA NB" took more iterations than "PU-LEA SVM", leading to greater reductions of the unlabeled sets, and, consequently, to a better identification of the subsets of reliable negative instances.

Finally, Figure 2 presents a summary of the best results obtained by each of the methods in all datasets. From this figure it is clear the advantage of the one-class SVM classifier when having only some examples of deceptive opinions for training, but also it is evident the advantage of the proposed method over the rest when having a considerable quantity of deceptive opinions for training. It is important to emphasize that the best result obtained by the proposed method (a F-meausre of 0.837 in the deceptive opinion class) is a very important results since it is comparable to the best result (0.89) reported for this collection/task, but when using 400 positive and 400 negative instances for training. Moreover, this result is also far better than the best human result obtained in this dataset, which, according to (Ott et al., 2011) it is around 60% of accuracy.

5 Conclusions and future work

In this paper we proposed a novel method for detecting deceptive opinion spam. This method adapts the PU-learning approach to this task. In contrast to traditional approaches that require large sets of labeled instances from both classes, deceptive and truthful

Original Training Set	Approach	Truthful			Deceptive			Itera-tion	Final Training Set
		P	R	F	P	R	F		
	ONE CLASS	0.500	0.688	0.579	*0.500*	*0.313*	*0.385*		
20-D	BASE NB	0.506	1.000	0.672	1.000	0.025	0.049		
	PU-LEA NB	0.506	1.000	0.672	1.000	0.025	0.049	5	20-D/493- U
520-U	BASE SVM	0.500	1.000	0.667	0.000	0.000	0.000		
	PU-LEA SVM	0.500	1.000	0.667	0.000	0.000	0.000	4	20-D/518-U
	ONE CLASS	0.520	0.650	0.578	*0.533*	*0.400*	*0.457*		
40-D	BASE NB	0.517	0.975	0.675	0.778	0.088	0.157		
	PU-LEA NB	0.517	0.975	0.675	0.778	0.088	0.157	4	40-D/479-U
520-U	BASE SVM	0.519	1.000	0.684	1.000	0.075	0.140		
	PU-LEA SVM	0.516	0.988	0.678	0.857	0.075	0.138	3	40-D/483-U
	ONE CLASS	0.500	0.500	0.500	*0.500*	*0.500*	*0.500*		
60-D	BASE NB	0.569	0.975	0.719	0.913	0.263	0.408		
	PU-LEA NB	0.574	0.975	0.722	0.917	0.275	0.423	3	60-D/449-U
520-U	BASE SVM	0.510	0.938	0.661	0.615	0.100	0.172		
	PU-LEA SVM	0.517	0.950	0.670	0.692	0.113	0.194	3	60-D/450-U

Table 1: Comparison of the performance of different classifiers when using 20, 40 and 60 examples of deceptive opinions for training; in this table D refers to deceptive opinions and U to unlabeled opinions.

Original Training Set	Approach	Truthful			Deceptive			Itera-tion	Final Training Set
		P	R	F	P	R	F		
	ONE CLASS	0.494	0.525	0.509	0.493	0.463	0.478		
80-D	BASE NB	0.611	0.963	0.748	0.912	0.388	0.544		
	PU-LEA NB	0.615	0.938	0.743	*0.868*	*0.413*	*0.559*	6	80-D/267-U
520-D	BASE SVM	0.543	0.938	0.688	0.773	0.213	0.333		
	PU-LEA SVM	0.561	0.925	0.698	0.786	0.275	0.407	3	80-D/426-U
	ONE CLASS	0.482	0.513	0.497	0.480	0.450	0.465		
100-D	BASE NB	0.623	0.950	0.752	0.895	0.425	0.576		
	PU-LEA NB	0.882	0.750	0.811	**0.783**	**0.900**	**0.837**	7	100-D/140-U
520-U	BASE SVM	0.540	0.938	0.685	0.762	0.200	0.317		
	PU-LEA SVM	0.608	0.913	0.730	0.825	0.413	0.550	4	100-D/325-U
	ONE CLASS	0.494	0.525	0.509	0.493	0.463	0.478		
120-D	BASE NB	0.679	0.950	0.792	0.917	0.550	0.687		
	PU-LEA NB	0.708	0.850	0.773	*0.789*	*0.781*	*0.780*	5	120-D/203-U
520-U	BASE SVM	0.581	0.938	0.718	0.839	0.325	0.468		
	PU-LEA SVM	0.615	0.738	0.670	0.672	0.538	0.597	6	120-D/169-U

Table 2: Comparison of the performance of different classifiers when using 80, 100 and 120 examples of deceptive opinions for training; in this table D refers to deceptive opinions and U to unlabeled opinions.

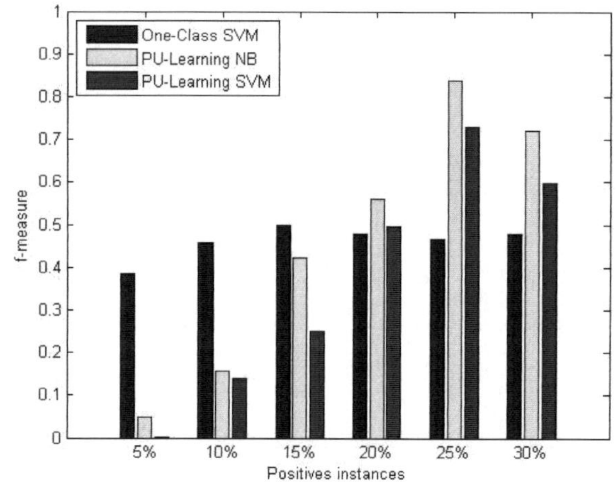

Figure 2: Summary of best F-measure results.

opinions, to build accurate classifiers, the proposed method only uses a small set of deceptive opinion examples and a set of unlabeled opinions. This characteristic represents a great advantage of our method over previous approaches since in real application scenarios it is very difficult to construct such large training sets and, moreover, it is almost impossible to determine the authenticity or truthfulness of the opinions.

The evaluation of the method in a set of hotel reviews indicated that the proposed method is very appropriate for the task of opinion spam detection. It achieved a F-meausre of 0.837 in the classification of deceptive opinions using only 100 positive examples and a bunch of unlabeled instances for training. This result is very relevant since it is comparable to previous results obtained by highly supervised methods in similar evaluation conditions.

Another important contribution of this work was the evaluation of a one-class classifier in this task. For the experimental results we can conclude that the usage of a one-class SVM classifier is very adequate for cases when there are only very few examples of deceptive opinions for training. In addition we could observe that this approach and the proposed method based on PU-learning are complementary. The one-class SVM classifier obtained the best results using less than 50 positive training examples, whereas the proposed method achieved the best results for the cases having more training examples.

As future work we plan to integrate the PU-learning and self-training approaches. Our idea is that iteratively adding some of the unlabeled instances into the original positive set may further improve the classification accuracy. We also plan to define and evaluate different stop criteria, and to apply this method in other related tasks such as email spam detection or phishing url detection.

Acknowledgments

This work is the result of the collaboration in the framework of the WIQEI IRSES project (Grant No. 269180) within the FP 7 Marie Curie. The work of the last author was in the framework the DIANA-APPLICATIONS-Finding Hidden Knowledge in Texts: Applications (TIN2012-38603-C02-01) project, and the VLC/CAMPUS Microcluster on Multimodal Interaction in Intelligent Systems.

References

H. Drucker, D. Wu and V.N. Vapnik. 2002. Support vector machines for spam categorization. Neural Networks, IEEE Transactions on, 10(5), pages 1048-1054.

Edgardo Ferretti, Donato Hernández Fusilier, Rafael Guzmán-Cabrera, Manuel Montes-y-Gómez, Marcelo Errecalde and Paolo Rosso. 2012. On the Use of PU Learning for Quality Flaw Prediction in Wikipedia. CLEF 2012 Evaluation Labs and Workshop, On line Working Notes, Rome, Italy, page 101.

Z. Gyongyi, H. Garcia-Molina and J. Pedersen. 2004. Combating web spam with trust rank. In Proceedings of the Thirtieth international conference on Very large data bases-Volume 30, pages 576-587. VLDB Endowment.

Hall Mark, Frank Eibe, Holmes Geoffrey, Pfahringer Bernhard, Reutemann Peter and Witten Ian H. 2009. The WEKA data mining software: an update. SIGKDD Explor. Newsl., pages 10-18. ACM.

N. Jindal and B. Liu. 2008. Opinion spam and analysis. In Proceedings of the international conference on Web search and web data mining, pages 219-230. ACM.

N. Jindal, B. Liu. and E. P. Lim. 2010. Finding unusual review patterns using unexpected rules. In CIKM, pages 219-230. ACM.

Raymond Y. K. Lau, S. Y. Liao, Ron Chi-Wai Kwok, Kaiquan Xu, Yunqing Xia and Yuefeng Li. 2011. Text mining and probabilistic modeling for online review spam detection. In Proceedings of the international conference on Web search and web data mining, Volume 2 Issue 4,Article 25. pages 1-30. ACM.

E.P. Lim, V.A. Nguyen, N. Jindal, B. Liu, and H.W. Lauw. 2010. Detecting product review spammers using rating behaviors. In CIKM,pages 939-948. ACM.

B. Liu, Y. Dai, X.L. Li, W.S. Lee and Philip Y. 2002. Partially Supervised Classification of Text Documents Proceedings of the Nineteenth International Conference on Machine Learning (ICML-2002), Sydney, July 2002, pages 387-394.

B. Liu, Y. Dai, X.L. Li, W.S. Lee and Philip Y. 2003. Building Text Classifiers Using Positive and Unlabeled Examples ICDM-03, Melbourne, Florida, November 2003, pages 19-22.

B. Liu. 2012. Sentiment Analysis and Opinion Mining. Synthesis Lecture on Human Language Technologies Morgan & Claypool Publishers

Manevitz, Larry M. and Yousef, Malik 2002. One-class svms for document classification. J. Mach. Learn. Res.,January 2002, pages 139-154. JMLR.org.

R. Mihalcea and C. Strapparava. 2009. The lie detector: Explorations in the automatic recognition of deceptive language. In Proceedings of the ACL-IJCNLP 2009 Conference Short Papers, pages 309-312. Association for Computational Linguistics.

Mukherjee Arjun, Liu Bing, Wang Junhui, Glance Natalie and Jindal Nitin. 2011. Detecting group review spam. Proceedings of the 20th international conference companion on World wide web, pages 93-94. ACM.

A. Ntoulas, M. Najork, M. Manasse and D. Fetterly. 2006. Detecting spam web pages through content analysis. Transactions on Management Information Systems (TMIS), pages 83-92. ACM.

Ott M., Choi Y., Cardie C. and Hancock J.T. 2011. Finding deceptive opinion spam by any stretch of the imagination. In Proceedings of the 49th Annual Meeting of the Association for Computational Linguistics: Human Language Technologies, Portland, Oregon, USA, Association for Computational Linguistics (2011), pages 309-319.

Reyes A. and Rosso P. 2012. Making Objective Decisions from Subjective Data: Detecting Irony in Customers Reviews. In Journal on Decision Support Systems, vol. 53, issue 4 (Special Issue on Computational Approaches to Subjectivity and Sentiment Analysis), pages 754-760. DOI: 10.1016/j.dss.2012.05.027

Sihong Xie, Guan Wang, Shuyang Lin and Philip S. Yu. 2012. Review spam detection via time series pattern discovery. Proceedings of the 21st international conference companion on World Wide Web, pages 635-636. ACM.

G. Wu, D. Greene and P. Cunningham. 2010. Merging multiple criteria to identify suspicious reviews. RecSys10, pages 241-244. ACM.

Bangzuo Zhang and Wanli Zuo. 2009. Reliable Negative Extracting Based on KNN for Learning from Positive and Unlabeled Examples Journal of Computers, Vol. 4 No. 1., January, 2009, pages 94-101.

L. Zhou, Y. Sh and D. Zhang. 2008. A Statistical Language Modeling Approach to Online Deception Detection. IEEE Transactions on Knowledge and Data Engineering, 20(8), pages 1077-1081.

Sexual predator detection in chats with chained classifiers

Hugo Jair Escalante
LabTL, INAOE
Luis Enrique Erro No. 1,
72840, Puebla, Mexico
hugojair@inaoep.mx

Esaú Villatoro-Tello*
Universidad Autónoma Metropolitana
Unidad Cuajimalpa
Mexico City, Mexico
villatoroe@inaoep.mx

Antonio Juárez
LabTL, INAOE
Luis Enrique Erro No. 1,
72840, Puebla, Mexico
antjug@inaoep.mx

Luis Villaseñor
LabTL, INAOE
72840, Puebla, Mexico
villasen@inaoep.mx

Manuel Montes-y-Gómez
LabTL, INAOE
72840, Puebla, Mexico
mmontesg@inaoep.mx

Abstract

This paper describes a novel approach for sexual predator detection in chat conversations based on sequences of classifiers. The proposed approach divides documents into three parts, which, we hypothesize, correspond to the different stages that a predator employs when approaching a child. Local classifiers are trained for each part of the documents and their outputs are combined by a chain strategy: *predictions of a local classifier are used as extra inputs for the next local classifier.* Additionally, we propose a ring-based strategy, in which the chaining process is iterated several times, with the goal of further improving the performance of our method. We report experimental results on the corpus used in the first international competition on sexual predator identification (PAN'12). Experimental results show that the proposed method outperforms a standard (global) classification technique for the different settings we consider; besides the proposed method compares favorably with most methods evaluated in the PAN'12 competition.

1 Introduction

Advances in communications' technologies have made possible to any person in the world to communicate with any other in different ways (e.g., text, voice, and video) regardless of their geographical locations, as long as they have access to internet. This undoubtedly represents an important and highly needed benefit to society. Unfortunately, this benefit also has brought some collateral issues that affect the security of internet users, as nowadays we are vulnerable to many threats, including: cyber-bullying, spam, fraud, and sexual harassment, among others.

A particularly important concern has to do with the protection of children that have access to internet (Wolak et al., 2006). Children are vulnerable to attacks from paedophiles, which "groom" them. That is, adults who meet underage victims online, engage in sexually explicit text or video chat with them, and eventually convince the children to meet them in person. In fact, one out of every seven children receives an unwanted sexual solicitation online (Wolak et al., 2006). Hence, the detection of cyber-sexual-offenders is a critical security issue that challenges the field of information technologies.

This paper introduces an effective approach for sexual predator detection (also called sexual predator identification) in chat conversations based on chains of classifiers. The proposed approach divides documents into three parts, with the hypothesis that different parts correspond to the different stages that predators adopt when approaching a child (Michalopoulos and Mavridis, 2011). Local classifiers are trained for each part of the documents and their outputs are combined by a chaining strategy. In the chain-based approach the predictions of a local classifier are used as extra inputs for the next local classifier. This strategy is inspired from chain-based classifiers developed for the task of multi-label classification (Read et al., 2011). A ring-based approach is proposed, in which the generation of chains of classifiers is iterated several times. We report experimental results in the corpus used in the first international competition on sexual predator identification (PAN-2012) (Inches and Crestani,

*Esaú Villatoro is also external member of LabTL at INAOE.

2012). Experimental results show that chain-based classifiers outperform standard classification methods for the different settings we considered. Furthermore, the proposed method compares favorably with alternative methods developed for the same task.

2 Sexual predator detection

We focus on the detection of sexual predators in chat rooms, among the many cyber-menaces targeting children. This is indeed a critical problem because most sexually-abused children have agreed voluntarily to met with their abuser (Wolak et al., 2006). Therefore, anticipatively detecting when a person attempts to approach a children, with malicious intentions, could reduce the number of abused children.

Traditionally, a term that is used to describe malicious actions with a potential aim of sexual exploitation or emotional connection with a child is referred as "Child Grooming" or "Grooming Attack" (Kucukyilmaz et al., 2008). Defined in (Harms, 2007) as: *"a communication process by which a perpetrator applies affinity seeking strategies, while simultaneously engaging in sexual desensitization and information acquisition about targeted victims in order to develop relationships that result in need fulfillment"* (e.g. physical sexual molestation).

The usual approach[1] to catch sexual predators is through police officers or volunteers, whom behave as fake children in chat rooms and provoke sexual offenders to approach them. Unfortunately, online sexual predators always outnumber the law enforcement officers and volunteers. Therefore, tools that can automatically detect sexual predators in chat conversations (or at least serve as support tool for officers) are highly needed.

A few attempts to automate processes related to the sexual predator detection task have been proposed already (Pendar, 2007; Michalopoulos and Mavridis, 2011; RahmanMiah et al., 2011; Inches and Crestani, 2012; Villatoro-Tello et al., 2012; Bogdanova et al., 2013). The problem of detecting conversations that potentially include a sexual predator approaching a victim has been approached, for example, by (RahmanMiah et al., 2011; Villatoro-Tello et al., 2012; Bogdanova et al., 2013). RahmanMiah et al. discriminated among child-exploitation, adult-adult and general-chatting conversations using a text categorization approach and psychometric information (RahmanMiah et al., 2011). Recently, Bogdanova et al. approached the same problem, the authors concluded that standard text-mining features are useful to distinguish general-chatting from child-exploitation conversations, but not for discriminating between child-exploitation and adult-adult conversations (Bogdanova et al., 2013). In the latter problem, features that model behavior and emotion resulted particularly helpful. N. Pendar approached the problem of distinguishing predators from victims within chat conversations previously confirmed as containing a grooming attack (Pendar, 2007). The author collapsed all of the interventions from each participant into a document and approached the problem as a standard text categorization task with two classes (victim vs. predator).

A more fine grained approximation to the problem was studied by (Michalopoulos and Mavridis, 2011). The authors developed a probabilistic method that classifies chat interventions into one of three classes: 1) *Gaining Access:* indicate predators intention to gain access to the victim; 2) *Deceptive Relationship:* indicate the deceptive relationship that the predator tries to establish with the minor, and are preliminary to a sexual exploitation attack; and 3) *Sexual Affair:* clearly indicate predator's intention for a sexual affair with the victim. These categories correspond to the different stages that a sexual offender adopt when approaching a child. As (Pendar, 2007), (Michalopoulos and Mavridis, 2011) approached this problem as one of text categorization (equating interventions to short-documents). They removed stop words and applied a spelling correction strategy, their best results were obtained with a Naïve Bayes classifier, reaching performance close to 96%. Thus giving evidence that the three categories can be recognized reasonably well. Which in turn gives evidence that modeling the three stages could be beneficial for recognizing sexual predators; for example, when it is not known whether a conversation contains or not a grooming attack. This is the underlying hypothesis behind the proposed method. We aim to use local classifiers, specialized in the different stages a predator approaches a

[1] Adopted for example by the Perverted Justice organization, http://www.perverted-justice.com/

child. Then, we combine the outputs of local classifiers with the goal of improving the performance on sexual predator detection in conversations including both: grooming attacks and well-intentioned conversations.

Because of the relevance of the problem, and of the interest of several research groups from NLP, it was organized in 2012 the first competition of sexual predator identification (Inches and Crestani, 2012). The problem approached in the competition was that of identifying sexual predators from conversations containing both: grooming attacks and well-intentioned conversations. The organizers provided a large corpus divided into development and evaluation data. Development (training) data were provided to participants for building their sexual-predator detection system. In a second stage, evaluation (testing) data were provided to participants, whom had to apply their system to that data and submit their results. Organizers evaluated participants using their predictions on evaluation data (labels for the evaluation data were not provided to participants during the competition).

Several research groups participated in that competition, see (Inches and Crestani, 2012). Some participants developed tailored features for detecting sexual predators (see e.g., (Eriksson and Karlgren, 2012)), whereas other researchers focused on the development of effective classifiers (Parapar et al., 2012). The winning approach implemented a two stage formulation (Villatoro-Tello et al., 2012): in a first step suspicious conversations where identified using a two class classifier. Suspicious conversations are those that potentially include a sexual predator (i.e., a similar approach to (RahmanMiah et al., 2011)). In a second stage, sexual predators were distinguished from victims in the suspicious conversations identified in the first stage (a similar approach to that of (Pendar, 2007)). For both stages a standard classifier and a bag-of-words representation was used.

The methods proposed in this paper were evaluated in the corpus used in the first international competition on sexual predator detection, PAN'12 (Inches and Crestani, 2012). As explained in the following sections, the proposed method uses standard representation and classification methods, therefore, the proposed methods can be improved if we use tailored features or learning techniques for sexual predator detection.

3 Chain-based classifiers for SPD

Chain-based classifiers were first proposed to deal with multi-label classification (Read et al., 2011). The goal was to incorporate dependencies among different labels, which are disregarded by most multi-label classification methods. The underlying idea was to increase the input space of classifiers with the outputs provided by classifiers trained for other labels. The authors showed important improvements over traditional methods.

In this paper, we use chain-based classifiers to incorporate dependencies among local classifiers associated to different segments of a chat conversation. The goal is building an effective predator-detection model made of a set of local models specialized at classifying certain segments of the conversation. Intuitively, we would like to have a local model associated to each of the stages in which a sexual predator approaches a child: *gaining access*, *deceptive relationship* and *sexual affair* (Michalopoulos and Mavridis, 2011). We associate a segment of the conversation to each of the three stages. The raw approach proposed in this work consists of dividing the conversation into three segments of equal length. The first, second and third segments of each conversation are associated to the first, second and third stages, respectively. Although, this approach is too simple, our goal was to determine whether having local classifiers combined via a chaining strategy could improve the performance on sexual predator detection.

We hypothesize that as the vocabulary used in different segments of the conversation is different, specialized models can result in better performance for classifying these local segments. Since local classifiers can only capture local information, it is desirable to somehow connect these classifiers in order to make predictions taking into account the whole conversation. One way to make local classifiers dependent is thought the chain-based methodology, where the outputs of one local classifier are feed as inputs for the next local classifier; the final prediction for the whole conversation can be obtained in several ways as described below.

The proposed approach is described in Figure 1. Since our goal is to detect sexual predators from chat conversations directly, we model each user (well-intentioned user, victim or sexual predator) by their set of interventions. Thus, we generate a single conversation for each user using their interventions, keeping the order in which such interventions happened. The approached problem is to classify these conversations into sexual-predator or any-other-type-of-user. In the following we call simply conversations to the generated per-user conversations.

Chat conversations are divided into three (equally-spaced) parts. Next, one local-classifier is trained for each part of the document according to a predefined order[2], where two out of the three classifiers (second and third) are not independent. Let p_1, p_2, and p_3 denote the segments of text that will be used for generating the first, second and third classifiers. The triplet $\{p_1, p_2, p_3\}$ can be any of the six permutations of 3 segments, this tripled determines the order in which classifiers will be built. Once that a particular order has been defined, a first local-classifier, f_1, is trained using the part p_1 from all of the training documents ($p_1 \in \{first, second, third\}$). Next, a second local-classifier, f_2, is trained by using the part p_2 from all of the training documents. f_2 is built by using both attributes extracted from part p_2 of conversations and the outputs of the first classifier over the training documents. Thus, classifier f_2 depends on classifier f_1, through the outputs of the latter model. A third local-classifier, f_3, is trained using attributes extracted from part p_3 from all conversations, the input space for training f_3 is augmented with the predictions of classifiers f_2 and f_1 over the training documents. Hence, the third classifier depends on the outputs of the first and second classifiers.

Once trained, the chain of local-classifiers can be used to make predictions for the whole conversation in different ways. When a test conversation needs to be classified it is also split into 3 parts. Part p_1 is feeded to classifier f_1, which generates a prediction for f_1. Next, part p_2 from the test document, together with the prediction for p_1 as generated by f_1 are feeded to classifier f_2. Likewise, the outputs of f_2 and f_1, together with part p_3 from the document are used as inputs for classifier f_3. Clearly, since we have predictions for the test document at the three stages of the chain (from $f_{1,2,3}$) we can make a prediction at any stage. The prediction from classifier f_3 is called *chain-prediction* as it is the outcome of the dependent local-classifiers.

[2]We hypothesize that building a chain of classifiers using different orders results in different performances, we evaluate this aspect in Section 4.

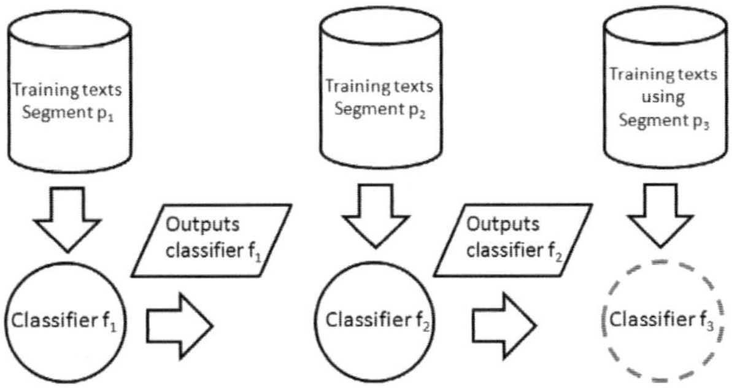

Figure 1: General diagram of the chain-based approach.

Additionally to local and chain-prediction, we propose a ring-like structure for chain-based classifiers in which the outputs of the third local-classifier are used again as inputs for another local model, where the order can be different to that used in the previous iteration. This process is iterated for a number of times, where we can make predictions at every link (local-classifier) of the ring. In addition, after a number of iterations we can make predictions by combining the outputs (like in an ensemble) generated by all of the classifiers considered in the ring up to that iteration. The underlying idea is to explore the performance of the chain as more local-models, that can use short and long term dependencies with other classifiers, are incorporated. Our hypothesis is that after incorporating a certain number of local-dependent-models, the predictions for the whole conversations will be steady and will improve the performance of the straight chain approach.

Algorithm 1 describes the proposed ring-based classifier. $\mathcal{E}$ denotes the set of extra inputs that have to be added to individual classifiers, which are the cumulative outputs of individual classifiers. $\mathcal{P}$ is a set of predefined permutations from which different orders can be took from, where $\mathcal{P}_i$ is the ith permutation. We denote with atts $(p_i, \mathcal{E})$ to the process of extracting attributes from documents' part p_i and merging them with attributes stored in $\mathcal{E}$. `atts` generates the representation that a classifier can use. `train` $[f(X)]$ denotes the process of training classifier f using inputs X. $\mathcal{M}_c$ stores the models trained through the ring process.

Algorithm 1 Ring-based classifier.

```
Require: g : # iterations; P : set of permutations;
  E = {}
  i = 0; c = 1;
  while i ≤ g do
    i++;
    {p1, p2, p3} ← P_i;
    for j = 1 → 3 do
      X ← atts [p_j, E]
      f*_j ← train [f_j(X)];
      M_c ← f*_j;
      E ← E ∪ f*_j(p_j, E);
      c++;
    end for

  end while
  return M_c : trained classifiers (ring-based approach);
```

When a test conversation needs to be labeled, the set of classifiers in $\mathcal{M}$ are applied to it using the same order in the parts that was used when generating the models. Each time a model is applied to the test instance, the prediction of such model is used to increase the input space that is to be used for the next model. We call the prediction given by the last model $\mathcal{M}_g$, *ring-prediction*. One should note that, as before, we can have predictions for the test conversation from every model $\mathcal{M}_i$. Besides, we can accumulate the predictions for the whole set of models $\mathcal{M}_{1,\ldots,g}$. Another alternative is to combine the predictions of the three individual classifiers in each iteration of the ring (every execution of the for-loop in Algorithm 1); this can be done, e.g., by weight averaging. In the next section we report the performance obtained by all these configurations.

4 Experiments and results

For the evaluation of the proposed approach we considered the data set used in the first international competition on sexual predator identification[3] (PAN-2012) (Inches and Crestani, 2012). Table 1 presents some features from the considered data set. The data set contains both chat conversations including sexual predators approaching minors and (authentic) conversations between users (which can or cannot be related to a sexual topic). The data set provided by the organizers contained too much noisy information that could harm the performance of classification methods (e.g., conversations with only one participant, conversations of a few characters long, etc.). Therefore, we applied a preprocessing that aimed to both remove noisy conversations and reducing the data set for scalability purposes. The filtering preprocessing consisted of eliminating: conversations with only one participant, conversations with less than 6 interventions per each participant, conversations that had long sequences of unrecognized characters (images, apparently). The characteristics of the data set after filtering are shown within parentheses in Table 1. It can be seen that the size of the data set was reduced considerably, although a few sexual predators were removed, we believe the information available from them was insufficient to recognize them.

[3]http://pan.webis.de/

Table 1: Features of the data set considered for experimentation (Inches and Crestani, 2012). We show the features of the raw data and in parentheses the corresponding features after applying the proposed preprocessing.

Feature	Development	Evaluation
# Convers.	66,928 (6,588)	155,129 (15,330)
# Users	97,690 (11,038)	218,702 (25,120)
# Sexual Pr.	148(136)	254 (222)

Conversations were represented using their bag-of-words. We evaluated the performance of different representations and found that better results were obtained with a Boolean weighting scheme. No stop-word removal nor stemming was applied, in fact, punctuation marks were conserved. We proceeded this way because we think in chat conversations every character conveys useful information to characterize users, victims and sexual predators. This is because of the highly unstructured and informal language used in chat conversations, as discussed in related works (Kucukyilmaz et al., 2008; RahmanMiah et al., 2011; Rosa and Ellen, 2009).

For indexing conversations we used the TMG toolbox (Zeimpekis and Gallopoulos, 2006). The resultant vocabulary was of 56, 964 terms. For building classifiers we used a neural network as implemented in the CLOP toolbox (Saffari and Guyon, 2006). Our choice is based on results from a preliminary study.

4.1 Performance of local classifiers

We first evaluate the performance of global and local classifiers separately. A global classifier is that generated using the content of the whole conversation, it resembles the formulation from (Pendar, 2007). Local classifiers were generated for each of the segments. Table 2 shows the performance of the global and local models. We report the average (of 5 runs) of precision, recall and F_1 measure for the positive class (sexual predators).

Table 2: Performance of global (row 2) and local classifiers (rows 3-6).

Setting	Precision	Recall	F_1 Measure
Global	95.14%	49.91%	65.42%
Segment 1	**96.16%**	**59.20%**	**73.23%**
Segment 2	96.25%	48.82%	64.72%
Segment 3	93.43%	51.87%	66.68%

It can be seen from Table 2 that the performance of the global model and that obtained for segments 2 and 3 are comparable to each other in terms of the three measures we considered. Interestingly, the best performance was obtained when the only the first segment of the conversation was used for classification. The difference is considerable, about 11.93% of relative improvement. This is a first contribution of our work: *using the first segment of a conversation can improve the performance obtained by a global classifier.* Since the first segment of conversations (barely) corresponds to the *gaining access* stage, the result provides evidence that sexual predators can be detected by the way they start approaching to their victims. That is, the way a well-intentioned person starts a conversation is somewhat different to that of sexual predators approaching a child. Also, it is likely that this makes a difference because for segments 2 and 3, conversations containing grooming attacks and well-intentioned conversations can be very similar (well-intentioned conversations can deal sexual thematic as well).

4.2 Chain-based classifiers

In this section we report the performance obtained by different settings of chain based classifiers. We first report the performance of the chain-prediction strategy, see Section 3. Figure 2 shows the precision, recall and F_1 measure, obtained by the chain-based classifier for the different permutations of the 3 segments (i.e., all possible orders for the segments). For each order, we report the initial performance (that obtained with the segment in the first order) and the chain-prediction, that is the prediction provided by the last classifier in the chain.

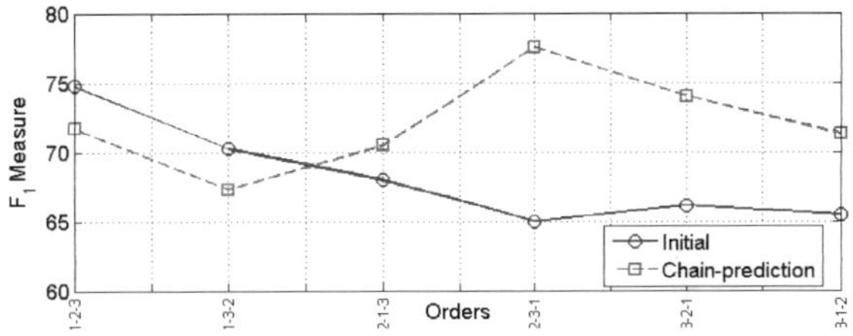

Figure 2: F_1 measure by the initial and chain-based classifier for different orders.

From Figure 2 it can be observed that the chain-prediction outperformed the initial classifier for most of the orders in terms of F_1 measure. For orders starting with segment 1 (1-2-3 and 1-3-2) chain-based classifiers worsen the initial performance. This is due to the high performance of local classifier for segment 1 (see Table 2), which cannot be improved with successive local classifiers. However, the best performance overall was obtained by the chain-based classifier with the order 2-3-1. The relative improvement of this configuration for the chain-based method over the global classifier (the one using the whole conversations) was of 18.52%. One should note that the second-best performance was obtained with the order 3-2-1. Hence, putting the most effective classifier (that for segment 1) at the end seems to have a positive influence in the chain-based classifier. We have shown evidence that chain-based classifiers outperform both the global classifier and any of the local methods. Also, the order of classifiers is crucial for obtaining acceptable results with the chain technique: *using the best classifier in the last position yields better performance; and, putting the best classifier at the beginning would lead the chain to worsen initial performance.*

4.3 Ring-based classifiers

In this section we report experimental results on sexual predator detection obtained with the ring-based strategy. Recall a ring-based classifier can be seen as a chain that is replicated several times with different orders, so we can have predictions for each of the local classifiers at each node of the ring/chain. Besides, we can obtain periodical/cumulative predictions from the chain and predictions derived from combining predictions from a subset of local classifiers in the chain. We explore the performance of all of these strategies in the rest of this section.

We implement ring-based classifiers by successively applying chain-based classifiers with different orders. We consider the following alternatives for detecting predators with ring-based classifiers:

- **Local.** We make predictions with *local classifiers* each time a local classifier is added to the ring (no dependencies are considered). We report the average performance (*segments avg.*) and the maximum performance (*segments max.*) obtained by local classifiers in each of the orders tried.

- **Chain-prediction.** We make predictions with *chain-based classifiers* each time a local classifier is added to the ring. We report the average performance (*chain-prediction avg.*) and the maximum performance (*chain-prediction max.*) obtained by chain-based classifiers per each of the orders tried.

- **Ensemble of chain-based classifiers.** We combine the outputs of the three *chain-based classifiers* built for each order; this method is referred to as *LC-Ensemble*.

- **Cumulative ensemble.** We combine the outputs (via averaging) of all the *chain-based classifiers* that have been built each time an order is added to the ring; we call this method *Cumulative-Ensemble*.

Besides reporting results for these approaches we also report the performance obtained by the global classifier (*Whole conversations*), see Table 2.

We iterated the ring-based classifier for a fixed number of orders. We tried 24 orders, repeating the following process two times: we tried the permutations of the 3 segments in lexicographical order, followed by the same permutations on inverted lexicographical order. So a total of 24 different orders were evaluated. Figure 3 shows the results obtained by the different settings we consider for a typical run of our approach.

Several findings can be drawn from Figure 3. With exception of the average of local classifiers (*segments avg.*), all of the methods outperformed consistently the global classifier (*whole conversations*). Thus confirming the competitive performance of local classifiers and that of chain-based variants. The best local classifier from each order (*segments max.*) achieved competitive performance, although it was outperformed by the average of chain-based classifiers (*chain-prediction avg.*). Since local classifiers are independent, no tendency on their performance can be observed as more orders are tried. On the contrary, the performance chain-based methods (as evidenced by the avg. and max of chain-predictions) improves for the first 8-9 orders and then remains steady. In fact, the best (per-order) chain-prediction (*chain-prediction max.*) obtained performance comparable to that obtained by ensemble methods. One should note, however, that in the *chain-prediction max.* formulation we report the best performance from each order tried, which might correspond to different segments in the different orders. Therefore, it is not clear how the select the specific order to use and the specific segment of the chain that will be used for making predictions, when putting in practice the method for a sexual-predator detection system. Notwithstanding, stable average predictions can be obtained when more than 6-8 orders are used (*chain-prediction avg.*), still the performance of this approach is lower than that of ensembles.

Clearly, the best performance was obtained with the ensemble methods: *chain-ensemble* and *cumulative-ensemble*. Both approaches obtained similar performance, although the *chain-ensemble* slightly outperformed *cumulative-ensemble*. The chain-ensemble considers dependencies within each order and not across orders, thus its performance after trying the 6 permutations of 3 segments did not vary significantly. This is advantageous as only 6 orders have to be evaluated to obtain competitive performance. Unfortunately, as with single chain-classifiers it may be unclear how to select the particular order to use to implement a sexual-predator detection system.

On the other hand, the *cumulative-ensemble* ob-

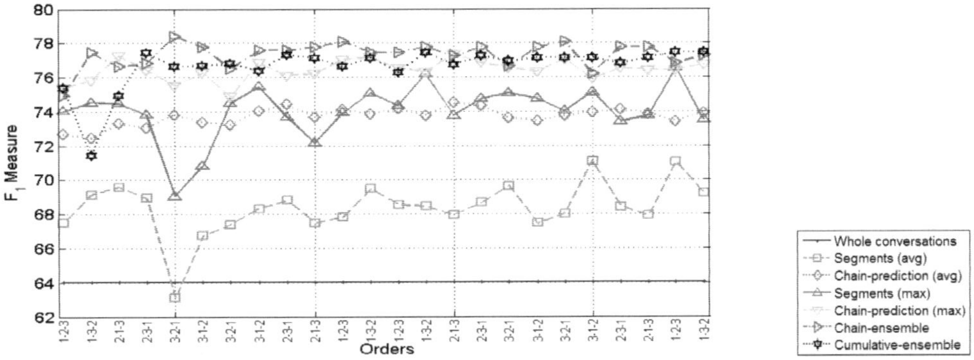

Figure 3: Performance of the different variants of ring-based classifiers for sexual predator detection.

tained stable performance after $\approx$ 12 orders were considered. Recall this method incorporates dependencies among the different orders tried. Although it requires the evaluation of more orders than the *chain-ensemble* to converge, this method is advantageous for a real application: *after a certain number of orders it achieves steady performance, and since it averages the outputs of all of the chain-classifiers evaluated up to a certain iteration, its performance does not rely on selecting a particular configuration.* In consequence, we claim the cumulative-ensemble offers the best tradeoff between performance, stability and model selection.

4.4 Comparison with related works

Table 3 shows a comparison of the configuration *cumulative-ensemble* against the top-ranked participants in the PAN'12 competition. We show the performance of the top-5 participants as described in (Inches and Crestani, 2012), additionally we report the average performance obtained by the methods of the 16 participating teams. We report, F_1 and $F_{0.5}$ measures, and the rank for each participant. We report $F_{0.5}$ measure because that was the leading evaluation measure for the PAN'12 competition.

From Table 3 it can be observed that the proposed method is indeed very competitive. *The results obtained by our method outperformed significantly the average performance (row 7) obtained by all of the participants in all of the considered measures.* In terms of F_1 measure our method would be ranked in the fourth position, while in terms of the $F_{0.5}$ measure our method would be ranked third.

Table 3: Comparison of the proposed method with related works evaluated in the PAN'12 competition (Inches and Crestani, 2012).

Participant	F_1	$F_{0.5}$	**Rk.**
(Villatoro-Tello et al., 2012)	87.34	93.46	1
(Inches and Crestani, 2012)	83.18	91.68	2
(Parapar et al., 2012)	78.16	86.91	3
(Morris and Hirst, 2012)	74.58	86.52	4
(Eriksson and Karlgren, 2012)	87.48	86.38	5
(Inches and Crestani, 2012)	49.10	51.06	-
Our method	78.98	89.14	-

5 Conclusions

We introduced a novel approach to sexual-predator detection in which documents are divided into 3 segments, which, we hypothesize, could correspond to the different stages in that a sexual predator approaches a child. Local classifiers are built for each of the segments, and the predictions of local classifiers are combined through a strategy inspired from chain-based classifiers. We report results on the corpus used in the PAN'12 competition, the proposed method outperforms a global approach. Results are competitive with related works evaluated in PAN'12. Future work includes applying the chain-based classifiers under the two-stage approach from Villatoro et al. (Villatoro-Tello et al., 2012).

Acknowledgments

This project was supported by CONACYT under project grant 134186. The authors thank INAOE, UAM-C and SNI for their support.

References

D. Bogdanova, P. Rosso, and T. Solorio. 2013. Exploring high-level features for detecting cyberpedophilia. In *Special issue on on Computational Approaches to Subjectivity, Sentiment and Social Media Analysis (WASSA 2012), Computer Speech and Language (accepted).*

G. Eriksson and J. Karlgren. 2012. Features for modelling characteristics of conversations. In P. Forner, J. Karlgren, and C. Womser-Hacker, editors, *Working notes of the CLEF 2012 Evaluation Labs and Workshop*, Rome, Italy. CLEF.

C. Harms. 2007. Grooming: An operational definition and coding scheme. *Sex Offender Law Report*, 8(1):1–6.

G. Inches and F. Crestani. 2012. Overview of the international sexual predator identification competition at PAN-2012. In P. Forner, J. Karlgren, and C. Womser-Hacker, editors, *Working notes of the CLEF 2012 Evaluation Labs and Workshop*, Rome, Italy. CLEF.

T. Kucukyilmaz, B. Cambazoglu, C. Aykanat, and F. Can. 2008. Chat mining: predicting user and message attributes in computer-mediated communication. *In Information Processing and Management*, 44(4):1448–1466.

D. Michalopoulos and I. Mavridis. 2011. Utilizing document classification for grooming attack recognition. In *Proceedings of the IEEE Symposium on Computers and Communications*, pages 864–869.

C. Morris and G. Hirst. 2012. Identifying sexual predators by svm classification with lexical and behavioral features. In P. Forner, J. Karlgren, and C. Womser-Hacker, editors, *Working notes of the CLEF 2012 Evaluation Labs and Workshop*, Rome, Italy. CLEF.

J. Parapar, D. E. Losada, and A. Barreiro. 2012. A learning-based approach for the identification of sexual predators in chat logs. In P. Forner, J. Karlgren, and C. Womser-Hacker, editors, *Working notes of the CLEF 2012 Evaluation Labs and Workshop*, Rome, Italy. CLEF.

N. Pendar. 2007. Toward spotting the pedophile telling victim from predator in text chats. In *Proceedings of the IEEE International Conference on Semantic Computing*, pages 235–241, Irvine California USA.

M. W. RahmanMiah, J. Yearwood, and S. Kulkarni. 2011. Detection of child exploiting chats from a mixed chat dataset as text classification task. In *Proceedings of the Australian Language Technology Association Workshop*, pages 157–165.

J. Read, B. Pfahringer, G. Holmes, and E. Frank. 2011. Classifier chains for multi-label classification. *Machine Learning Journal*, 85(3):333–359.

K. D. Rosa and J. Ellen. 2009. Text classification methodologies applied to micro-text in military chat. In *Proceedings of the eight IEEE International Conference on Machine Learning and Applications*, pages 710–714.

A. Saffari and I Guyon. 2006. Quick start guide for CLOP. Technical report, Graz-UT and CLOPINET, May.

E. Villatoro-Tello, A. Juárez-González, H. J. Escalante, M. Montes-Y-Gómez, and L. Villaseñor-Pineda. 2012. A two-step approach for effective detection of misbehaving users in chats. In P. Forner, J. Karlgren, and C. Womser-Hacker, editors, *Working notes of the CLEF 2012 Evaluation Labs and Workshop*, Rome, Italy. CLEF.

J. Wolak, K. Mitchell, and D. Finkelhor. 2006. Online victimization of youth: Five years later. Bulleting 07-06-025, National Center for Missing and Exploited Children, Alexandia, Alexandria, VA.

D. Zeimpekis and E. Gallopoulos, 2006. *Grouping Multidimensional Data: Recent Advances in Clustering*, chapter TMG: A MATLAB toolbox for generating term-document matrices from text collections, pages 187–210. Springer.

Subjectivity and Sentiment Analysis of Modern Standard Arabic and Arabic Microblogs

Ahmed Mourad and Kareem Darwish
Qatar Computing Research Institute
Qatar Foundation
Doha, Qatar
{amourad, kdarwish}@qf.org.qa

Abstract

Though much research has been conducted on Subjectivity and Sentiment Analysis (SSA) during the last decade, little work has focused on Arabic. In this work, we focus on SSA for both Modern Standard Arabic (MSA) news articles and dialectal Arabic microblogs from Twitter. We showcase some of the challenges associated with SSA on microblogs. We adopted a random graph walk approach to extend the Arabic SSA lexicon using Arabic-English phrase tables, leading to improvements for SSA on Arabic microblogs. We used different features for both subjectivity and sentiment classification including stemming, part-of-speech tagging, as well as tweet specific features. Our classification features yield results that surpass Arabic SSA results in the literature.

1 Introduction

Subjectivity and Sentiment Analysis has gained considerable attention in the last few years. SSA has many applications ranging from identifying consumer sentiment towards products to voters' reaction to political adverts. A significant amount of work has focused on analyzing English text with measurable success on news articles and product reviews. There has been recent efforts pertaining to expanding SSA to languages other than English and to analyzing social text such as tweets. To enable effective SSA for new languages and genres, two main requirements are necessary: (a) subjectivity lexicons that broadly cover sentiment carrying words in the genre or language; and (b) tagged corpora to train subjectivity and sentiment classifiers. These two are often scarce or nonexistent when expanding to new languages or genres. In this paper we focus on performing SSA on Arabic news articles and microblogs. There has been some recent work on Arabic SSA. However, the available resources continue to lag in the following ways:
(1) The size of existing subjectivity lexicons is small, with low coverage in practical application.
(2) The available tagged corpora are limited to the news domain, with no publicly available tagged corpora for tweets.
To address the issue of limited lexicons, we applied two methods to build large coverage lexicons. In the first, we used Machine Translation (MT) to translate an existing English subjectivity lexicon. In the second, we employed a random graph walk method to automatically expand a manually curated Arabic lexicon. For the later method, we used Arabic-English MT phrase tables that include both Modern Standard Arabic (MSA) as well as dialectal Arabic. As for tagged corpora, we annotated a new corpus that includes 2,300 Arabic tweets. We describe in detail the process of collecting tweets and some of the major attributes of tweets.

The contribution of this paper is as follows:
- We introduce strong baselines that employ Arabic specific processing including stemming, POS tagging, and tweets normalization. The baseline outperforms state-of-the-art subjectivity classification for the news domain.
- We provide a new annotated dataset for Arabic tweet SSA.
- We employ a random graph walk algorithm to ex-

pand SSA lexicons, leading to improvements for SSA for Arabic tweets.

The remainder of this paper is organized as follows: Section 2 surveys related work; section 3 introduces some of the challenges associated with Arabic SSA; section 4 describes the lexicons we used; section 5 presents the experimental setup and results; and section 6 concludes the paper and discusses future work.

2 Related Work

There has been a fair amount work on SSA. Liu (2010) offers a thorough survey of SSA research. He defines the problem of sentiment analysis including associated SSA terms such as object, opinion, opinion holder, emotions, sentence subjectivity, etc. He also discusses the more popular two stage sentiment and subjectivity classification approach at different granularities (document and sentence levels) using different machine learning approaches (supervised and unsupervised) along with different ways to construct the required data resources (corpora and lexicon). In our work, we classify subjectivity and sentiment in a cascaded fashion following Wilson et al. (2005).

2.1 Subjectivity Analysis

One of most prominent features for subjectivity analysis is the existence of words in a subjectivity lexicon. Mihalcea et al. (2007) translated an existing English subjectivity lexicon from Wiebe and Riloff (2005) using a bilingual dictionary. They also used a subjectivity classifier to automatically annotate the English side of an English-Romanian parallel corpus and then project the annotations to the Romanian side. The projected annotations were used to train a subjectivity classifier. In follow on work, Banea et al. (2010) used MT to exploit annotated SSA English corpora for other languages, including Arabic. They also integrated features from multiple languages to train a combined classifier. In Banea et al. (2008), they compared the automatic annotation of non-English text that was machine translated into English to automatically or manually translating annotated English text to train a classifier in the target language. In all these cases, they concluded that translation can help avail the need for building language specific resources. In performing both subjectivity and sentiment classification, researchers have used word, phrase, sentence, and topic level features. Wilson et al. (2005) report on such features in detail, and we use some of their features in our baseline runs. For Arabic subjectivity classification, Abdul-Mageed et al. (2011) performed sentence-level binary classification. They used a manually curated subjectivity lexicon and corpus that was drawn from news articles (from Penn Arabic tree bank). They used features that are akin to those developed by Wilson et al. (2005). In later work, Abdul-Mageed et al. (2012) extended their work to social content including chat sessions, tweets, Wikipedia discussion pages, and online forums. Unfortunately, their tweets corpus is not publicly available. They added social media features such as author information (person vs. organization and gender). They also explored Arabic specific features that include stemming, POS tagging, and dialect vs. MSA. Their most notable conclusions are: (a) POS tagging helps and (b) Most dialectal Arabic tweets are subjective. Concerning work on subjectivity classification on English tweets, Pak and Paroubek (2010) created a corpus of tweets for SSA. They made a few fundamental assumptions that do not generalize to Arabic well, namely:

- They assumed that smiley and sad emoticons imply positive and negative sentiment respectively. Due to the right-to-left orientation of Arabic text, smiley and sad emoticons can be easily interchanged by mistake in Arabic.
- They also assumed that news tweets posted by newspapers Twitter accounts are neutral. This assumption is not valid for Arabic news articles because many Arabic newspapers are overly critical or biased in their reporting of news. Thus, the majority of news site tweets have sentiment. Consider the following headline:

اللّجنة الدينية تهاجم استمرار تحكم أمن الدولة في تعيين أئمة المساجد

meaning: Religious Council critical of State Security over interference in hiring of clerics.

- They constructed their tweet sets to be uniformly distributed between subjective and objective classes. However, our random sample of Arabic tweets showed that 70% of Arabic tweets are subjective. So this kind of training is misleading especially for a Naïve Bayesian classifier that utilizes the prior probability of classes.

2.2 Sentiment Analysis

Abbasi et al. (2008) focused on conducting sentiment classification at document level. They used syntactic, stylistic, and morphological (for Arabic) features to perform classification. Abdul-Mageed et al. (2011) performed sentence-level sentiment classification for MSA. They concluded that the appearance of a positive or negative adjective, based on their lexicon, is the most important feature. In later work, Abdul-Mageed et al. (2012) extended their work to social text. They concluded that: (a) POS tags are not as effective in sentiment classification as in the subjectivity classification, and (b) most dialectal Arabic tweets are negative. Lastly, they projected that extending/adapting polarity lexicon to new domains; e.g. social media; would result in higher gains. Kok and Brockett (2010) introduced a random-walk-base approach to generate paraphrases from parallel corpora. They proved to be more effective in generating more paraphrases by traversing paths of lengths longer than 2. El-Kahky et al. (2011) applied graph reinforcement on transliteration mining problem to infer mappings that were unseen in training. We used this graph reinforcement method in our work.

3 Challenges for SSA of Arabic

Arabic SSA faces many challenges due to the poorness of language resources and to Arabic-specific linguistic features.

Lexicon: Lexicons containing words with prior polarity are crucial feature for SSA. The most common English lexicon that has been used in literature is the Multi-Perspective Question Answering (MPQA) lexicon, which contains 8,000 words. Some relied on the use of MT to translate English lexicons to languages that lack SSA resources (Mihalcea et al., 2007). A lexicon that is translated into Arabic may have poor coverage due to the morphological and orthographic complexities of Arabic. Arabic nouns and verbs are typically derived from a set of 10,000 roots that are cast into stems using templates that may add infixes, double letters, or remove letters. Stems can accept the attachment of prefixes or suffixes, such as prepositions, determiners, pronouns, etc. The number of possible Arabic surface forms is in the order of billions. In this work, we employed stemming and graph reinforcement to improve the converge of lexicons.

Negation: Negation in dialects can be expressed in many ways. In MSA, the word ليس (meaning "not") is typically used to negate adjectives. Dialects use many words to negate adjectives including: ماهو, مش, مو, ما, منو, etc. These words can have other meanings also. For example, ماهو also means "what is". As for verbs, some dialects like Egyptian and Levantine use a negation construct akin to the "ne ... pas" construct in French. All these make detecting negation hard. We use word n-gram features to overcome this problem.

Emoticons: Another challenge has to do with the limited usefulness of emoticons, because Arabic's smileys and sad emoticons are often mistakenly interchanged. Thus, many tweets have words and emoticons that are contradictory in sentiment. For example:

بسم الله عليك من الألم :(

meaning: with the help of God over your pain (positive) : followed by a sad face

أنا عندي أخت حسبي الله عليها :)

meaning: I have a sister from which I seek the protection of Allah (negative) : followed by a smilie

Use of dialects: Though most Arabic speakers can read and understand MSA, they generally use different Arabic dialects in their daily interactions including online social interaction [1]. There are 6 dominant dialects, namely Egyptian, Moroccan, Levantine, Iraqi, Gulf, and Yemeni. Dialects introduce many new words into the language, particularly stopwords (ex. ماحد and شنو mean "no one" and "what" respectively). Dialects lack spelling standards (ex. ماعرفتش and معرفتش are varying spellings of "I did not know" in Egyptian). Different dialects make different lexical choices for concepts (ex. باهي and صافي mean "good" in Morrocan and Libyan respectively). Due to morphological divergence of dialectal text from MSA, word prefixes and suffixes could be different. For example, Egyptian and Levantine tend to insert the letter ب ("ba") before verbs in present tense. Building lexicons that cover multiple dialects is cumbersome. Further, using MT to build SSA lexicons would be suboptimal because most MT systems perform poorly on dialects of Ara-

[1] http://en.wikipedia.org/wiki/Varieties_of_Arabic

bic.

Tweet specific phenomena: Tweets may contain transliterated words ("LOL" → لول) and non-Arabic words, particularly hashtags such as #syria. Tweets are often characterized by the informality of language and the presence of name mentions (@user_mention), hashtags, and URL's. Further, tweets often contain a significant percentage of misspelled words.

Contradictory language: Often words with negative sentiment are used to express positive sentiment:

تتظاهر الأنثي بالبرود وعدم الاهتمام بك، وتبدء بقول

ألفاظ قد توءلمك .. اعلم أنها كانت تعشقك الي حد الألم

meaning: a female pretends to be cold and uninterested and may even use hurtful words. Know that she painfully loves you.

Other observations: We also observed the following:

- Users tend to express their feelings through extensive use of Quranic verses, Prophetic sayings, proverbs, and poetry.
- Of the annotated tweets in our corpus, nearly 13.5% were sarcastic.
- People primarily use tweets to share their thoughts and feelings and to report facts to a lesser extent. In the set we annotated, 70% of the tweets were subjective and 30% were objective. Of the subjective tweets (positive and negative only), the percentage of positive tweets was 66% compared to 34% for negative tweets.

4 SSA Lexicon

We employed two lexicons that were available to us, namely:

- The MPQA lexicon, which contains 8,000 English words that were manually annotated as strong subjective (subjective in most contexts) or weak subjective (subjective in some contexts) and with their prior polarity (positive, negative, neutral, or both). We used the Bing online MT system [2] to translate the MPQA lexicon into Arabic.
- The ArabSenti lexicon (Abdul-Mageed et al., 2011) containing 3,982 adjectives that were extracted from news data and labeled as positive, negative, or neutral. We optionally used graph reinforcement to expand the ArabSenti lexicon using MT phrase tables, which were modeled as a bipartite graph (El-Kahky et al., 2011). As shown in Figure 1, given a seed lexicon, graph reinforcement is then used to enrich the lexicon by inferring additional mappings. Specifically, given the word with the dotted outline, it may map to the words "unfair" and "unjust" in English that in turn map to other Arabic words, which are potentially synonymous to the original word. We applied a single graph reinforcement iteration over two phrase tables that were generated using Moses (Koehn et al., 2007). The two phrase tables were:

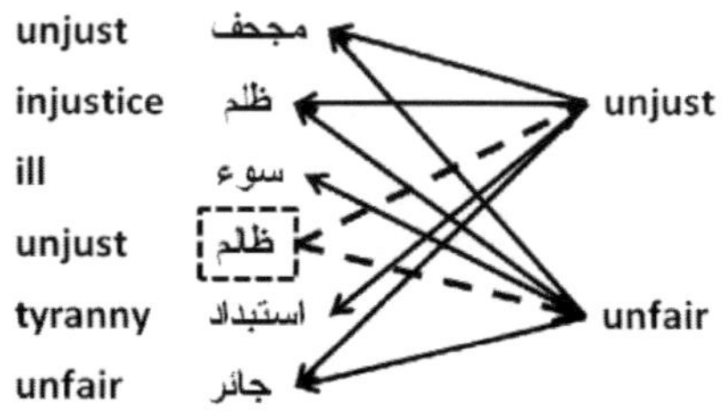

Figure 1: Example mappings seen in phrase table

- an **English-MSA** phrase table, which was trained on a set of 3.69 million parallel sentences containing 123.4 million English tokens. The sentences were drawn from the UN parallel data along with a variety of parallel news data from LDC and the GALE project. The Arabic side was stemmed (by removing just prefixes) using the Stanford word segmenter (Green and DeNero, 2012).
- an **English-Dialect** phrase table, which was trained on 176K short parallel sentences containing 1.8M Egyptian, Levantine, and Gulf dialectal words and 2.1M English words (Zbib et al., 2012). The Arabic side was also stemmed using the Stanford word segmenter.

More formally, Arabic seed words and their English translations were represented using a bipartite graph G = (S, T, M), where S was the set of Arabic words, T was the set of English words, and M was the set of mappings (links or edges) between S and T. First, we found all possible English translations $T' \subseteq T$ for each Arabic word $s_i \subseteq S$ in the seed lexicon. Then, we found all possible Arabic translations $S' \subseteq S$ of the English translations T'. The mapping score $m(s_j \subseteq S'|s_i)$ would be computed

[2]http://www.bing.com/translator/

as:

$$1 - \prod_{\forall s_j, s_i \in S, t \in T'} (1 - \frac{p(t|s_i)}{\sum_t p(s_i|t)} \frac{p(s_j|t)}{\sum_{s_j} p(t|s_j)}) \quad (1)$$

where the terms in the denominator are normalization factors and the product computes the probability that a mapping is not correct given all the paths from which it was produced. Hence, the score of an inferred mapping would be boosted if it was obtained from multiple paths, because the product would have a lower value.

5 Experimental Setup

5.1 Corpus, Classification, and Processing

For subjectivity and sentiment classification experiments on Arabic MSA news, we used the translated MPQA dataset and the ArabSenti dataset respectively. As for SSA on Arabic tweets, to the best of our knowledge, there is no publicly available dataset. Thus, we built our own. We crawled Twitter using the Twitter4j API (Yanamoto, 2011) using the query "lang:ar" to restrict tweets to Arabic ones only. In all, we collected 65 million unique Arabic tweets in the time period starting from January to December 2012; we made sure that duplicate tweets were ignored during crawling. Then we randomly sampled 2300 tweets (nearly 30k words) from the collected set and we gave them to two native Arabic speakers to manually annotate. If the two annotators disagreed on the annotation of a tweet, they discussed it to resolve the disagreement. If they couldn't resolve the disagreement, then the tweet was discarded, which would somewhat affect the SSA effectiveness numbers. They applied one of five possible labels to the tweets, namely: neutral, positive, negative, both, or sarcastic. For subjectivity analysis, all classes other than neutral were considered subjective. As for sentiment analysis, we only considered positive and negative tweets. For both subjectivity and sentiment classification experiments, we used 10-fold cross validation with 90/10 training/test splits. We used the NLTK (Bird, 2006) implementation of the Naïve Bayesian classifier for all our experiments. In offline experiments, the Bayesian classifier performed slightly better than an SVM classifier. The classifier assigned a sentence or tweet the class $c \in C$ that maximizes:

$$\underset{c \in C}{argmax} P(c) \prod_{i=1}^{n} P(f_i|c) \quad (2)$$

where f is the feature vector and C is the set of pre-defined classes. As for stemming and POS Tagging, we used an in-house reimplementation of AMIRA (Diab, 2009). We report accuracy as well as precision, recall and F-measure for each class.

5.2 Baseline: SSA for MSA

5.2.1 Subjectivity Classification

As mentioned in section 2, we employed some of the SSA features that were shown to be successful in the literature (Wiebe and Riloff, 2005; Wilson et al., 2005; Yu and Hatzivassiloglou, 2003) to construct our baseline objective-subjective classifier. We used the automatically translated MPQA and the ArabSenti lexicons. We tokenized and stemmed all words in the dataset and the lexicon. Part of the tokenization involved performing letter normalization where the variant forms of alef (آ, أ, and إ) were normalized to the bare alef (ا), different forms of hamza (ؤ and ئ) were normalized to hamza (ء), ta marbouta (ة) was normalized to ha (ه), and alef maqsoura (ى) was normalized to ya (ي). We used the following features:

Stem-level features:

- *Stem* is a binary features that indicates the presence of the stem in the sentence.

- *Stem prior polarity* as indicated in the translated MPQA and ArabSenti lexicons (positive, negative, both or neutral). Stems and their prior polarity were reportedly the most important features in Wilson et al. (2005).

- *Stem POS*, which has been shown to be effective in the work done by (Wiebe and Riloff, 2005; Yu and Hatzivassiloglou, 2003). Although Abdul-Mageed et al. (2011) used a feature to indicate if a stem is an adjective or not, other tags, such as adverbs, nouns, and verbs, may be good indicators of sentiment. Thus, we used a feature that indicates the POS tag of a stem as being: adjective, adverb, noun, IV, PV, or other, concatenated with the stem. For example, the stem "play" may be assigned "play-noun" if it appears as a noun in a sentence. We chose this reduced POS set based on the frequency distribution

	Acc	Prec		Rec		F-Meas	
		Obj	Subj	Obj	Subj	Obj	Subj
Banea et al. (2010)	72.2	72.6	72.0	60.8	81.5	66.2	76.4
Baseline-MPQA	77.2	83.4	74.2	61.4	90.0	70.7	81.4
Baseline-ArabSenti	76.7	82.4	73.9	60.9	89.5	70.0	80.9
Expanded-ArabSenti-MSA	76.7	83.2	73.6	60.0	90.2	69.7	81.0
Expanded-ArabSenti-MSA+Dialect	76.7	82.9	73.7	60.4	89.9	69.9	81.0

Table 1: Baseline Results for MSA Subjectivity Classifier.

	Acc	Prec		Rec		F-Meas	
		Pos	Neg	Pos	Neg	Pos	Neg
Baseline-MPQA	80.6	75.4	84.0	78.0	82.5	76.5	83.2
Baseline-ArabSenti	80.5	75.4	84.6	78.6	81.5	76.8	82.9
Expanded-ArabSenti-MSA	80.0	74.9	83.9	77.8	81.4	76.2	82.6
Expanded-ArabSenti-Dialect	79.2	73.7	82.8	76.0	81.2	74.6	81.9

Table 2: Baseline Results for MSA Polarity Classifier.

of POS tags and subjectivity classes in the training data.
- *Stem context* as the stem bi-gram containing the stem along with the previous stem. We experimented with higher order stem n-grams, but bigrams yielded the best results.

Sentence features: These features have been shown to be effective by Wiebe and Riloff (2005). They include:
- *Counts of stems belonging to so-called reliability classes* (Wiebe and Riloff, 2005), which are basically either strong-subjective and weak-subjective tokens (as indicated in the SSA lexicon).
- *Counts of POS tags* where we used the counts of the POS tags that used for stem features (adjective, adverb, noun, IV, and PV).

We compared our baseline results with the results reported by Banea et al. (2010) for Arabic subjectivity classification. We used their Arabic MPQA corpus that has been automatically translated from English and then projected subjectivity labels with the same training/test splits. The 9,700 sentences in this corpus are nearly balanced with a 55/45 subjective/objective ratio. Table 1 shows the results for MSA subjectivity classification compared to the results of Banea et al. (2010). Our baseline system improved upon the results of Banea et al. (2010) by 5% (absolute) in accuracy with significant gains in both precision and recall. Using MPQA or ArabSenti lexicons yielded comparable results with MPQA yielding marginally better results. We think that much of improvement that we achieve over the results of Banea et al. (2010) could be attributed to stemming and POS tagging.

5.2.2 Polarity Classification

For polarity classification experiments, we used the positive and negative sentences from the ArabSenti dataset (Abdul-Mageed and Diab, 2011). From the 2,855 sentences in ArabSenti, 45% were objective, 17.2% were positive, 24.1% were negative and the rest were both. We employed the following features:

Stem-level features:
- *Stem*, *Stem prior polarity*, and *Stem POS tag* as in subjectivity classification
- *Stem context* where we considered a stem and the two preceding stems. In offline experiments, we tried looking at more and less context and using the two previous stems yielded the best results. The intuition to use stem context is to compensate for the difficulties associated with 'negation' in Arabic (as mentioned earlier section 3).

Sentence-level features: We used only one binary feature that checks for the occurrence of positive adjectives in the sentence. We experimented with other features that aggregate other POS tags with their prior polarity including negative adjectives and all led to worse classification results.

Table 2 reports on the baseline results of doing sentiment classification. The results of using either MPQA or ArabSenti lexicons were comparable.

	Acc	Prec		Rec		F-Meas	
		Obj	Subj	Obj	Subj	Obj	Subj
Baseline-Majority-Class	70.0	0.0	70.0	0.0	100.0	0.0	83.0
Baseline-MSA	55.1	53.8	56.4	54.5	55.8	54.1	56.1
Baseline-MPQA	64.8	44.9	81.4	66.5	64.0	53.5	71.5
Baseline-ArabSenti	63.9	43.8	80.8	65.9	62.9	52.5	70.7
Expanded-ArabSenti-MSA	64.1	44.2	81.1	66.3	63.3	52.8	71.0
Expanded-ArabSenti-Dialect	63.1	43.2	80.3	65.5	62.1	51.9	70.0

Table 3: Baseline Results for Arabic Tweets Subjectivity Classifier.

	Acc	Prec		Rec		F-Meas	
		Pos	Neg	Pos	Neg	Pos	Neg
Baseline-MSA	54.8	63.2	45.7	55.5	53.8	59.1	49.4
Baseline-MPQA	72.2	85.9	57.0	69.0	77.8	76.3	65.5
Baseline-Arabsenti	71.1	83.9	55.9	69.2	74.8	75.8	63.8
Expanded-ArabSenti-MSA	72.5	86.1	57.7	69.1	79.3	76.5	66.4
Expanded-ArabSenti-Dialect	71.3	85.5	56.3	68.0	77.8	75.6	65.1

Table 4: Baseline Results for Arabic Tweets Polarity Classifier.

5.3 Baseline: SSA of Arabic Microblogs

5.3.1 Subjectivity Classification

We have four baselines for subjectivity classification of Arabic tweets, namely:
Baseline-Majority-Class for which we considered all the tweets to be subjective, where "subjective" was the majority class.
Baseline-MSA for which we used the aforementioned MSA subjectivity classifier using the MPQA lexicon (section 5.2).
Baseline-MPQA and **Baseline-ArabSenti** for which we used microblog specific features and the MPQA and ArabSenti lexicons respectively. We used the following features:

Stem-level features:
- *Stems*, where we normalized words using the scheme described by Darwish et al. (2012). Their work extended the basic Arabic normalization to handle non-Arabic characters that were borrowed from Farsi and Urdu for decoration decorate and words elongation and shortening. After normalization, words were stemmed.
- *MSA or dialect*, which is a binary feature that indicates whether the stem appears in a large MSA stem list (containing 82,380 stems) which was extracted from a large Arabic news corpus from Aljazeera.net.
- *Stem prior polarity* and *Stem POS* as those for MSA subjectivity classification.

Tweets-specific features: Following Barbosa and Feng (2010) and Kothari et al. (2013), we took advantage of tweet specific features, namely:
- Presence of hashtag (#tag).
- Presence of user mention (@some_user) and position in the tweet (start, end and middle).
- Presence of URL and position in the tweet (start, end and middle).
- Presence of retweet symbol "RT" and position in the tweet (start, end and middle).
"RT" and URL's usually appear in the beginning and end of tweets respectively, particularly when retweeting news articles. A change in their position may indicate that the person retweeting added text to the tweet, often containing opinions or sentiment.

Language-independent features: These are binary features that look for non-lexical markers that may indicate sentiment. They are:
- Usage of decorating characters. e.g. گ instead of ك.
- Elongation (detecting both repeated uni-gram & bi-gram character patterns. e.g. لووول (looool), هاهاها (hahaha).
- Punctuation; exclamation and question marks.
- Elongated punctuation marks (e.g. ???, !!!!!)
- Emoticons (e.g. :), :(, :P ... etc.).

Sentence-level features: We used the counts of so-called reliability classes, which count the number of strong-subjective and weak-subjective words.

Table 3 shows the results for subjectivity analysis on tweets. Baseline-Majority-Class was the best given that most Arabic tweets were subjective. Tweet-specific features were not discriminative enough to outperform Baseline-Majority-Class. Thus, assuming that all tweets are subjective seems to be the most effective option. However, it is worth noting that using a classifier that was trained on dialectal tweets yielded better results than using a classifier that was trained on news in MSA. Again using either lexicon made little difference.

5.3.2 Polarity Classification

Our work on MSA showed that *stem* and *stem prior polarity* are the most important features for this task. We used these two features, and we added a third binary feature that indicates the presence of positive emoticons. Negative emoticons appeared infrequently in both training and test sets. Hence using a feature that indicates the presence of negative emoticons would be unreliable. Again we used the MPQA or ArabSenti lexicons, both of which were constructed from news domain (**Baseline-MPQA** and **Baseline-ArabSenti** respectively). For reference, we used the sentiment classifier trained on the MSA news set as a reference (**Baseline-MSA**). Table 4 shows the results for sentiment classification on tweets. Training a classifier with in-domain data (tweets) enhanced classification effectiveness significantly with a gain of 17.4% (absolute) in accuracy and 17.2% and 16.1% (absolute) improvement in F-measure for positive and negative classes respectively. We saw that MPQA led to slightly better results than ArabSenti.

5.4 Lexicon Expansion

We chose to expand the ArabSenti lexicon using graph reinforcement instead of the MPQA lexicon because the ArabSenti was curated manually. The MPQA lexicon had many translation errors and automatic expansion would have likely magnified the errors. We repeated all our **Baseline-ArabSenti** experiments using the expanded ArabSenti lexicon. We expanded using the English-MSA (**Expanded-ArabSenti-MSA**) and the English-Dialect (**Expanded-ArabSenti-Dialect**) phrase tables.

Table 1 reports on the expansion results for MSA news subjectivity classification. The expanded lexicon marginally lowered classification effectiveness. This is surprising given that the number of tokens that matched the lexicon increased more than five fold compared to the baseline (105k matches for the baseline and 567k and 550k matches for the English-MSA and English-Dialect phrase tables respectively). As shown in Table 2, we observed a similar outcome for the expanded lexicon results, compared to baseline results, for MSA sentiment classification. Though expansion had little effect on classification, we believe that the expanded lexicon can help generalize the lexicon to new out-of-domain data.

Tables 3 and 4 report subjectivity and sentiment classification of Arabic tweets respectively. Lexicon expansion had some positive impact on subjectivity classification with improvements in both accuracy, precision, and recall. Lexicon expansion had a larger effect on sentiment classification for tweets with improvement accuracy, precision, and recall with improvements ranging between 1-3% (absolute). The coverage of the lexicon increased nearly 4-folds compared to the baseline (19k matches for baseline compared to 75k matches with expansion for subjectivity, and 7k matches for baseline compared to 28k matches with expansion for sentiment classification). For both subjectivity and sentiment classification, using the English-MSA phrase table was better than using the English-Dialect phrase table. This is not surprising given the large difference in size between the two phrase tables.

6 Conclusion and Future Work

In this paper we presented a strong baseline system for performing SSA for Arabic news and tweets. In our baseline, we employed stemming and POS tagging, leading to results that surpass state-of-the-art results for MSA news subjectivity classification. We also introduced a new tweet corpus for SSA, which we plan to release publicly. We also employed tweet specific language processing to improve classification. Beyond our baseline, we employed graph reinforcement based on random graph walks to expand the SSA lexicon. The expanded lexicon had much broader coverage than the original lexicon. This led to improvements in both subjectivity and sentiment classification for Arabic tweets.

For future work, we plan to explore other features that may be more discriminative. We would like to investigate automatic methods to increase the size of SSA training data. This can be achieved by either utilizing bootstrapping methods or applying MT on large English tweets corpora. Another problem that deserves thorough inspection is the identification of polarity modifiers such as negation.

References

Ahmed Abbasi, Hsinchun Chen, and Arab Salem. 2008. Sentiment analysis in multiple languages: Feature selection for opinion classification in web forums. *ACM Transactions on Information Systems (TOIS)*, 26(3):12, 2008.

Muhammad Abdul-Mageed, Mona Diab, and Mohammed Korayem. 2011. Subjectivity and sentiment analysis of modern standard arabic. In *Proceedings of the 49th Annual Meeting of the Association for Computational Linguistics: Human Language Technologies*, pages 587–591, 2011.

Muhammad Abdul-Mageed and Mona T. Diab. 2011. Subjectivity and sentiment annotation of modern standard arabic newswire. *ACL HLT 2011*, page 110, 2011.

Muhammad Abdul-Mageed, Sandra Kübler, and Mona Diab. 2012. Samar: A system for subjectivity and sentiment analysis of arabic social media. *WASSA 2012*, page 19, 2012.

Carmen Banea, Rada Mihalcea, Janyce Wiebe, and Samer Hassan. 2008. Multilingual subjectivity analysis using machine translation. In *Proceedings of the Conference on Empirical Methods in Natural Language Processing*, pages 127–135.

Carmen Banea, Rada Mihalcea, and Janyce Wiebe. 2010. Multilingual subjectivity: are more languages better? In *Proceedings of the 23rd International Conference on Computational Linguistics*, pages 28–36. Association for Computational Linguistics, 2010.

Luciano Barbosa and Junlan Feng. 2010. Robust sentiment detection on twitter from biased and noisy data. In *Proceedings of the 23rd International Conference on Computational Linguistics: Posters*, pages 36–44. Association for Computational Linguistics.

Steven Bird. 2006. NLTK: the natural language toolkit. In *Proceedings of the COLING/ACL on Interactive presentation sessions*, pages 69–72. Association for Computational Linguistics, 2006.

Kareem Darwish, Walid Magdy, and Ahmed Mourad. 2012. Language processing for arabic microblog retrieval. In *Proceedings of the 21st ACM international conference on Information and knowledge management*, pages 2427–2430. ACM, 2012.

Mona Diab. 2009. Second Generation Tools (AMIRA 2.0): Fast and Robust Tokenization, POS tagging, and Base Phrase Chunking. In *2nd International Conference on Arabic Language Resources and Tools*, 2009.

Ali El-Kahky, Kareem Darwish, Ahmed Saad Aldein, Mohamed Abd El-Wahab, Ahmed Hefny, and Waleed Ammar. 2011. Improved transliteration mining using graph reinforcement. In *Proceedings of the Conference on Empirical Methods in Natural Language Processing*, pages 1384–1393. Association for Computational Linguistics, 2011.

Spence Green and John DeNero. 2012. A Class-Based Agreement Model for Generating Accurately Inflected Translations. *ACL* 2012.

Philipp Koehn, Hieu Hoang, Alexandra Birch, Chris Callison-Burch, Marcello Federico, Nicola Bertoldi, Brooke Cowan, Wade Shen, Christine Moran, Richard Zens, and others. 2007. Moses: Open source toolkit for statistical machine translation. In *Annual meeting-association for computational linguistics*.

Stanley Kok and Chris Brockett. 2010. Hitting the right paraphrases in good time *HLT-NAACL-2010*, pages 145–153.

Alok Kothari, Walid Magdy, Kareem Darwish, Ahmed Mourad, and Ahmed Taei. 2013. Detecting Comments on News Articles in Microblogs *ICWSM*, pages 145–153.

Bing Liu. 2010. Sentiment analysis and subjectivity. *Handbook of Natural Language Processing*, pages 627–666, 2010.

Rada Mihalcea, Carmen Banea, and Janyce Wiebe. 2007. Learning multilingual subjective language via cross-lingual projections. In *ACL-2007*, volume 45, page 976, 2007.

Alexander Pak and Patrick Paroubek. 2010. Twitter as a corpus for sentiment analysis and opinion mining. In *Proceedings of LREC*, volume 2010, 2010.

Janyce Wiebe and Ellen Riloff. 2005. Creating subjective and objective sentence classifiers from unannotated texts. In *Proceedings of CICLing 2005*.

Theresa Wilson, Janyce Wiebe, and Paul Hoffmann. 2005. Recognizing contextual polarity: An exploration of features for phrase-level sentiment analysis. *Computational linguistics*, 35(3):399–433, 2009.

Yusuke Yanamoto. 2011. Twitter4j: A java library for the twitter api, 2011.

Hong Yu and Vasileios Hatzivassiloglou 2003. Towards answering opinion questions: Separating facts from opinions and identifying the polarity of opinion sentences In *EMNLP-2003*, pages 129–136. Association for Computational Linguistics.

Rabih Zbib, Erika Malchiodi, Jacob Devlin, David Stallard, Spyros Matsoukas, Richard Schwartz, John

Makhoul, Omar F. Zaidan and Chris Callison-Burch. 2012. Machine translation of arabic dialects. In *Proceedings of NAACL.*

Sentiment Analysis in Czech Social Media Using Supervised Machine Learning

Ivan Habernal
NTIS – New Technologies for the Information Society, Faculty of Applied Sciences, University of West Bohemia, Univerzitní 8, 306 14 Plzeň Czech Republic
habernal@kiv.zcu.cz

Tomáš Ptáček
Department of Computer Science and Engineering, Faculty of Applied Sciences University of West Bohemia, Univerzitní 8, 306 14 Plzeň Czech Republic
tigi@kiv.zcu.cz

Josef Steinberger
NTIS – New Technologies for the Information Society, Faculty of Applied Sciences, University of West Bohemia, Univerzitní 8, 306 14 Plzeň Czech Republic
jstein@kiv.zcu.cz

Abstract

This article provides an in-depth research of machine learning methods for sentiment analysis of Czech social media. Whereas in English, Chinese, or Spanish this field has a long history and evaluation datasets for various domains are widely available, in case of Czech language there has not yet been any systematical research conducted. We tackle this issue and establish a common ground for further research by providing a large human-annotated Czech social media corpus. Furthermore, we evaluate state-of-the-art supervised machine learning methods for sentiment analysis. We explore different pre-processing techniques and employ various features and classifiers. Moreover, in addition to our newly created social media dataset, we also report results on other widely popular domains, such as movie and product reviews. We believe that this article will not only extend the current sentiment analysis research to another family of languages, but will also encourage competition which potentially leads to the production of high-end commercial solutions.

1 Introduction

Sentiment analysis has become a mainstream research field in the past decade. Its impact can be seen in many practical applications, ranging from analyzing product reviews (Stepanov and Riccardi, 2011) to predicting sales and stock markets using social media monitoring (Yu et al., 2013). The users' opinions are mostly extracted either on a certain polarity scale, or binary (positive, negative); various levels of granularity are also taken into account, e.g., document-level, sentence-level, or aspect-based sentiment (Hajmohammadi et al., 2012).

Most of the research in automatic sentiment analysis of social media has been performed in English and Chinese, as shown by several recent surveys, i.e., (Liu and Zhang, 2012; Tsytsarau and Palpanas, 2012). For Czech language, there have been very few attempts, although the importance of sentiment analysis of social media became apparent, i.e., during the recent presidential elections [1]. Many Czech companies also discovered a huge potential in social media marketing and started launching campaigns, contests, and even customer support on Facebook—the dominant social network of the Czech online community with approximately 3.5 million users.[2] However, one aspect still eludes many of them: automatic analysis of customer sentiment of products, services, or even a brand or a company name. In many cases, sentiment is still labeled manually, according to our information from one of the leading Czech companies for social media monitoring.

Automatic sentiment analysis in the Czech environment has not yet been thoroughly targeted by the research community. Therefore it is necessary to create a publicly available labeled dataset as well as to evaluate the current state of the art for two reasons. First, many NLP methods must deal with high flection and rich syntax when processing the Czech language. Facing these issues may lead to novel

[1] http://www.mediaguru.cz/2013/01/analyza-facebook-rozhodne-o-volbe-prezidenta/ [in Czech]

[2] http://www.czso.cz/csu/redakce.nsf/i/uzivatele_facebooku [in Czech]

approaches to sentiment analysis as well. Second, freely accessible and well-documented datasets, as known from many shared NLP tasks, may stimulate competition which usually leads to the production of cutting-edge solutions.[3]

This article focuses on document-level sentiment analysis performed on three different Czech datasets using supervised machine learning. As the first dataset, we created a Facebook corpus consisting of 10,000 posts. The dataset was manually labeled by two annotators. The other two datasets come from online databases of movie and product reviews, whose sentiment labels were derived from the accompanying star ratings from users of the databases. We provide all these labeled datasets under Creative Commons BY-NC-SA licence[4] at `http://liks.fav.zcu.cz/sentiment`, together with the sources for all the presented experiments.

The rest of this article is organized as follows. Section 2 examines the related work with a focus on the Czech research and social media. Section 3 thoroughly describes the datasets and the annotation process. In section 4, we list the employed features and describe our approach to classification. Finally, section 5 contains the results with a thorough discussion.

2 Related work

There are two basic approaches to sentiment analysis: dictionary-based and machine learning-based. While dictionary-based methods usually depend on a sentiment dictionary (or a polarity lexicon) and a set of handcrafted rules (Taboada et al., 2011), machine learning-based methods require labeled training data that are later represented as features and fed into a classifier. Recent attempts have also investigated semi-supervised methods that incorporate auxiliary unlabeled data (Zhang et al., 2012).

2.1 Supervised machine learning for sentiment analysis

The key point of using machine learning for sentiment analysis lies in engineering a representative set of features. Pang et al. (2002) experimented with unigrams (presence of a certain word, frequencies of words), bigrams, part-of-speech (POS) tags, and adjectives on a Movie Review dataset. Martineau and Finin (2009) tested various weighting schemes for unigrams based on TFIDF model (Manning et al., 2008) and proposed delta weighting for a binary scenario (positive, negative). Their approach was later extended by Paltoglou and Thelwall (2010) who proposed further improvement in delta TFIDF weighting.

The focus of the current sentiment analysis research is shifting towards social media, mainly targeting Twitter (Kouloumpis et al., 2011; Pak and Paroubek, 2010) and Facebook (Go et al., 2009; Ahkter and Soria, 2010; Zhang et al., 2011; López et al., 2012). Analyzing media with very informal language benefits from involving novel features, such as emoticons (Pak and Paroubek, 2010; Montejo-Ráez et al., 2012), character n-grams (Blamey et al., 2012), POS and POS ratio (Ahkter and Soria, 2010; Kouloumpis et al., 2011), or word shape (Go et al., 2009; Agarwal et al., 2011).

In many cases, the gold data for training and testing the classifiers are created semi-automatically, as in, e.g., (Kouloumpis et al., 2011; Go et al., 2009; Pak and Paroubek, 2010). In the first step, random samples from a large dataset are drawn according to presence of emoticons (usually positive and negative) and are then filtered manually. Although large high-quality collections can be created very quickly using this approach, it makes a strong assumption that every positive or negative post must contain an emoticon.

Balahur and Tanev (2012) performed experiments with Twitter posts as part of the CLEF 2012 RepLab[5]. They classified English and Spanish tweets by a small but precise lexicon, which contained also slang, combined with a set of rules that capture the manner in which sentiment is expressed in social media.

---

[3] E.g., named entity recognition based on Conditional Random Fields emerged from CoNLL-2003 named entity recognition shared task.

[4] `http://creativecommons.org/licenses/by-nc-sa/3.0/`

[5] `http://www.limosine-project.eu/events/replab2012`

Since the limited space of this paper does not allow us to present detailed evaluation from the related work, we recommend an in-depth survey by Tsytsarau and Palpanas (2012) for actual results obtained from the abovementioned methods.

2.2 Sentiment analysis in Czech environment

Veselovská et al. (2012) presented an initial research on Czech sentiment analysis. They created a corpus which contains polarity categories of 410 news sentences. They used the Naive Bayes classifier and a classifier based on a lexicon generated from annotated data. The corpus is not publicly available, moreover, due to the small size of the corpus no strong conclusions can be drawn.

Steinberger et al. (2012) proposed a semi-automatic 'triangulation' approach to creating sentiment dictionaries in many languages, including Czech. They first produced high-level gold-standard sentiment dictionaries for two languages and then translated them automatically into the third language by a state-of-the-art machine translation service. Finally, the resulting sentiment dictionaries were merged by taking overlap from the two automatic translations.

A multilingual parallel news corpus annotated with opinions towards entities was presented in (Steinberger et al., 2011). Sentiment annotations were projected from one language to several others, which saved annotation time and guaranteed comparability of opinion mining evaluation results across languages. The corpus contains 1,274 news sentences where an entity (the target of the sentiment analysis) occurs. It contains 7 languages including Czech. Their research targets fundamentally different objectives from our research as they focus on news media and aspect-based sentiment analysis.

3 Datasets

3.1 Social media dataset

The initial selection of Facebook brand pages for our dataset was based on the 'top' Czech pages, according to the statistics from SocialBakers.[6] We focused on pages with a large Czech fan base and a sufficient number of Czech posts. Using Facebook Graph API and Java Language Detector[7] we acquired 10,000 random posts in the Czech language from nine different Facebook pages. The posts were then completely anonymized as we kept only their textual contents.

Sentiment analysis of posts at Facebook brand pages usually serves as a marketing feedback of user opinions about brands, services, products, or current campaigns. Thus we consider the sentiment target to be the given product, brand, etc. Typically, users' complaints hold negative sentiment, whereas joy or happiness about the brand is taken as positive. We also added another class called *bipolar* which represents both positive and negative sentiment in one post.[8] In some cases, the user's opinion, although being somehow positive, does not relate to the given page.[9] Therefore the sentiment is treated as neutral in these cases, according to our above-mentioned assumption.

The complete 10k dataset was independently annotated by two annotators. The inter-annotator agreement (Cohen's κ) between these two annotators reaches 0.66 which represents a substantial agreement level (Pustejovsky and Stubbs, 2013), therefore the task can be considered as well-defined.

The gold data were created based on the agreement of the two annotators. They disagreed in 2,216 cases. To solve these conflicts, we involved a third super-annotator to assign the final sentiment label. However, even after the third annotator's labeling, there was still no agreement for 308 labels. These cases were later solved by a fourth annotator. We discovered that most of these conflicting cases were classified as either neutral or bipolar. These posts were often difficult to label because the author used irony, sarcasm or the context or previous posts. These issues remain open.

The Facebook dataset contains of 2,587 positive, 5,174 neutral, 1,991 negative, and 248 bipolar posts, respectively. We ignore the bipolar class later in all experiments. The sentiment distribution among the

[6] `http://www.socialbakers.com/facebook-pages/brands/czech-republic/`

[7] `http://code.google.com/p/jlangdetect/`

[8] For example *"to bylo moc dobry ,fakt jsem se nadlabla :-D skoda ze uz neni v nabidce"—"It was very tasty, I really stuffed myself :-D sad it's not on the menu anymore"*.

[9] Certain campaigns ask the fans for, i.e., writing a poem—these posts are mostly positive (or funny, at least) but are irrelevant for the desired task.

source pages is shown in Figure 1. The statistics reveal negative opinions towards cell phone operators and positive opinions towards, e.g., perfumes and ZOO.

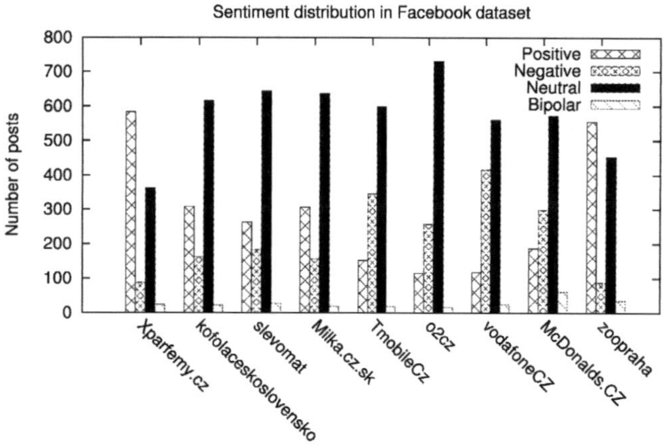

Figure 1: Social media dataset statistics

3.2 Movie review dataset

Movie reviews as a corpus for sentiment analysis has been used in research since the pioneering research conducted by Pang et al. (2002). Therefore we covered the same domain in our experiments as well. We downloaded 91,381 movie reviews from the Czech Movie Database[10] and split them into 3 categories according to their star rating (0–2 stars as negative, 3–4 stars as neutral, 5–6 stars as positive). The dataset contains of 30,897 positive, 30,768 neutral, and 29,716 negative reviews, respectively.

3.3 Product review dataset

Another very popular domain for sentiment analysis deals with product reviews (Hu and Liu, 2004). We crawled all user reviews from a large Czech e-shop Mall.cz[11] which offers a wide range of products. The product reviews are accompanied with star ratings on the scale 0–5. We took a different strategy for assigning sentiment labels. Whereas in the movie dataset the distribution of stars was rather uniform, in the product review domain the ratings were skewed towards the higher values. After a manual inspection we discovered that 4-star ratings mostly correspond to neutral opinions and 3 or less stars denote mostly negative comments. Thus we split the dataset into three categories according to this observation. The final dataset consists of 145,307 posts (102,977 positive, 31,943 neutral, and 10,387 negative).

4 Classification

4.1 Preprocessing

As pointed out by Laboreiro et al. (2010), tokenization significantly affects sentiment analysis, especially in case of social media. Although Ark-tweet-nlp tool (Gimpel et al., 2011) was developed and tested in English, it yields satisfactory results in Czech as well, according to our initial experiments on the Facebook corpus. Its significant feature is proper handling of emoticons and other special character sequences that are typical for social media. Furthermore, we remove stopwords using the stopword list from Apache Lucene project.[12]

In many NLP applications, a very popular preprocessing technique is stemming. We tested Czech light stemmer (Dolamic and Savoy, 2009) and High Precision Stemmer[13]. Another widely-used method for reducing the vocabulary size, and thus the feature space, is lemmatization. For Czech language the only currently available lemmatizer is shipped with Prague Dependency Treebank (PDT) toolkit (Hajič et al., 2006). However, we use our in-house Java HMM-based implementation using the PDT training data as we need a better control over each preprocessing step.

Part-of-speech tagging is done using our in-house Java solution that exploits Prague Dependency Treebank (PDT) data as well. However, since PDT is trained on news corpora, we doubt it is suitable for tagging social media that are written in very informal language (consult, i.e., (Gimpel et al., 2011) where similar issues were tackled in English).

Since the Facebook dataset contains a huge number of grammar mistakes and misspellings (typically *'i/y'*,*'ě/je/ie'*, and others), we incorporated phonetic transcription to International Phonetic Alphabet (IPA) in order to reduce the effect of these mistakes. We rely on eSpeak[14] implementation. An-

[10] `http://www.csfd.cz/`

[11] `http://www.mall.cz`

[12] `http://lucene.apache.org/core/`

[13] Publication pending; please visit `http://liks.fav.zcu.cz/HPS/`.

[14] `http://espeak.sourceforge.net`

Pipe 1	**Pipe 2**	**Pipe 3**
Tokenizing		
ArkTweetNLP		
POS tagging		
PDT		
Stem (S)		**Lemma (L)**
none (n)		PDT (p)
light (l)		
HPS (h)		
Stopwords		
remove		
Casing (C)	**Phonetic (P)**	–
keep (k)	eSpeak (e)	
lower (l)		

Table 1: The preprocessing pipes (top-down). Various combinations of methods can be denoted using the appropriate labels, e.g. "SnCk" means *1. tokenizing, 2. POS-tagging, 3. no stemming, 4. removing stopwords, and 5. no casing*, or "Lp" means *1. tokenizing, 2. POS-tagging, 3. lemmatization using PDT, and 4. removing stopwords*.

other preprocessing step might involve removing diacritics, as many Czech users type only using unaccented characters. However, posts without diacritics represent only about 8% of our datasets, thus we decided to keep diacritics unaffected.

The complete preprocessing diagram and its variants is depicted in Table 1. Overall, there are 10 possible preprocessing 'pipe' configurations.

4.2 Features

N-gram features We use presence of unigrams and bigrams as binary features. The feature space is pruned by minimum n-gram occurrence which was empirically set to 5. Note that this is the baseline feature in most of the related work.

Character n-gram features Similarly to the word n-gram features, we added character n-gram features, as proposed by, e.g., (Blamey et al., 2012). We set the minimum occurrence of a particular character n-gram to 5, in order to prune the feature space. Our feature set contains 3-grams to 6-grams.

POS-related features Direct usage of part-of-speech n-grams that would cover sentiment patterns has not shown any significant improvement in the related work. Still, POS tags provide certain characteristics of a particular post. We implemented various POS features that include, e.g., the number of nouns, verbs, and adjectives (Ahkter and Soria, 2010), the ratio of nouns to adjectives and verbs to adverbs (Kouloumpis et al., 2011), and number of negative verbs.

Emoticons We adapted the two lists of emoticons that were considered as positive and negative from (Montejo-Ráez et al., 2012). The feature captures number of occurrences of each class of emoticons within the text.

Delta TFIDF variants for binary scenarios Although simple binary word features (presence of a certain word) reach surprisingly good performance, they have been surpassed by various TFIDF-based weighting, such as Delta TFIDF (Martineau and Finin, 2009), or Delta BM25 TFIDF (Paltoglou and Thelwall, 2010). Delta-TFIDF still uses traditional TFIDF word weighting but treats positive and negative documents differently. However, all the existing related works which use this kind of features deal only with binary decisions (positive/negative), thus we filtered out neutral documents from the datasets.[15] We implemented the most promising weighting schemes from (Paltoglou and Thelwall, 2010), namely *Augmented TF*, *LogAve TF*, *BM25 TF*, *Delta Smoothed IDF*, *Delta Prob. IDF*, *Delta Smoothed Prob. IDF*, and *Delta BM25 IDF*.

4.3 Classifiers

All evaluation tests were performed using two classifiers, Maximum Entropy (MaxEnt) and Support Vector Machines (SVM). Although Naive Bayes classifier is also widely used in the related work, we did not include it as it usually performs worse than SVM or MaxEnt. We used a pure Java framework for machine learning[16] with default settings (linear kernel for SVM).

5 Results

For each combination from the preprocessing pipeline (refer to Table 1) we assembled various sets of features and employed two classifiers. In the first

[15] Opposite to leave-one-out cross validation in (Paltoglou and Thelwall, 2010), we still use 10-fold cross validation in all experiments.

[16] `http://liks.fav.zcu.cz/ml`

scenario, we classify into all three classes (positive, negative, and neutral).[17] In the second scenario, we follow a strand of related research, e.g., (Martineau and Finin, 2009; Celikyilmaz et al., 2010), that deals only with positive and negative classes. For these purposes we filtered out all the neutral documents from the datasets. Furthermore, in this scenario we evaluate only features based on weighted delta-TFIDF, as, e.g., in (Paltoglou and Thelwall, 2010). We also involved only MaxEnt classifier into the second scenario.

All tests were conducted in the 10-fold cross validation manner. We report macro F-measure, as it allows comparing classifier results on different datasets. Moreover, we do not report micro F-measure (accuracy) as it tends to prefer performance on dominant classes in highly unbalanced datasets (Manning et al., 2008), which is, e.g., the case of our Product Review dataset where most of the labels are positive.

5.1 Social media

Table 2 shows the results for the 3-class classification scenario on the Facebook dataset. The row labels denote the preprocessing configuration according to Table 1. In most cases, maximum entropy classifier significantly outperforms SVM. The combination of all features (the last column) yields the best results regardless to the preprocessing steps. The reason might be that the involved character n-gram feature captures subtle sequences which represent subjective punctuation or emoticons, that were not covered by the *emoticon* feature. On average, the best results were obtained when HPS stemmer and lowercasing or phonetic transcription were involved (lines *ShCl* and *ShPe*). This configuration significantly outperforms other preprocessing techniques for token-based features (see column *Unigr + bigr + POS + emot.*).

In the second scenario we evaluated various TFIDF weighting schemes for binary sentiment classification. The results are shown in Table 3. The three-character notation consists of term frequency, inverse document frequency, and normalization. Due to a large number of possible combinations, we report only the most successful ones, namely *Augmented*—a and *LogAve*—L term frequency, followed by *Delta Smoothed*—$\Delta(t')$, *Delta Smoothed Prob.*—$\Delta(p')$, and *Delta BM25*—$\Delta(k)$ inverse document frequency; normalization was not involved. We can see that the baseline (the first column *bnn*) is usually outperformed by any weighted TFIDF technique. Moreover, using any kind of stemming (the row entitled *various**) significantly improves the results. For the exact formulas of the delta TFIDF variants please refer to (Paltoglou and Thelwall, 2010).

We also tested the impact of TFIDF word features when added to other features from the first scenario (refer to Table 2). Column *FS1* in Table 3 displays results for a feature set with the simple binary presence-of-the-word feature (binary unigrams). In the last column *FS2* we replaced this binary feature with TFIDF weighted feature $a\Delta(t')n$. It turned out that the weighed form of word feature does not improve the performance, when compared with simple binary unigram feature. Furthermore, a set of different features (words, bigrams, POS, emoticons, character n-grams) significantly outperforms a single TFIDF weighted feature.

We also report the effect of the dataset size on the performance. We randomly sampled 10 subsets from the dataset (1k, 2k, etc.) and tested the performance; still using 10-fold cross validation. We took the most promising preprocessing configuration (*ShCl*) and MaxEnt classifier. As can be seen in Figure 2, while the dataset grows to approx 6k–7k items, the performance rises for most combinations of features. At 7k-items dataset, the performance begins to reach its limits for most combinations of features and hence adding more data does not lead to a significant improvement.

5.1.1 Upper limits of automatic sentiment analysis

To see the upper limits of the task itself, we also evaluate the annotator's judgments. Although the gold labels were chosen after a consensus of at least two people, there were many conflicting cases that must have been solved by a third or even a fourth person. Thus even the original annotators do not achieve 1.00 F-measure on the gold data.

We present 'performance' results of both annotators and of the best system as well (MaxEnt classi-

[17] We ignore the bipolar posts in the current research.

Facebook dataset, 3 classes

	Unigrams		Unigr + bigrams		Unigr + bigr + POS features		Unigr + bigr + POS + emot.		Unigr + bigr + POS + emot. + char n-grams	
	MaxEnt	SVM	MaxEnt	SVM	MaxEnt	SVM	MaxEnt	SVM	MaxEnt	SVM
SnCk	0.63	0.64	0.63	0.64	0.66	0.64	0.66	0.64	**0.69**	0.67
SnCl	0.63	0.64	0.63	0.64	0.66	0.63	0.66	0.63	**0.69**	0.68
SlCk	0.65	0.67	0.66	0.67	0.68	0.66	0.67	0.66	**0.69**	0.67
SlCl	0.65	0.67	0.65	0.67	0.68	0.66	**0.69**	0.66	**0.69**	0.67
ShCk	0.66	0.67	0.66	0.67	0.68	0.67	0.67	0.67	**0.69**	0.67
ShCl	0.66	0.66	0.66	0.67	**0.69**	0.67	**0.69**	0.67	**0.69**	0.67
SnPe	0.64	0.65	0.64	0.65	0.67	0.65	0.67	0.65	0.68	0.68
SlPe	0.65	0.67	0.65	0.67	0.68	0.67	0.67	0.66	0.68	0.67
ShPe	0.66	0.67	0.66	0.67	**0.69**	0.66	**0.69**	0.66	0.68	0.67
Lp	0.64	0.65	0.63	0.65	0.67	0.64	0.67	0.65	0.68	0.67

Table 2: Results on the Facebook dataset, classification into 3 classes. Macro F-measure, 95% confidence interval $= \pm 0.01$. Bold numbers denote the best results.

Facebook dataset, positive and negative classes only

	bnn	$a\Delta(t')n$	$a\Delta(p')n$	$a\Delta(k)n$	$L\Delta(t')n$	$L\Delta(p')n$	$L\Delta(k)n$	FS1	FS2
SnCk	0.83	0.86	0.86	0.86	0.85	0.86	0.86	**0.90**	0.89
SnCl	0.84	0.86	0.86	0.86	0.86	0.86	0.86	**0.90**	**0.90**
various*	0.85	<u>0.88</u>	<u>0.88</u>	<u>0.88</u>	<u>0.88</u>	<u>0.88</u>	<u>0.88</u>	**0.90**	**0.90**
SnPe	0.84	0.86	0.86	0.86	0.86	0.86	0.86	**0.90**	**0.90**
Lp	0.84	0.86	0.85	0.85	0.86	0.86	0.86	0.88	0.88

* same results for ShCk, ShCl, SlCl, SlPe, SlCk, and ShPe
FS1: Unigr + bigr + POS + emot. + char n-grams
FS2: $a\Delta(t')n$ + bigr + POS + emot. + char n-grams

Table 3: Results on the Facebook dataset for various TFIDF-weighted features, classification into 2 classes. Macro F-measure, 95% confidence interval $= \pm 0.01$. Underlined numbers show the best results for TFIDF-weighted features. Bold numbers denote the best overall results.

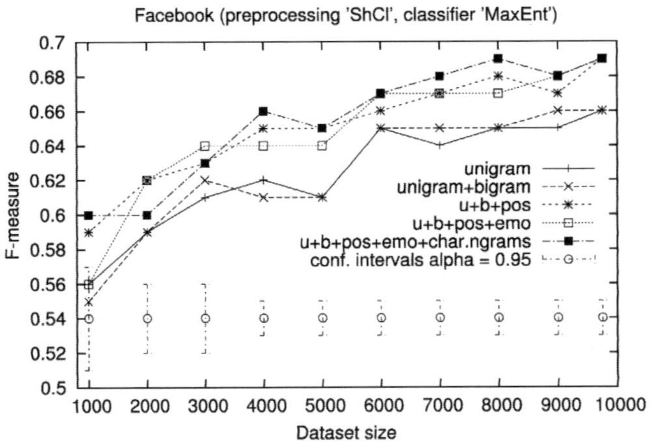

Figure 2: Performance wrt. data size. Using *ShCl* preprocessing and MaxEnt classifier.

fier, all features, *ShCl* preprocessing). Table 4 shows the results as confusion matrices. For each class (*p*—positive, *n*—negative, *0*—neutral) we also report precision, recall, and F-measure. The row headings denote gold labels, the column headings represent values assigned by the annotators or the system.[18] The annotators' results show what can be expected from a 'perfect' system that would solve the task the way a human would.

In general, both annotators judge all three classes with very similar F-measure. By contrast, the system's F-measure is very low for negative posts (0.54 vs. ≈ 0.75 for neutral and positive). We offer the following explanation. First, many of the negative posts surprisingly contain happy emoticons, which

[18]Even though the task has three classes, the annotators also used 'b' for 'bipolar and '?' for 'cannot decide'.

	Annotator 1							
	0	**n**	**p**	**?**	**b**	**P**	**R**	**Fm**
0	4867	136	115	2	54	.93	.94	.93
n	199	1753	6	0	33	.93	.88	.90
p	175	6	2376	0	30	.95	.92	.93
							Macro Fm:	.92

	Annotator 2							
	0	**n**	**p**	**?**	**b**	**P**	**R**	**Fm**
0	4095	495	573	3	8	.95	.79	.86
n	105	1878	6	0	2	.79	.94	.86
p	100	12	2468	3	4	.81	.95	.88
							Macro Fm:	.86

	Best system					
	0	**n**	**p**	**P**	**R**	**Fm**
0	4014	670	490	.74	.78	.76
n	866	1027	98	.57	.52	.54
p	563	102	1922	.77	.74	.75
					Macro Fm:	.69

Table 4: Confusion matrices for three-class classification. 'Best system' configuration: all features (unigram, bigram, POS, emoticons, character n-grams), *ShCl* preprocessing, and MaxEnt classifier. 95% confidence interval $= \pm 0.01$.

could be a misleading feature for the classifier. Second, the language of the negative posts in not as explicit as for the positive ones in many cases; the negativity is 'hidden' in irony, or in a larger context (i.e., *"Now I'm sooo satisfied with your competitor :))"*). This remains an open issue for the future research.

5.2 Product and movie reviews

For the other two datasets, the product reviews and movie reviews, we slightly changed the configuration. First, we removed the character n-grams from the feature sets, otherwise the feature space would become too large for feasible computing. Second, we abandoned SVM as it became computationally infeasible for such a large datasets.

Table 5 (left-hand part) presents results on the product reviews. The combination of unigrams and bigrams works best, almost regardless of the preprocessing. By contrast, POS features rapidly decrease the performance. We suspect that POS features do not carry any useful information in this case and by introducing a lot of 'noise' they cause that the optimization function in the MaxEnt classifier fails to find a global minimum.

In the right-hand part of Table 5 we can see the results on the movie reviews. Again, the bigram feature performs best, paired with combination of HPS stemmer and phonetic transcription (*ShPe*). Adding POS-related features causes a large drop in performance. We can conclude that for larger texts, the bigram-based feature outperforms unigram features and, in some cases, a proper preprocessing may further significantly improve the results.

6 Conclusion

This article presented an in-depth research of supervised machine learning methods for sentiment analysis of Czech social media. We created a large Facebook dataset containing 10,000 posts, accompanied by human annotation with substantial agreement (Cohen's κ 0.66). The dataset is freely available for non-commercial purposes.[19] We thoroughly evaluated various state-of-the-art features and classifiers as well as different language-specific preprocessing techniques. We significantly outperformed the baseline (unigram feature without preprocessing) in three-class classification and achieved F-measure 0.69 using a combination of features (unigrams, bigrams, POS features, emoticons, character n-grams) and preprocessing techniques (unsupervised stemming and phonetic transcription). In addition, we reported results in two other domains (movie and product reviews) with a significant improvement over the baseline.

To the best of our knowledge, this article is the only of its kind that deals with sentiment analysis in Czech social media in such a thorough manner. Not only it uses a dataset that is magnitudes larger than any from the related work, but also incorporates state-of-the-art features and classifiers. We believe that the outcomes of this article will not only help to set the common ground for sentiment analysis for the Czech language but also help to extend the research outside the mainstream languages in this research field.

Acknowledgement

This work was supported by grant no. SGS-2013-029 Advanced computing and information

[19] We encourage other researchers to download our dataset for their research in the sentiment analysis field.

	Product reviews, 3 classes				Movie reviews, 3 classes			
	FS1	FS2	FS3	FS4	FS1	FS2	FS3	FS4
SnCk	0.70	0.74	0.52	0.49	0.76	0.77	0.71	0.61
SnCl	0.71	**0.75**	0.51	0.52	0.76	0.77	0.71	0.70
SlCk	0.67	**0.75**	0.59	0.55	0.78	0.78	0.73	0.72
SlCl	0.67	**0.75**	0.56	0.57	0.78	0.78	0.71	0.71
ShCk	0.67	**0.75**	0.57	0.57	0.78	0.78	0.74	0.72
ShCl	0.67	0.74	0.55	0.57	0.77	0.78	0.73	0.73
SnPe	0.69	0.74	0.50	0.55	0.77	0.78	0.69	0.72
SlPe	0.67	**0.75**	0.55	0.57	0.78	0.78	0.73	0.73
ShPe	0.68	0.74	0.56	0.59	0.78	**0.79**	0.74	0.73
Lp	0.66	**0.75**	0.56	0.57	0.77	0.77	0.68	0.70

Table 5: Results on the product and movie review datasets, classification into 3 classes. FSx denote different feature sets. FS1 = Unigrams; FS2 = Uni + bigrams; FS3 = Uni + big + POS features; FS4 = Uni + big + POS + emot. Macro F-measure, 95% confidence interval ± 0.002 (products), ± 0.003 (movies). Bold numbers denote the best results.

systems and by the European Regional Development Fund (ERDF), project "NTIS - New Technologies for Information Society", European Center of Excellence, CZ.1.05/1.1.00/02.0090. The access to computing and storage facilities owned by parties and projects contributing to the National Grid Infrastructure MetaCentrum, provided under the programme "Projects of Large Infrastructure for Research, Development, and Innovations" (LM2010005) is highly acknowledged.

References

Apoorv Agarwal, Boyi Xie, Ilia Vovsha, Owen Rambow, and Rebecca Passonneau. 2011. Sentiment analysis of twitter data. In *Proceedings of the Workshop on Languages in Social Media*, LSM '11, pages 30–38, Stroudsburg, PA, USA. Association for Computational Linguistics.

Julie Kane Ahkter and Steven Soria. 2010. Sentiment analysis: Facebook status messages. Technical report, Stanford University. Final Project CS224N.

Alexandra Balahur and Hristo Tanev. 2012. Detecting entity-related events and sentiments from tweets using multilingual resources. In *Proceedings of the 2012 Conference and Labs of the Evaluation Forum Information Access Evaluation meets Multilinguality, Multimodality, and Visual Analytics*.

Ben Blamey, Tom Crick, and Giles Oatley. 2012. R U : -) or : -(? character- vs. word-gram feature selection for sentiment classification of OSN corpora. In *Proceedings of AI-2012, The Thirty-second SGAI International Conference on Innovative Techniques and Applications of Artificial Intelligence*, pages 207–212. Springer.

A. Celikyilmaz, D. Hakkani-Tür, and Junlan Feng. 2010. Probabilistic model-based sentiment analysis of twitter messages. In *Spoken Language Technology Workshop (SLT), 2010 IEEE*, pages 79–84. IEEE.

Ljiljana Dolamic and Jacques Savoy. 2009. Indexing and stemming approaches for the czech language. *Information Processing and Management*, 45(6):714–720, November.

Kevin Gimpel, Nathan Schneider, Brendan O'Connor, Dipanjan Das, Daniel Mills, Jacob Eisenstein, Michael Heilman, Dani Yogatama, Jeffrey Flanigan, and Noah A. Smith. 2011. Part-of-speech tagging for twitter: annotation, features, and experiments. In *Proceedings of the 49th Annual Meeting of the Association for Computational Linguistics: Human Language Technologies: short papers - Volume 2*, HLT '11, pages 42–47, Stroudsburg, PA, USA. Association for Computational Linguistics.

Alec Go, Richa Bhayani, and Lei Huang. 2009. Twitter sentiment classification using distant supervision. CS224N Project Report, Stanford.

Jan Hajič, Jarmila Panevová, Eva Hajičová, Jarmila Panevová, Petr Sgall, Petr Pajas, Jan Štěpánek, Jiří Havelka, and Marie Mikulová. 2006. Prague dependency treebank 2.0. Linguistic Data Consortium, Philadelphia.

Mohammad Sadegh Hajmohammadi, Roliana Ibrahim, and Zulaiha Ali Othman. 2012. Opinion mining and sentiment analysis: A survey. *International Journal of Computers & Technology*, 2(3).

Minqing Hu and Bing Liu. 2004. Mining and summarizing customer reviews. In *Proceedings of the tenth*

ACM SIGKDD international conference on Knowledge discovery and data mining, KDD '04, pages 168–177, New York, NY, USA. ACM.

Efthymios Kouloumpis, Theresa Wilson, and Johanna Moore. 2011. Twitter sentiment analysis: The good the bad and the OMG! In *Proceedings of the Fifth International Conference on Weblogs and Social Media, Barcelona, Catalonia, Spain, July 17-21, 2011*. The AAAI Press.

Gustavo Laboreiro, Luís Sarmento, Jorge Teixeira, and Eugénio Oliveira. 2010. Tokenizing micro-blogging messages using a text classification approach. In *Proceedings of the fourth workshop on Analytics for noisy unstructured text data*, AND '10, pages 81–88, New York, NY, USA. ACM.

Bing Liu and Lei Zhang. 2012. A survey of opinion mining and sentiment analysis. In *Mining Text Data*, pages 415–463. Springer.

Roque López, Javier Tejada, and Mike Thelwall. 2012. Spanish sentistrength as a tool for opinion mining peruvian facebook and twitter. In *Artificial Intelligence Driven Solutions to Business and Engineering Problems*, pages 82–85. ITHEA, Sofia, Bulgaria.

Christopher D. Manning, Prabhakar Raghavan, and Hinrich Schütze. 2008. *Introduction to Information Retrieval*. Cambridge University Press, New York, NY, USA.

Justin Martineau and Tim Finin. 2009. Delta TFIDF: An improved feature space for sentiment analysis. In *Proceedings of the Third International Conference on Weblogs and Social Media, ICWSM 2009, San Jose, California, USA*. The AAAI Press.

A. Montejo-Ráez, E. Martínez-Cámara, M. T. Martín-Valdivia, and L. A. Ureña López. 2012. Random walk weighting over sentiwordnet for sentiment polarity detection on twitter. In *Proceedings of the 3rd Workshop in Computational Approaches to Subjectivity and Sentiment Analysis*, WASSA '12, pages 3–10, Stroudsburg, PA, USA. Association for Computational Linguistics.

Alexander Pak and Patrick Paroubek. 2010. Twitter as a corpus for sentiment analysis and opinion mining. In Nicoletta Calzolari, Khalid Choukri, Bente Maegaard, Joseph Mariani, Jan Odijk, Stelios Piperidis, Mike Rosner, and Daniel Tapias, editors, *Proceedings of the International Conference on Language Resources and Evaluation, LREC 2010*. European Language Resources Association.

Georgios Paltoglou and Mike Thelwall. 2010. A study of information retrieval weighting schemes for sentiment analysis. In *Proceedings of the 48th Annual Meeting of the Association for Computational Linguistics*, ACL '10, pages 1386–1395, Stroudsburg, PA, USA. Association for Computational Linguistics.

Bo Pang, Lillian Lee, and Shivakumar Vaithyanathan. 2002. Thumbs up?: sentiment classification using machine learning techniques. In *Proceedings of the ACL-02 conference on Empirical methods in natural language processing - Volume 10*, EMNLP '02, pages 79–86, Stroudsburg, PA, USA. Association for Computational Linguistics.

James Pustejovsky and Amber Stubbs. 2013. *Natural Language Annotation for Machine Learning*. O'Reilly Media, Sebastopol, CA 95472.

Josef Steinberger, Polina Lenkova, Mijail Alexandrov Kabadjov, Ralf Steinberger, and Erik Van der Goot. 2011. Multilingual entity-centered sentiment analysis evaluated by parallel corpora. In *Proceedings of the 8th International Conference on Recent Advances in Natural Language Processing*, RANLP'11, pages 770–775.

Josef Steinberger, Mohamed Ebrahim, Maud Ehrmann, Ali Hurriyetoglu, Mijail Alexandrov Kabadjov, Polina Lenkova, Ralf Steinberger, Hristo Tanev, Silvia Vázquez, and Vanni Zavarella. 2012. Creating sentiment dictionaries via triangulation. *Decision Support Systems*, 53:689—694.

E.A. Stepanov and G. Riccardi. 2011. Detecting general opinions from customer surveys. In *Data Mining Workshops (ICDMW), 2011 IEEE 11th International Conference on*, pages 115–122.

Maite Taboada, Julian Brooke, Milan Tofiloski, Kimberly Voll, and Manfred Stede. 2011. Lexicon-based methods for sentiment analysis. *Computational Linguistics*, 37(2):267–307.

Mikalai Tsytsarau and Themis Palpanas. 2012. Survey on mining subjective data on the web. *Data Mining and Knowledge Discovery*, 24(3):478–514, May.

Kateřina Veselovská, Jan Hajič Jr., and Jana Šindlerová. 2012. Creating annotated resources for polarity classification in Czech. In *Proceedings of KONVENS 2012*, pages 296–304. ÖGAI, September. PATHOS 2012 workshop.

Liang-Chih Yu, Jheng-Long Wu, Pei-Chann Chang, and Hsuan-Shou Chu. 2013. Using a contextual entropy model to expand emotion words and their intensity for the sentiment classification of stock market news. *Knowledge Based Syst*, 41:89–97.

Kunpeng Zhang, Yu Cheng, Yusheng Xie, Daniel Honbo, Ankit Agrawal, Diana Palsetia, Kathy Lee, Wei keng Liao, and Alok N. Choudhary. 2011. SES: Sentiment elicitation system for social media data. In *Data Mining Workshops (ICDMW), 2011 IEEE 11th Conference on, Vancouver, BC, Canada, December 11, 2011*, pages 129–136. IEEE.

Dan Zhang, Luo Si, and Vernon J. Rego. 2012. Sentiment detection with auxiliary data. *Information Retrieval*, 15(3-4):373–390.

Tagging Opinion Phrases and their Targets in User Generated Textual Reviews

Narendra Gupta
AT&T Labs - Research, Inc.
Florham Park, NJ 07932 - USA
ngupta@research.att.com

Abstract

We discuss a tagging scheme to tag data for training information extraction models which can extract the features of a product/service and opinions about them from textual reviews, and which can be used across different domains with minimal adaptation. A simple tagging scheme results in a large number of domain dependent opinion phrases and impedes the usefulness of the trained models across domains. We show that by using minor modifications to this simple tagging scheme the number of domain dependent opinion phrases are reduced from 36% to 17%, which leads to models more useful across domains.

1 Introduction

A large number of opinion-rich reviews about most products and services are available on the web. These reviews are often summarized by star ratings to help consumers in making buying decisions. While such a summarization is very useful, often consumers like to know about specific features of the product/service. For example in the case of restaurants consumers might want to know what people think about their chicken dish. There are many research papers on both supervised (Li et al., 2010) and unsupervised(Liu et al., 2012),(Hu and Liu, 2004), (Popescu and Etzioni, 2005), (Baccianella et al., 2009) methods for extracting reviewer's opinions and their targets (features of products/services) from textual reviews. Unsupervised methods are preferred as they can be used across domains, however their performance is limited by the assumptions they make about lexical and syntactic properties of opinion and target phrases. We would like to use supervised methods to develop information extraction models that can also be used across domains with minimum adaptation. We hope to succeed in our goal because: a) even though there are domain specific opinion phrases, we believe a large proportion of opinion phrases can be used across the domains with the same semantic interpretation; b) target phrases mostly contain domain dependent words, but have domain independent syntactic relationships with opinion phrases. Obviously for a domain containing large number of domain dependent opinion phrases, our models will perform poorly and additional domain adaptation will be necessary.

In this paper we discuss a tagging scheme to manually tag the necessary training data. In section 2 we show that simply tagging opinion and target phrases, forces a large number of opinion phrases to contain domain dependent vocabulary. This makes them domain dependent, even when domain independent opinion words are used. In section 3 we propose a modification to the simple tagging scheme and show that this modification allows tagging of opinion phrases without forcing them to contain domain dependent vocabulary. We also identify many linguistic structures used to express opinions that cannot be captured even with our modified tagging scheme. In section 4 we experimentally show the improvement in the coverage of tagged domain independent opinion phrases due to our proposed modification. In section 5 we discuss the relationship with other work. We conclude this paper in section 6 by summarizing the contribution of this work.

2 A Simple Tagging Scheme

Our goal is to only extract author's *current opinions* by using the smallest possible representation. *Past opinions* or those of other agents are not of interest.

As shown in Table 1, in this *simple tagging scheme* we tag opinions, their targets, and pronominal references in each sentence without considering the review or the domain the sentence is part of[1]. Opinion phrases are further categorized to represent their polarity and their domain dependence[2].

There are two relations in this scheme viz. $Target(Opinionphrase, Target|Referencephrase)$, and $Reference(Referencephrase, Targetphrase)$.

Finally, we tag only the *contiguous non-overlapping spans* in the sentences.

Phrase Type		Domain Dependent	Tag Symbol
Opinion	Positive	No	P
		Yes	PD
	Negative	No	N
		Yes	ND
	Neutral	Yes	UD
Target		Yes	T
Pronomial Reference		No	R

Table 1: Different types of phrases to be tagged.

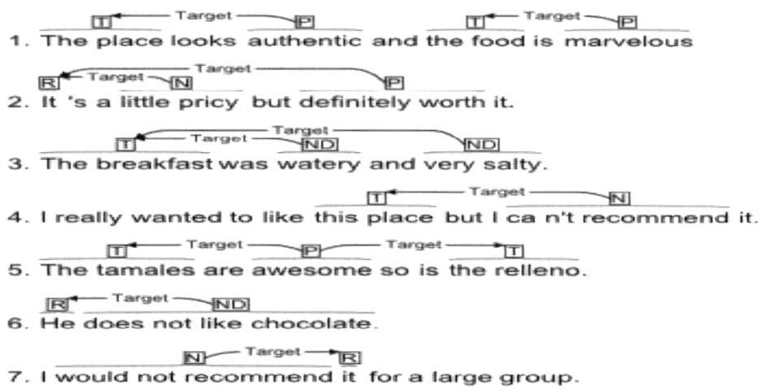

Figure 1: Examples tagged by the simple tagging scheme.

Figure 1[3] shows examples of tagged sentences using the simple tagging scheme. It illustrates: a) a sentence can have multiple "Target" relationships b) pronominal references can be used as targets; c) many opinion phrases can have the same target and vice versa; d) opinion phrases are not always adjectives and/or adverbs; e) in the sixth sentence "his" opinion about chocolate is not tagged instead, author's opinion about the opinion holder is tagged; f) in the last sentence fragmented opinion phrase "not recommend for a large group" is not tagged.

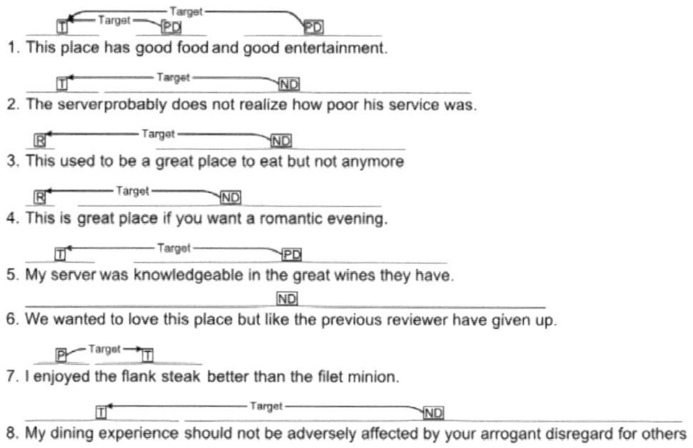

Figure 2: Examples where the simple tagging scheme is not discriminating enough.

Figure 2 shows examples where our simple tagging scheme is not discriminating enough. As a result majority of the opinion phrases are tagged as domain dependent. Example 1, 2 show that the tagging scheme cannot express attributes of a target. Therefore, they are lumped with the opinion phrases, making them domain dependent. In example 5 the opinion about "wines they have" is embedded in the tagged opinion phrase. In example 6 the fact that "we do not love this place" is not captured. Example 7 shows that our scheme can only tag one of the two targets of a comparative opinion expression. Example 8 shows a complex opinion expression involving multiple agents, opinions, expectations, analogies and modalities. To accurately represent opinions expressed in the infinitely many compositions, natural languages offer, a more complex representation is required. Instead of solving this knowledge representation problem, we introduce two additional tags and relations, and show that our modified tagging scheme is able to capture opinions expressed through some commonly used expressions.

3 A Modified Tagging Scheme

In our modified tagging scheme, we add 2 more tags and relations. We add an "Embedded Target"

[1]Once context independent information is extracted from individual sentences, post processing (not discussed in this paper) can aggregate information (e.g. resolve all identified pronominal references) within the context of the entire review.

[2]An opinion phrase is domain independent if its interpretation remains unchanged across domains

[3]Figures showing examples annotations are extracted from Brat Annotation Tool (http://brat.nlplab.org/). In Brat tags are displayed as square boxes and relations as directed arcs.

(symbol ET) tag to represent attributes of the targets, embedded in the opinion phrases tagged by the *simple tagging scheme.* These attributes could have any relationship e.g. part-of, feature-of and instance-of, with the target of the opinion. More specifically in the *modified tagging scheme* we break the opinion phrases as tagged in the simple tagging scheme into opinion phrases and the embedded target phrases.We also add a "Negation" (symbol NO) tag to capture the negation of an opinion which often is located far from the opinion phrases (example 3 and 6 in Figure 2). The corresponding relations in our modified scheme are $Embeddedtarget(OpinionPhrase, EmbeddedTarget)$ and $Negation(NegationPhrase, OpinionPhrase)$.

Figure 3: Example sentences tagged with modified tagging scheme.

Figure 3 shows the examples in Figure 2 tagged with the modified tagging scheme. From this tagging we can put together fragmented components of opinion and target phrases (Table 2) using the rule: $Target(Op, Tp)\&Emb\_Target(Op, ETp) \rightarrow Target(Op, Tp : ETp)$ i.e. if Tp is tagged as target phrase of the opinion phrase Op and ETp is tagged as its embedded target phrase then $Tp : ETp$[4] is the target of the opinion phrase Op. Similarly if a relation $Negation(Np, Op)$ exists, the complete specification of the opinion is derived by adding the negation phrase Np to the opinion phrase Op .

As can be seen in Table 2, the modified tagging scheme is able to capture the opinions and their targets more precisely than the simple tagging scheme. In addition, opinion phrases become mostly domain independent. Still, there is some information loss. For example in sentence 4 "for" rela-

Sentence	Opinion phrase	Target Phrase
1	good	This place: food
	good	This place: entertainment
2	does not realize how poor	The server: service
3	not anymore: a great	This: place to eat
4	great	This: place
	romantic	This: evening
5	knowledgeable	My server: wine
	great	they: wine
6	have given up: love	this place

Table 2: Tagged information in Figure 3.

tionship between the two opinion phrases is ignored ("place is great *for* romantic evening"), instead we extract "This:place" is "great" and "This[5]:evening" is "Romantic". This although not exact, captures the essence of the reviewer's opinion without additional complexity in the tagging scheme. In the rest of this section, we describe other natural language structures used to express opinions and also show how they are handled in our tagging scheme.

3.1 Ambiguous Targets

In many situations it is difficult to distinguish between the target and the embedded target. In Figure 4 two possible tags on a sentence are shown. In the

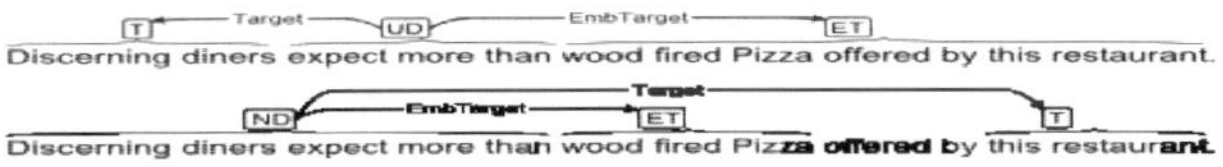

Figure 4: Examples sentences showing ambiguity in tagging targets and embedded targets.

first version, the neutral opinion about the "discerning diners" is tagged. In the second version, domain dependent negative opinion about "this restaurant" is tagged. If the context of tagging i.e. interest in opinions about the restaurants, was known, this ambiguity is resolved. In our context free tagging, we resolve this ambiguity by preferring the subject of the sentence as the main target of the opinions.

3.2 Conditional Opinions

Opinions are also expressed in conditional form and sometimes, like in example 1 and 2 in Figure 5, it is difficult to separate the opinion phrases from the target/embedded target phrases and the only choice is to tag entire sentence/segement as domain dependent neutral. Even though in the first sentence opinion about the loud music is expressed, and in the sec-

[4]The colon in this expression is intended to join specifications of the target.

[5]Anphora resoultion will bind "This" to the reviewed restaurant.

ond sentence opinion about the food of the restaurant is expressed, they cannot be tagged as such even with our modified scheme. Examples 3 and 4 as

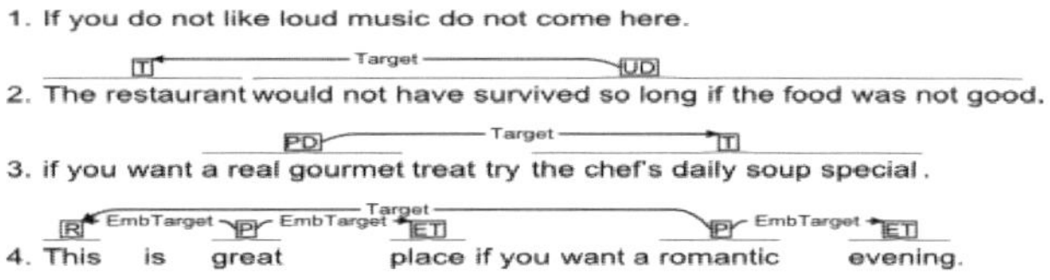

Figure 5: Examples of conditional opinion phrases.

shown in Figure 5 however, can be segmented into opinions and their targets/embedded targets. These examples illustrate that when there are no negations in the conditional opinions they typically can be segmented into opinion and target phrases.

3.3 Opinion Referencing Other Opinion Phrases

Figure 6 shows examples where opinions about other opinions are expressed. In the first example, the opinion "most impressive" reinforces other opinions; such reinforcement cannot be represented in our tagging scheme. In the second example, however, the pronoun "it" references the magazine's opinion, which is ignored in our tagging scheme.

Figure 6: Examples where opinion expressions reference other opinion expressions.

3.4 Implicit Target Switch

In the first part of the sentence shown in Figure 7 an opinion about "this: steak" is expressed and in the second part an opinion about "this: ambiance" is expressed. Clearly if "this" refers to a steak, it cannot have ambiance. It must be the ambiance of the restaurant serving the steak. Our tagging scheme does not capture this implicit target switching.

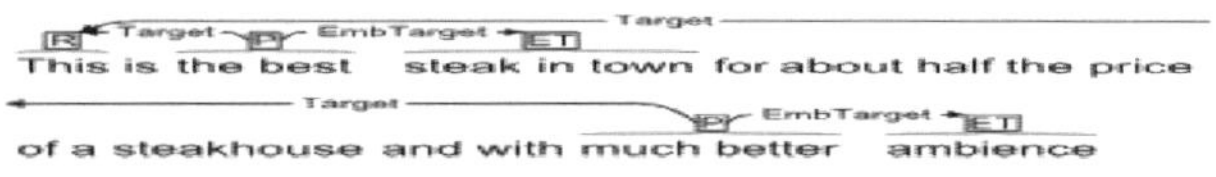

Figure 7: Example of implicit target switching.

4 Coverage experiment

Table 3 shows the counts of domain dependent opinion phrases tagged on a small sample of data from 3 different domains, using both simple and modified schemes. The number of domain dependent opinion phrases in case of the modified tagging scheme is reduced by more than half. Even for the MP3 players with a large domain dependent vocabulary, 73% of opinion phrases are tagged as domain independent. This will make models trained on different domains useful even for MP3 players.

Domain	Num. Sentences	Number of Tagged Opinion Phrases		
		Total	Domain Dependent	
			Simple	Modified
Restaurant	68	101	31(30%)	13(13%)
Hotels	147	111	39(35%)	15(14%)
MP3 Plyr.	350	287	103(36%)	48(17%)

Table 3: Comparison of simple and modified scheme.

5 Relationship to other work

Kessler et al. (2010)[6] have tagged automobile data (JDPA Corpus) with sentiment expressions (our opinion phrases) and mentions (our target and embedded target phrases). JDPA representation is more extensive than ours. It explicitly represents many relationships among mentions and a number of modifiers of sentiment expressions. The strength of our scheme however, is in the way we choose the targets. In JDAP, mentions are tagged as targets of their *modifying* sentiment expressions. In our scheme we tag the main object as the target of opinions. For some cases both JDPA and our schemes result in equivalent representations, but for others we believe our scheme results in a more accurate representation.

As can be verified for Example 1 in Figure 2 both schemes result in an equivalent representation. For example in Figure 8, on the other hand our scheme represents the opinion expressions more accurately then JDPA. This example contains an opinion about any good camera. Therefore, the target of the opinion in our scheme is "good camera" and not "camera" by itself, and the opinion is "must have a great zoom", "zoom" being embedded target we can drive *Target(must have a great, good camera:zoom)*. In JDPA this will be represented as *Target(good,camera), Target(must have a great,zoom),*

[6] Author is thankful to the reviewers of the paper to point out this reference.

part-of(camera, zoom). Notice that JDPA explicitly represents that the "camera is good", which is not true, and is not represent in our scheme.

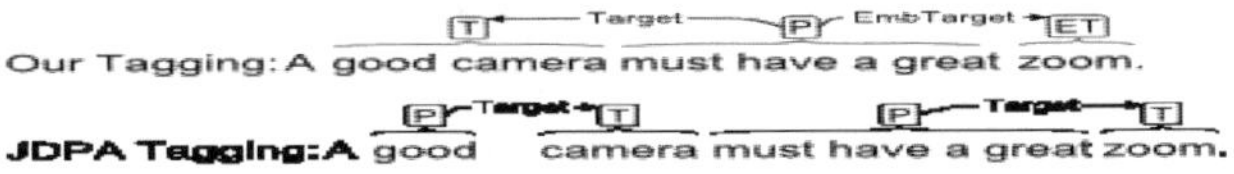

Figure 8: Example where our scheme captures the opinions more accurately than JDPA.

The tagged data by Hu and Liu (2004)(H-L data) is the another data that has opinions and their targets labeled. It has been used by many researchers to benchmark their work. We randomly selected reviews from the H-L data and tagged them with our modified tagging scheme (Figure 9). Several observations can be made from Table 4, showing information tagged by our scheme and by the labels in the H-L data. First, not all opinion and targets are tagged in the H-L data. Instead of tagging the opinion phrases directly, the H-L data relies on labeler's assessments for polarity strengths of the opinion. In the H-L data even the targets may or may not be present in the sentence (example 2). Again the H-L data relies on the labeler's assessment of what the target is. Clearly in the H-L data the labeling is performed with a specific context in mind while our scheme makes no such assumption. The main reason for this difference is that Hu and Liu (2004) used this data only to test their un-supervised technique, while our motivation is to use the tagged data for supervised training of models that could be used across domains. With the contextual assumptions made in the labeling, the models trained by using the H-L data will perform very poorly when used across domains.

Modified Tagging Scheme			H-L Label	
Opinion	Pol.	Target	Pol.	Target
incredibly overpriced	neg	apple i-pod		
not(regret)	pos	the purchase	3	player
Not(any doubts)	pos	this player		
easy	pos	software: to use	2	software
much cheaper	pos	player	2	price
good looking	pos	player		
beautiful	pos	blue back-lit screen		
good	pos	this→lack of a viewing hole for ..		
not(damaged/scratched)	pos	the face		
fast	pos	transfer rate		
suck	neg	the stock ones→headphones	-3	headphone
will out sell	pos	this player		

Table 4: Side by side comparison of tagged information with our modified tagging scheme and H-L data

Wiebe et al. (2005) describe the MPQA tagging

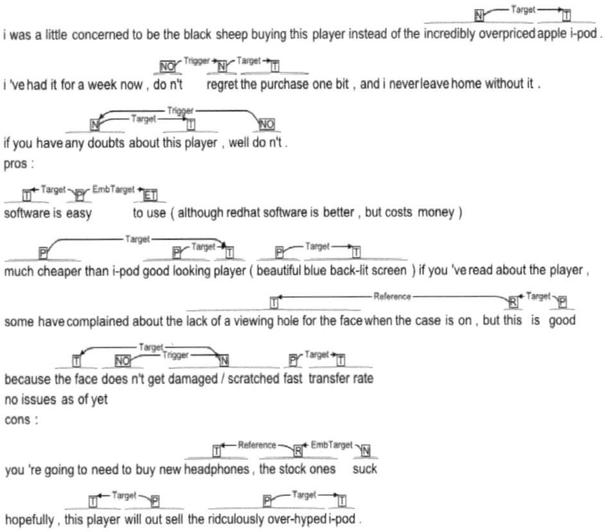

Figure 9: Tagging a review from Hu and Liu (2004) data using the our modified tagging scheme.

scheme for identifying private states of agents, including those of the author and any other agent referred in the text. The MPAQ tags *direct subjective expressions* (DSE) e.g. "faithful" and "criticized", and *expressive subjective elements* (ESE) e.g. "highway robbery" and "illegitimate", to identify the private states. We only tag author's opinions. For example in ""The US fears a spill-over," said Xirao-Nima" the MPQA will identify the private states of "US" and of "Xirao-Nima". We, however, will not tag this sentence since the author is not expressing any opinion.

Opinions are part of an agent's private state, but not all private states are opinions. For example in the sentence "I am happy" the author is describing his private state and not an opinion. In the MPQA the author's private state will be identified by "happy" but, in our tagging scheme this sentence will not be tagged. However, in the sentence "I am happy with their service" author is expressing an opinion about "their service" and will be tagged in our scheme.

Another difference between MPQA and our scheme is that MPQA tags only the private states of agents, causing some inconsistencies as illustrated by the following example. In the sentence "The U.S. is full of absurdities", "absurdities" is tagged as a private state of the U.S. At the same time in sentence "The report is full of absurdities", "absurdities" is tagged as a private state of the author, and "the report" is relegated to its target. In our tagging scheme both "the US" and "the report" are consistently tagged as targets of the opinion phrase "absurdities". Because of these differences we believe that the MPQA data is less suitable for opinion mining research.

6 Conclusion

We discussed a tagging scheme to tag data for training information extraction models to extract from textual reviews the features of a product/service and opinions about them, and which can be used across domains with minimal adaptation. We demonstrated that a) by using a simple tagging scheme a large proportion of opinion phrases are tagged as domain dependent, defeating our goal to train models usable across domains; b) even when a domain independent vocabulary is used, a more complex tagging scheme is needed to fully disambiguate opinion and target phrases. Instead of addressing this complex representation problem, we show that by introducing two additional tags the number of domain dependent opinion phrases is reduced from 36% to 17%. This will lead to information extraction models that perform better when used across domains.

7 Acknowledgments

Author is thankful to Amanda Stent and to the anonymous reviewers for their comments and suggestions, which significantly contributed to improving the quality of the publication.

References

Baccianella, Stefano, Andrea Esuli, and Fabrizio Sebastiani. 2009. Multi-facet rating of product reviews. In *Proceedings of the 31th European Conference on IR Research on Advances in Information Retrieval (ECIR 09)*. pages 462–472.

Hu, Minqing and Bing Liu. 2004. Mining and summarizing customer reviews. In *Proceedings of the ACM SIGKDD Conference on Knowledge Discovery and Data Mining (KDD)*. pages 168–177.

Kessler, Jason S., Miriam Eckert, Lyndsay Clark, and Nicolas Nicolov. 2010. The icwsm 2010 jdpa sentiment corpus for the automotive domain. In *Proceedings of the 4th International AAAI Conference on Weblogs and Social Media Data Challenge Workshop (ICWSM-DCW 2010)*.

Li, Fangtao, Chao Han, Minlie Huang, Xiaoyan Zhu, Yingju Xia, Shu Zhang, and Hao Yu. 2010. Structure-aware review mining and summarization. In *Proceedings of the 23rd International Conference on Computational Linguistics (COLING 2010)*. pages 653–661.

Liu, Kang, Liheng Xu, and Jun Zhao. 2012. Opinion target extraction using word-based translation model. In *Proceedings of the 2012 Joint Conference on Empirical Methods in Natural Language Processing and Computational Natural Language Learning, EMNLP-CoNLL 2012*. pages 1346–1356.

Popescu, Ana-Maria and Oren Etzioni. 2005. Extracting product features and opinions from reviews. In *Proceedings of the Human Language Technology Conference and the Conference on Empirical Methods in Natural Language Processing (HLT/EMNLP)*.

Wiebe, Janyce, Theresa Wilson, and Claire Cardie. 2005. Annotating expressions of opinions and emotions in language. *Language Resources and Evaluation* 39(2-3):165–210.

From newspaper to microblogging: What does it take to find opinions?

Wladimir Sidorenko and **Jonathan Sonntag** and **Manfred Stede**
Applied Computational Linguistics
University of Potsdam/Germany
sidarenk|sonntag|stede@uni-potsdam.de

Nina Krüger and **Stefan Stieglitz**
Dept. of Information Systems
University of Münster/Germany
nina.krueger|stefan.stieglitz@uni-muenster.de

Abstract

We compare the performance of two lexicon-based sentiment systems – SentiStrength (Thelwall et al., 2012) and SO-CAL (Taboada et al., 2011) – on the two genres of newspaper text and tweets. While SentiStrength has been geared specifically toward short social-media text, SO-CAL was built for general, longer text. After the initial comparison, we successively enrich the SO-CAL-based analysis with tweet-specific mechanisms and observe that in some cases, this improves the performance. A qualitative error analysis then identifies classes of typical problems the two systems have with tweets.

1 Introduction: Twitter, SentiStrength and SO-CAL

In recent years, microblogging has been an attractive new target for sentiment analysis. The question studied in this paper is how the methods used for "standard" newspaper text can be transferred to microblogs. We focused on the Twitter network because of its widespread use, and because Twitter communication, in response to emerging issues, is fast and especially ad hoc, making it an effective platform for the sharing and discussion of crisis-related information (Bruns/Burgess, 2011). Furthermore, Twitter is characterized by a high topicality of content (Milstein al., 2008).

Specifically, we present experiments involving two sentiment analysis systems that both employ a combination of polarity lexicon and sentiment composition rules: (i) SentiStrength (Thelwall et al., 2012), a system that is geared toward short social-media text, and (ii) SO-CAL (Taboada et al., 2011), 'Semantic Orientation Calculator', a general-purpose system that was designed primarily to work on the level of complete texts. While both are lexicon-based approaches, there are certain differences in the roles of the various submodules. For our purposes here, it is important that SentiStrength was designed to cope specifically with "user-generated content". Among the features of the system, as stated by Thelwall et al., the following four are especially important for tweets: (i) a simple spelling correction algorithm deletes repeated letters when the word is not found in the dictionary; (ii) repeated letters lead to a boost in sentiment value; (iii) an emoticon list supplements the polarity lexicon; (iv) positive sentences ending in an exclamation mark receive an additional boost, and multiple exclamation marks further strengthen the polarity.

SO-CAL, on the other hand, does not include social-media-specific measures. In contrast, it was designed for determining semantic orientation on the text level; in our experiments here, we are thus using it for the non-intended purpose of sentence-level sentiment, on tweet "sentences".

Next, we review related work on twitter sentiment analysis (Section 2), and describe the data sets for our experiments in Section 3. Then we investigate the relative performance of SentiStrength and SO-CAL on newspaper text and on tweets (Section 4), including experiments with preprocessing steps. In Section 5, we present observations from a qualitative evaluation, and we interpret the results and conclude in Section 6.

2 Related work

Following the work on "standard" text, sentiment classification on tweets is often treated as a two-step task, e.g., (Barbosa/Feng, 2010): subjectivity classification followed by polarity classification. For subjectivity classification, (Pak/Paroubek, 2010) found that the distribution of POS tags is a useful feature, due to, for example, the presence of modal verbs in subjective tweets.

For polarity assignment, one approach is to automatically build large sets of training data and then train classifiers on token n-grams; in this vein, (Pak/Paroubek, 2010) found that in their approach, bigrams outperform unigrams and trigrams, and they report f-measures around 0.6 for the three-way pos/neg/neutral classification. The other, non-learning, approach is to rely on a polarity wordlist (or a collection of several, as in (Joshi et al., 2011; Mukherjee et al., 2012)). Mukherjee et al. report an accuracy of 66.69% for pos/neg, and 56.17% for pos/neg/neut classification.

Typical preprocessing steps employed by the approaches discussed are the correction of misspellings, the replacement of URLs and hashtags, the translation of emoticons and of slang words. Sometimes, stop word removal and stemming is used; sometimes deliberately not. Few authors evaluate the influence of the various measures; one exception is (Mukherjee et al., 2012).

A recent branch of research deals with fine-grained target-specific analysis (as proposed recently by (Jiang et al., 2011)). In our work, however, we tackle the more coarse-grained problem of assigning a single sentiment value to a complete tweet. However, we will return to the issue of target-specificity in our conclusions.

An interesting result from analysing the state of the art is that apparently no consensus has been reached yet on the question of "extra difficulty" of tweet sentiment analysis. While everybody agrees that tweets are noisy and can pose considerable difficulty to any standard linguistically-inspired analysis tool, it is not clear to what extent this is a problem for sentiment analysis. Some authors argue that the noise renders the task more difficult than the analysis of longer text, while others maintain that the brevity of tweets is in fact an advantage, because – as (Bermingham/Smeaton, 2010) put it, "the short document length introduces a succinctness to the content", and thus "the focused nature of the text and higher density of sentiment-bearing terms may benefit automated sentiment analysis techniques." In their evaluation, the classification of microblogs indeed yields better results than that of blogs.

In correspondence with this open question, there are only few investigations so far on the performance differences for existing sentiment tools operating on newspaper versus social media text. To shed more light on the issue, we chose to run a set of comparative experiments with the two aforementioned lexicon/rule-based systems, on both newspaper and twitter corpora.

3 Data sets

MPQA The well-known MPQA corpus[1] (Wiebe et al., 2005) of newspaper text has fine-grained annotations of 'private states' at phrase level. For our purposes these need to be reduced to a more coarse-grained labelling of sentence-level sentiment. To avoid ambiguity, we ignored those sentences that include both positive and negative sentiment annotations. From the remaining sentences, we selected 100 positive and negative sentences each, where the former target-specific sentiment is now taken to represent sentence-level sentiment. The data set is a difficult one, given that we are dealing with isolated sentences from newspaper reports.

Qantas To track Twitter data we used a self-developed prototype (see (Stieglitz/Kaufhold, 2011)). We concentrate our analysis on Qantas, an Australian leading carrier for long-haul air travel, for which we assume substantial interest in public communication. We furthermore expect that – caused by some management crises in 2011 – online communication around Qantas-related topics is characterized by a strong emotional investment of stakeholders.

The tracking tool captures all those tweets that contain the keyword 'Qantas' in their content, in the username of the sender, or in a URL. After spam removal, we had a dataset of some 27,000 tweets, collected between mid-May and mid-November 2011.

[1] `http://mpqa.cs.pitt.edu/`

Topic	#pos	#neut	#neg	#irrelevant
Apple	219	581	377	164
Google	218	604	61	498
Microsoft	93	671	138	513
Twitter	68	647	78	611

Table 1: Distribution of tweets and labels across subcorpora

For evaluation purposes, 300 Tweets have been manually annotated by two annotators in parallel, using a polarity scale ranging from -2 to 2. 190 Tweets of those (63%) received identical labels, and we used only this set in our experiments described below. That means we also discarded cases of "minor" disagreement such as a -1/-2 annotation.

Sanders The Sanders corpus[2] is a corpus consisting of 5513 tweets of various languages which have been annotated for sentiment. The tweets have been sampled by the search terms „@apple", „#google", „#microsoft" and „#twitter". Each tweet is accompanied by a date-time stamp and the target of its polarity. Possible polarity values are *positive*, *negative*, *neutral* (simple factual statements / questions without strong emotions / neither positive nor negative / both positive and negative), and *irrelevant* (spam / non-English). The positive and negative tweets thus contain judgements on the companies or their products/services. Along with the corpus comes an annotation scheme and statistics about the corpus. Some numbers of the size and distribution within the corpus are given in Table 1.

According to the annotation guidelines, positive and negative labels were only assigned to clear cases of sentiment. Ambigious tweets have been annotated as neutral.

4 Experiments and results

4.1 Performance on MPQA sentences

In order to establish a basis for the comparison, we first ran a small comparative evaluation on "standard" text, i.e., on the sentences from the MPQA newspaper corpus. The results, given in Table 2, show that both systems perform considerably better on negative than on positive sentences, and overall there is a slight advantage for SO-CAL.

	SentiStrength	SO-CAL
acc pos	0.2727	0.4717
acc neg	0.7071	0.6542
weighted avg	0.4899	0.5634

Table 2: Accuracy on MPQA sentences

	Senti-Strength	SO-CAL	SO-CAL preproc.
Qantas			
acc	0.3754	0.3953	0.3887
acc pos	0.3091	0.2545	0.2545
acc neg	0.2857	0.2857	0.2857
acc neut	0.6164	0.6781	0.6644
avg sentiment	1.1075	1.2756	1.3316
Sanders total			
acc	0.5945	0.5899	0.5790
acc pos	0.6171	0.5694	0.6032
acc neg	0.4572	0.5301	0.5519
acc neut	0.6230	0.6092	0.5802
avg sentiment	0.8517	1.3761	1.5233
Sanders twitter			
acc	0.4985	0.5804	0.5387
acc pos	0.4286	0.3750	0.4821
acc neg	0.4590	0.4754	0.5246
acc neut	0.5099	0.6121	0.5245
avg sentiment	0.8393	1.4054	1.6978

Table 3: Accuracy on tweet corpora

4.2 Performance on Qantas and Sanders tweets

In Table 3, we show the system performance on the Twitter corpora: Qantas, the complete Sanders corpus, and the Sanders subcorpus with target "Twitter". We ran evaluations on all four separate subcorpora, but only "Twitter" showed interesting differences from the results for the total corpus, and that is why they are included in the table. The "acc" row gives the overall weighted accuracy. "Avg sentiment" is the absolute value of the sentiment strength determined by SentiStrength and SO-CAL; notice that these should not be compared between the two systems, as they do not operate on the same scale. (We will return to the role of sentiment strength in Section 6.)

[2] `http://www.sananalytics.com/lab/twitter-sentiment/`

4.3 Preprocessing steps

Since SO-CAL was not intended for analyzing Twitter data, we implemented three preprocessing steps to study whether noise effects of this text genre can be reduced. Similarly to the steps suggested by (Mukherjee et al., 2012), we first unified all URLs, e-mail addresses and user names by replacing them with unique tokens. Additionally, in step 1 all hash marks were stripped from words, and emoticons were mapped to special tokens representing their emotion categories. These special tokens were then added to the polarity lexicons used by SO-CAL.

In step 2, social media specific slang expressions and abbreviations like *"2 b"* (for *"to be"*) or *"imsry"* (for *"I am sorry"*) were translated to their appropriate standard language forms. For this, we used a dictionary of 5,424 expressions that we gathered from publicly available resources.[3]

In the last step, we tackled two typical spelling phenomena: the omission of final *g* in gerund forms (*goin*), and elongations of characters (*suuuper*). For the former, we appended the character *g* to words ending with *-in* if these words are unknown to vocabulary,[4] while the corresponding 'g'-forms are in-vocabulary words (IVW). For the latter problem, we first tried to subsequently remove each repeating character until we hit an IVW. For cases resisting this treatment, we adopted the method suggested by (Brody/Diakopoulos, 2011) and generated a squeezed form of the prolongated word, subsequently looking it up in a probability table that has previously been gathered from a training corpus.

Altogether, SO-CAL does not benefit from preprocessing in the Qantas corpus, but it does help for the pos/neg tweets from the Sanders corpus, especially for the Twitter subcorpus. The observation that the accuracy on neutral tweets decreases while the average sentiment increases will be discussed in Section 6. We also measured the effects of the three individual steps in isolation, and the only noteworthy result is that SentiStrength, when subjected to our "extra" preprocessing, benefits slightly from slang normalization for the Qantas corpus, and from noise cleaning for some parts of the Sanders corpus.

[3] `http://www.noslang.com/dictionary/`, `http://onlineslangdictionary.com/`, `http://www.urbandictionary.com/`

[4] For vocabulary check, we used the open Hunspell dictionary (`http://hunspell.sourceforge.net/`).

5 Qualitative evaluation

Having computed the success rates, we then performed a small qualitative evaluation: What are the main reasons for the misclassifications on tweets? In addition, we wanted to know why the Qantas corpus yielded much worse results than the Sanders corpus, and thus we looked into its results.

5.1 Problems for SO-CAL

We chose SO-CAL's judgements as the basis for this evaluation and randomly selected 120 tweets from the Sanders corpus that were not correctly classified. The distribution across the manual annotations pos/neg/neut was 40/40/40.

In Table 4, we provide a classification of the reasons for problems. The first group are cases where we would not agree with the annotation and thus cannot blame SO-CAL. The second group includes problems that are beyond the scope of the system and hence, strictly speaking, not its fault. Among the typos, there are cases of misspelled opinion words, but also a few where the typo leads to problems with SO-CALs linguistic analysis and in consequence to a misclassification. The slang words include items like "wow!" but also shorthands such as "thx". Most important are "domain formulae": expressions that require inferences in order to identify the sentiment. An example is "I now use X instead of TARGET". We encounter these most often in negative tweets, where complaints are expressed, as in "My phone can send but not receive texts."

In the third group, we find problems that are or could be in the scope of SO-CAL. Occasionally, negation or irrealis rules misfire. Gaps in the lexicon are noticeable especially on the positive side (examples: "loving", "better", "thanks to"). 'Lexical ambiguity' refers to words that may or may not carry polarity; by far the most frequent example here is "new", which SO-CAL labels positive, but in technology-related tweets often is neutral. Also in neutral tweets, we often find high complexity, i.e., cases where both positive and negative judgements are mixed. And finally, a fair number of problems stems from sentiment expressed on the wrong target of the tweet.

Problem	Pos	Neg	Neut
Annotation ambig.	15%	0%	2%
Typo	3%	5%	10%
Slang words	12%	10%	0%
Sarcasm	0%	2%	0%
Domain formula	23%	60%	5%
Wrong rule	3%	5%	3%
Lexicon gap	30%	12%	0%
Lexical ambiguity	5%	5%	50%
Complexity	0%	0%	18%
Wrong target	8%	0%	12%

Table 4: SO-CAL error types on 120 Sanders tweets

Problem	Pos	Neg	Neut
Annotation ambig.	45%	25%	12%
Typo	18%	0%	0%
Slang words	0%	0%	0%
Sarcasm	0%	16%	0%
Domain formula	9%	42%	4%
Wrong rule	9%	0%	10%
Lexicon gap	9%	16%	0%
Lexical ambiguity	0%	0%	16%
Complexity	9%	0%	16%
Spam / news	0%	0%	41%

Table 5: Error types on 75 Qantas tweets

5.2 Observations on the Qantas corpus

The analysis of 75 Qantas tweets that have been misclassified by both SentiStength and SO-CAL yielded the results in Table 5: Again, many annotation cases are ambiguous, and domain formulae are the major problem with negative tweets. Sarcasm is much more frequent than in the Sanders corpus. The central problem for neutral tweets stems from the fact that spam and tweets containing headlines and URLs of news messages have been annotated as neutral, but these may very well contain polarity-bearing words, which are then detected by the systems.

6 Interpretation and Conlusions

News versus tweets. Since the Sanders corpus is much larger than Qantas, we regard it as the tweet representative for the comparison to MPQA (a difficult data set, as argued above). For positive text, both SentiStrength and SO-CAL yield better results on tweets, while for negative texts, the results on tweets are much lower than on news sentences. Within the news genre, however, both systems perform much better on negative than on positive text. So we conclude a "polarity flip" in the performance of both systems when going from news to tweets.

Differences among tweets. Based on the Sanders corpus, the SentiStrength and SO-CAL results are a little better than those reported by (Mukherjee et al., 2012), who achieved 56.17% accuracy for the three-way classification. As SO-CAL does not include tweet-specific analysis, we may conclude that the utility of such genre-specific measures is in fact limited. – An interesting question is why the "Twitter" subcorpus of Sanders behaves so different from the others: While overall accuracy is the same, the figures for the three categories differ widely. Also, SO-CAL here benefits heavily from preprocessing on the non-neutral tweets. One factor is the large proportion of neutral tweets (see Table 1); besides, we find that these tweets are not as target-related as those for Apple, Google, Microsoft; it seems that users often drop a '#twitter' without actually talking *about* Twitter or its service.

Preprocessing. Of the four measures taken by SentiStrength to account for tweet problems (see Sct. 1), SO-CAL already implements the exclamation mark boost; the other three were added in our own preprocessing, but we did only minimal spellchecking. Overall, SO-CAL does not profit as much as we had expected, but we find a fair improvement (0.57–0.6) for the positive Sanders tweets. For neutral tweets, performance actually decreases.

The role of targets An interesting observation is that adding preprocessing to SO-CAL leads to detecting "more" sentiment: The average sentiment values increase for all the corpora in Table 3. At the same time, the accuracy on neutral tweets decreases, which indicates that "spurious" sentiment is being detected. The most likely reason is that SO-CAL indeed profits from tweet-preprocessing but then detects sentiment that is unrelated to the target and therefore not annotated in the gold data. An important direction for future work therefore is to pay more attention to target-specific sentiment identification, cf. (Jiang et al., 2011).

Acknowledgments

This work was funded by German Ministry for Education and Research (BMBF), grant 01UG1232D.

References

L. Barbosa and J. Feng. 2010. Robust sentiment detection on twitter from biased and noisy data. Proc. of COLING (Posters), Beijing.

A. Bermingham and A. Smeaton. 2010. Classifying Sentiment in Microblogs: Is Brevity an Advantage? Proc. of the 20th ACM Conference on Information and Knowledge Management (CIKM), Toronto.

S. Brody and N. Diakopoulos. 2011. Cooooooooooooooollllllllllllll!!!!!!!!!!!!!! Using Word Lengthening to Detect Sentiment in Microblogs. Proceedings of the 2011 Conference on Empirical Methods in Natural Language Processing (EMNLP), pp. 562–570, Edinburgh.

A. Bruns and J.E. Burgess. 2011. The Use of Twitter Hashtags in the Formation of Ad Hoc Publics. 6th European Consortium for Political Research General Conference, Reykjavik, Iceland, pp. 25-27.

L. Jiang, M. Yu, M. Zhou, X. Liu and T. Zhao. 2011. Target-dependent twitter sentiment classification. Proc. of the 49th Annual Meeting of the ACL, pp. 151-160, Portland/OR.

A. Joshi, Balamurali A R, P. Bhattacharyya and R. Mohanty. 2011. C-Feel-It: a sentiment analyzer for micro-blogs. Proc. of the ACL-HLT 2011 System Demonstrations, pp. 127-132, Portland/OR.

S. Milstein, A. Chowdhury, G. Hochmuth, B. Lorica and R. Magoulas. 2008. Twitter and the Micro-Messaging Revolution: Communication, Connections, and Immediacy - 140 Characters at a Time.

S. Mukherjee, A. Malu, A.R. Balamurali and P. Bhattacharyya. 2012. TwiSent: a multistage system for analyzing sentiment in twitter. Proc. of the 21st ACM Conference on Information and Knowledge Management (CIKM).

A. Pak and P. Paroubek. 2010. Twitter as a corpus for sentiment analysis and opinion mining. Proc. of LREC, Valletta/Malta.

S. Stieglitz and C. Kaufhold. 2011. Automatic Full Text Analysis in Public Social Media – Adoption of a Software Prototype to Investigate Political Communication. Proc. of the 2nd International Conference on Ambient Systems, Networks and Technologies (ANT-2011) / The 8th International Conference on Mobile Web Information Systems (MobiWIS 2011), Procedia Computer Science 5, Elsevier, 776-781.

M. Taboada, J. Brooke, M. Tofiloski, K. Voll, and M. Stede. 2011. Lexicon-based methods for sentiment analysis. *Computational Linguistics*, 37(2):267–307.

M. Thelwall, K. Buckley, and G. Paltoglou. 2012. Sentiment strength detection for the social Web. *Journal of the American Society for Information Science and Technology*, 63(1):163–173.

J. Wiebe, T. Wilson, and C. Cardie. 2005. Annotating expressions of opinions and emotions in language. *Language Resources and Evaluation*, 39(2–3):165–210.

Bilingual Experiments on an Opinion Comparable Corpus

E. Martínez-Cámara
SINAI research group
University of Jaén
E-23071, Jaén (Spain)
emcamara@ujaen.es

M. T. Martín-Valdivia
SINAI research group
University of Jaén
E-23071, Jaén (Spain)
maite@ujaen.es

M. D. Molina-González
SINAI research group
University of Jaén
E-23071, Jaén (Spain)
mdmolina@ujaen.es

L. A. Ureña-López
SINAI research group
University of Jaén
E-23071, Jaén (Spain)
laurena@ujaen.es

Abstract

Up until now most of the methods published for polarity classification are applied to English texts. However, other languages on the Internet are becoming increasingly important. This paper presents a set of experiments on English and Spanish product reviews. Using a comparable corpus, a supervised method and two unsupervised methods have been assessed. Furthermore, a list of Spanish opinion words is presented as a valuable resource.

1 Introduction

Opinion Mining (OM) is defined as the computational treatment of opinion, sentiment, and subjectivity in text. The OM discipline combines Natural Language Processing (NLP) with data mining techniques and includes a large number of tasks (Pang and Lee, 2008). One of the most studied tasks is polarity classification of reviews. This task focuses on determining which is the overall sentiment-orientation (positive or negative) of the opinions contained within a given document.

Two main appraoches are followed by researches to tackle the OM task. On the one hand, the Machine Learning (ML) approach (also known as the supervised approach) is based on using a collection of data to train the classifiers (Pang et al., 2002). On the other hand, (Turney, 2002) proposed an unsupervised method based on the semantic orientation of the words and phrases in the reviews. Both methodologies have their advantages and drawbacks. For example, the ML approach depends on the availability of labelled data sets (training data), which in many cases are impossible or difficult to achieve, partially due to the novelty of the task. On the contrary, the unsupervised method requires a large amount of linguistic resources which generally depend on the language, and often this approach obtains lower recall because it depends on the presence of the words comprising the lexicon in the document in order to determine the polarity of opinion.

Although opinions and comments on the Internet are expressed in any language, most of research in OM is focused on English texts. However, languages such as Chinese, Spanish or Arabic, are ever more present on the web. Thus, it is important to develop resources for these languages. The work presented herein is mainly motivated by the need to develop polarity classification systems and resources in languages other than English. We present an experimental study over the SFU Review Corpus (Taboada, 2008), a comparable corpus that includes opinions of several topics in English and in Spanish. We have followed this line of work: Firstly, we have taken as baseline a supervised experiment using Support Vector Machine (SVM). Then we have tried different unsupervised strategies. The first one uses the method presented in (Montejo-Ráez et al., 2012). This approach combines SentiWordNet scores with a random walk analysis of the concepts found in the text over the WordNet graph in order to determine the polarity of a tweet. This method obtained very good results in short texts (tweets) and so, we want to try it using larger document. Although we have carried out several experiments using different parameters and modifications, the results are not as good as we hoped. For this, we have tried a very simple experiment using a list of opinionated words in order to classify the polarity of the reviews. For English we have used the Bin Liu English lexicon (BLEL) (Hu and Liu, 2004) and for Spanish we have automatically translated the BLEL lexicon into Spanish. In addition, we have also checked manually and improved the Spanish list.

The paper is organized as follows: Section 2 briefly describes papers that study non-English sentiment polarity classification and, specifically work related to Spanish OM. In Section 3 we explain the resources used in the unsupervised methods assessed. Section 4 presents the experiments carried out and discusses the main results obtained. Finally, we outline conclusions and further work.

2 Related Work

There are some interesting papers that have studied the problem using non-English collections. Denecke (2008) worked on German comments collected from Amazon. These reviews were translated into English using standard machine translation software. Then the translated reviews were classified as positive or negative, using three different classifiers: LingPipe7, SentiWordNet (Baccianella et al., 2010) with classification rule, and SentiWordNet with machine learning. Ghorbel and Jacot (2011) used a corpus with movie reviews in French. They applied a supervised classification combined with SentiWordNet in order to determine the polarity of the reviews. In (Rushdi-Saleh et al., 2011a) a corpus of movies reviews in Arabic annotated with polarity was presented and several supervised experiments were performed. Subsequently, they generated the parallel EVOCA corpus (English version of OCA) by translating the OCA corpus automatically into English. The results showed that they are comparable to other English experiments, since the loss of precision due to the translation process is very slight, as can be seen in (Rushdi-Saleh et al., 2011b).

Regarding Spanish, there are also some interesting studies. Banea et al. (2008) showed that automatic translation is a viable alternative for the construction of resources and tools for subjectivity analysis in a new target language. In (Brooke et al., 2009) several experiments are presented dealing with Spanish and English resources. They conclude that although the ML techniques can provide a good baseline performance, it is necessary to integrate language-specific knowledge and resources in order to achieve an improvement. Cruz et al. (2008) manually recollected the MuchoCine (MC) corpus to develop a sentiment polarity classifier based on the semantic orientation of the phrases and words. The corpus contains annotated Spanish movie reviews from the MuchoCine website. The MC corpus was also used in (Martínez-Cámara et al., 2011) to carry out several experiments with a supervised approach applying different ML algorithms. Finally, (Martín-Valdivia et al., 2012) also dealt with the MC corpus to present an experimental study of supervised and unsupervised approaches over a Spanish-English parallel corpus.

3 Resources for the unsupervised methods

In order to tackle the unsupervised experiments we have chosen several well-known resources in the OM research community. In addition, we have also generated a new Spanish linguistic resource.

Comparable corpora are those consisted of texts in two or more languages about the same topic, but they are not the translated version of the texts in the source language. For the experiments, we chose the comparable corpus SFU Review Corpus. The SFU Review Corpus is composed of reviews of products in English and Spanish. The English version (Taboada and Grieve, 2004) has 400 reviews (200 positive and 200 negative) of commercial products downloaded in 2004 from the Epinions web which are divided into eight categories: books, cars, computers, cookware, hotels, movies, music and phones. Each category includes 25 positive reviews and 25 negative reviews. Recently, the authors of SFU Review Corpus have made available the Spanish version of the corpus[1]. The Spanish reviews are divided into the same eight categories, and also each category has 25 positive and 25 negative reviews.

In the unsupervised experiments we have analysed the performance of two approaches, the first one is based on lexicon and the other one in a graph-based method. We have selected the BLEL lexicon (Hu and Liu, 2004) to carry out the experiment based

[1] http://www.sfu.ca/~mtaboada/download/downloadCorpusSpa.html

on lexicon on the English version of the corpus. The lexicon is composed by 6,787 opinion words that indicate positive or negative opinions, which 2,005 are positive and 4,782 are negative. With the aim of following the same approach over the Spanish version, firstly we have translated the BLEL lexicon with the Reverso machine translator, and them we have checked manually the resultant list. The Spanish Opinion Lexicon[2] (SOL) is composed by 2,509 positive and 5,627 negative words, thus in total SOL has 8,136 opinion words. If a review has more or the same positive words than negative the polarity is positive, otherwise negative.

The graph-based method is a modular system which is made up of different components and technologies. The method was first presented in (Montejo-Ráez et al., 2012) with a good performance over a corpus of English tweets. The main idea of the algorithm is to represent each review as a vector of polarity scores of the senses in the text and senses related to the context of the first ones. Besides, the polarity score is weighted with a measure of importance. Taking a review as input, the workflow of the algorithm is the following:

1. Disambiguation: To get the corresponding sense of the words that are in the text is required to disambiguate them. Thus, the output of this first step is one unique synset from WordNet[3] (Miller, 1995) for each term. The input of the algorithm is the set of words with a POS-Tag allowed in WordNet. The graph nature of the WordNet structure is the basis for the UKB disambiguation method proposed by (Agirre and Soroa, 2009). The UKB disambiguation algorithm apply PageRank (Page et al., 1999) on the WordNet graph starting from term nodes, where each term node points to all its possible senses or synsets. The output of the process is a ranked list of synsets for each input word, and the highest rank synset is chosen as candidate sense.

   For the Spanish disambiguation process we have chosen the Spanish WordNet version offered by the project Multilingual Central Repository (MCR) (Gonzalez-Agirre et al., 2012). The Spanish WordNet of MCR has 38,702 synsets while WordNet has 117,659, i.e. the MCR covers the 32.89% of WordNet.

2. PPV: Once the synsets for the reviews are computed, the following step performs a second run of PageRank described in (Agirre and Soroa, 2009). Using the *Personalized PageRank*, a set of Personalized PageRank Vectors (PPVs) is obtained. This vector is a list of synsets with their ranked values. The key of this approach is to take from this vector additional synsets not related directly to the set of synsets disambiguated in the first step. The result is a longer list of pair <*synset, weight*> where the weight is the rank value obtained by the propagation of the weights of original synsets across the WordNet graph.

3. Polarity: The following step is to calculate the polarity score. For this purpose it is necessary a semantic resource to take the polarity score for each retrieved synset in the two previous steps. The semantic resource selected is SentiWordNet (Baccianella et al., 2010). According to these values, the three following equations have been applied to obtain the final polarity value:

$$p(r) = \frac{1}{|r|}\sum_{s\in r}\frac{1}{|s|}\sum_{i\in s}(p_i^+ - p_i^-)w_i \quad (1)$$

$$p(r) = \frac{1}{|r|}\sum_{s\in r}\frac{1}{|s|}\sum_{i\in s}f(p_i)$$
$$f(p_i) = \begin{cases} p_i^+ & \text{if } p_i^+ > p_i^- \\ p_i^- & \text{if } p_i^+ <= p_i^- \end{cases} \quad (2)$$

$$p(r) = \frac{1}{|r|}\sum_{s\in r}\frac{1}{|s|}\sum_{i\in s}f(p_i)$$
$$f(p_i) = \begin{cases} 1 & \text{if } i \in \text{[positive words]} \\ -1 & \text{if } i \in \text{[negative words]} \\ p_i^+ & \text{if } p_i^+ > p_i^- \\ p_i^- & \text{if } p_i^+ <= p_i^- \end{cases} \quad (3)$$

where $p(r)$ is the polarity of the review; $|r|$ is the number of sentences in the review r; s is a sentence in r, being itself a set of synsets; i is a synset in s; p_i^+ is the positive polarity of synset i; p_i^- is the negative polarity of synset i and w_i is the weight of synset i.

[2]http://sinai.ujaen.es/wiki/index.php/SOL

[3]We have used the 3.0 release of WordNet.

4 Experiments and Results

Systems based on supervised approach are the most successfully in the OM literature. Therefore, we began the set of experiments applying a machine learning algorithm to the SFU corpus. Also, we have carried out a set of unsupervised experiments following a lexicon-based approach and a graph-based algorithm. For all the experiments the evaluation measures have been: precision, recall, F1 and Accuracy (Acc.). The validation approach followed for the supervised approach has been the well-known 10-cross-validation.

The algorithm chose for the supervised experiments is SVM (Cortes and Vapnik, 1995) because is one of the most successfully used in OM. LibSVM[4] (Chang and Lin, 2011) was the implementation selected to carry out several experiments using SVM. We have evaluated unigrams and bigrams as minimum unit of information. Also, the influence of stemmer have been assessed. The weight scheme for representing each unit of information is TF-IDF. The same configuration has been applied to English and Spanish version of SFU corpus. Table 1 and Table 2 show the results for English version and Spanish version respectively.

	Precision	Recall	F1	Acc.
Unigrams	79.07%	78.50%	78.78%	78.50%
Unigrams & stemmer	79.82%	79.50%	79.66%	79.50%
Bigrams	78.77%	78.25%	78.51%	78.25%
Bigrams & stemmer	**80.64%**	**80.25%**	**80.44%**	**80.25%**

Table 1: SVM results for English SFU corpus

	Precision	Recall	F1	Acc.
Unigrams	73.65%	73.25%	73.45%	73.25%
Unigrams & stemmer	**74.10%**	**73.75%**	**73.92%**	**73.75%**
Bigrams	74.02%	73.50%	73.76%	73.50%
Bigrams & stemmer	73.90%	73.50%	73.70%	73.50%

Table 2: SVM results for Spanish SFU corpus

The results show one of the differences between the works published in SA, the use of unigrams or bigrams. In (Pang et al., 2002) is asserted that the reviews should be represented with unigrams, but in (Dave et al., 2003) bigrams and trigrams outperformed the unigrams features. In our case, regarding the results reached without using a stemmer, the use of unigrams as minium unit of information achieves better result than the use of bigrams when the language is English, but bigrams outperform unigrams when the texts are in Spanish. On the other hand, the best result both in English and Spanish is reached when a stemmer algorithm is applied. So, one conclusion of the supervised experiments is that the use of stemmer enhances the polarity classification in reviews. The following conclusion is that in English the presence of pair of words separate better the positive and negative classes, while in Spanish the use of unigrams is enough to classify the polarity when a stemmer algorithm is used.

The set of unsupervised experiments begins with a lexicon-based method. The method consists of find the presence in the reviews of opinion words which are included in a lexicon of opinion words. BLEL has been used for the English reviews, and SOL for the Spanish reviews. The results are presented in Table 3.

	Precision	Recall	F1	Acc.
BLEL lexicon	69.56%	64.42%	66.89%	64.75%
SOL	66.91%	61.94%	64.33%	62.25%

Table 3: Lexicon-based approch results

The differences in the results between the English and Spanish version of SFU Review Corpus are lower when a lexicon is used instead of a machine learning algorithm is applied. In a lexicon-based method is very important the recall value, because it indicates whether the set of words covers the vocabulary of the corpus. The recall value is upper 60% regarding English and Spanish, although is not an excellent value, is good for the two small and independent-domain lexicons. In the case of Spanish the supervised method is only 15.59% better regarding Accuracy. The results show that may be considered the use of a lexicon-based method for Spanish due to the few computer resources needed. Moreover, it must be highlighted the performance of SOL, so it is the first time that this resource is used to resolve a polarity classification problem.

[4]http://www.csie.ntu.edu.tw/~cjlin/libsvm/

The graph-based method has been described as a modular and flexible algorithm. Due to its modular nature we have carried out several experiments:

1. **wnet_ant+_eq1_[en|es]**: As baseline, we have run the algorithm with the same configuration as is described in (Montejo-Ráez et al., 2012), i.e. using the equation 1.

2. **wnet_ant-_eq1_[en|es]**: We have assessed the algorithm with a version of WordNet without the antonym relation.

3. **wnet_ant+_eq2_[en|es]**: The equation to calculate the polarity is 2

4. **wnet_ant-_eq2_[en|es]**: The same as wnet_ant+_eq2_[en|es] but the antonym relation is not considered.

5. **wnet_ant+_eq3_[en|es]**: The same as wnet_ant+_eq2_[en|es] but the equation 3 is used to calculate the polarity.

6. **wnet_ant-_eq3_[en|es]**: The same as wnet_ant+_eq3_[en|es] but the antonym relation is not considered.

Furthermore, one of the key elements of the algorithm is the possibility of setting the number of related synsets to get from WordNet. In all of the experiments we have evaluated from an expansion of 0 sysnsets to 100 synsets. In Table 4 are the best results obtained with the English and the Spanish version of SFU corpus.

Regarding the results, only for English is evident that the selection of the right equation to calculate the polarity score is important. On the other hand, the initial assumption that the relation of antonym could complicate the calculation of the final polarity, and the use of a graph of WordNet without antonym could enhance the results cannot be demonstrated because these experiments have reached the same results as the obtained ones using the graph with the relation of antonym. The equation 3, which includes additional information (in this case the BLEL lexicon) to calculate the final polarity score, outperforms the original way to get the polarity score (equation 1). The equation 3 for the English version of the corpus reaches 5.84% and 8.4% better results than equation 1 regarding F1 and Accuracy respectively.

The results obtained with the Spanish reviews are a bit different. In this case, the results are always improved when the antonym relation is not taking into account. So the first conclusion is the relation of antonym is not convenient for the calculation of the polarity value on Spanish texts. The process of expansion with related senses has not been relevant for the final results on the English reviews, but when the language of the reviews is Spanish the expansion is more decisive. For the *wnet_ant-_eq3_es* experiment the best result has been reached considering 71 related senses, so we can conclude that for Spanish the context should be considered. Although the best results is obtained with the configuration *wnet_ant+_eq3_es*, it must be highlighted the precision value of 68.03% reached by the configuration *wnet_ant+_eq2_es*. In some OM experiments is more important the precision of the system than the recall or other evaluation measures, so for Spanish reviews should be taken account this configuration too.

Regarding English and Spanish results, Table 4 shows similar performance, i.e. the graph-based algorithm obtained better results when the antonym is not considered and the use of a lexicon of opinion words enhances considerably the results.

The supervised approach clearly outperforms the two unsupervised approaches. The results obtained by the two unsupervised approaches are closer. The lexicon based method has a better performance on English reviews regarding the four different evaluation measures considered. Thus, the lexicon method not only has better results but also it is simpler, faster and more efficient than the graph-based method. Nevertheless, the graph-based method on Spanish reviews outperforms in precision regarding the configuration *wnet_ant+_eq2_es* and in the other three measures take into account the configuration *wnet_ant+_eq3_es*. However, the graph-based method is only 1.64% better regarding the precision value, and 0.54% better regarding F1. Therefore, we also considered the lexicon-based approach as the more suitable approach than the graph-based one.

	Expansion	Precision	Recall	F1	Accuracy
wnet_ant+_eq1_en	2	66.86%	57.25%	61.68%	57.25%
wnet_ant-_eq1_en	2	66.86%	57.25%	61.68%	57.25%
wnet_ant+_eq2_en	0	65.27%	55.5%	59.99%	55.50%
wnet_ant-_eq2_en	0	65.27%	55.5%	59.99%	55.50%
wnet_ant+_eq3_en	3	68.83%	62.50%	65.51%	62.50%
wnet_ant-_eq3_en	**3**	**68.83%**	**62.50%**	**65.51%**	**62.50%**
wnet_ant+_eq1_es	0	65.42%	54.5%	59.46%	54.5%
wnet_ant-_eq1_es	19	64.39%	57.75%	60.89%	57.75%
wnet_ant+_eq2_es	0	68.03%	52.75%	59.42%	52.75%
wnet_ant-_eq2_es	70	64.62%	58.00%	61.13%	58.00%
wnet_ant+_eq3_es	71	65.91%	63.50%	64.68%	63.05%
wnet_ant-_eq3_es	**71**	**65.91%**	**63.50%**	**64.68%**	**63.05%**

Table 4: Results of the graph-based algorithm

5 Conclusion and future work

In this work, we have presented a set of experiments with a comparable corpora in English and Spanish. As it is usual, the supervised experiment has outperforms the unsupervised ones. The unsupervised experiments have included the evaluation of two different approaches: lexicon-based and graph-based. In the lexicon-based approach we have presented a new resource for the Spanish OM research community, being an important contribution of this paper. The results reached with SOL are very closed to the ones obtained with graph-based methods. Although, for short texts the graph-based method performed well, for the kind of reviews used in these experiments is not as good. Due to the fact that for English the BLEL lexicon has reached better results, for Spanish the results of SOL are nearly the same ones obtained by the graph method, and the use of a lexicon is more efficient, we conclude that the lexicon-based method is most suitable.

Currently we are improving the SOL lexicon, and also we are adding domain information to the words in SOL. Furthermore, one of our main objectives is the treatment of the negation because we considered that is essential for OM.

Acknowledgments

This work has been partially supported by a grant from the Fondo Europeo de Desarrollo Regional (FEDER), TEXT-COOL 2.0 project (TIN2009-13391-C04-02) and ATTOS project (TIN2012-38536-C03-0) from the Spanish Government. Also, this paper is partially funded by the European Commission under the Seventh (FP7 - 2007-2013) Framework Programme for Research and Technological Development through the FIRST project (FP7-287607). This publication reflects the views only of the authors, and the Commission cannot be held responsible for any use which may be made of the information contained therein.

References

Eneko Agirre and Aitor Soroa. 2009. Personalizing pagerank for word sense disambiguation. In *Proceedings of the 12th Conference of the European Chapter of the Association for Computational Linguistics*, EACL '09, pages 33–41, Stroudsburg, PA, USA. Association for Computational Linguistics.

Stefano Baccianella, Andrea Esuli, and Fabrizio Sebastiani. 2010. Sentiwordnet 3.0: An enhanced lexical resource for sentiment analysis and opinion mining. In Nicoletta Calzolari (Conference Chair), Khalid Choukri, Bente Maegaard, Joseph Mariani, Jan Odijk, Stelios Piperidis, Mike Rosner, and Daniel Tapias, editors, *Proceedings of the Seventh International Conference on Language Resources and Evaluation (LREC'10)*, Valletta, Malta, may. European Language Resources Association (ELRA).

Carmen Banea, Rada Mihalcea, Janyce Wiebe, and Samer Hassan. 2008. Multilingual subjectivity analysis using machine translation. In *Proceedings of the Conference on Empirical Methods in Natural Language Processing*, EMNLP '08, pages 127–135, Stroudsburg, PA, USA. Association for Computational Linguistics.

Julian Brooke, Milan Tofiloski, and Maite Taboada. 2009. Cross-linguistic sentiment analysis: From english to spanish. In *Proceedings of the International Conference RANLP-2009*, pages 50–54, Borovets,

Bulgaria, September. Association for Computational Linguistics.

Chih-Chung Chang and Chih-Jen Lin. 2011. Libsvm: A library for support vector machines. *ACM Trans. Intell. Syst. Technol.*, 2(3):27:1–27:27, May.

Corinna Cortes and Vladimir Vapnik. 1995. Support-vector networks. *Machine Learning*, 20:273–297.

Fermín L. Cruz, Jose A. Troyano, Fernando Enriquez, and Javier Ortega. 2008. Clasificación de documentos basada en la opinión: experimentos con un corpus de críticas de cine en español. *Procesamiento del Lenguaje Natural*, 41:73–80.

Kushal Dave, Steve Lawrence, and David M. Pennock. 2003. Mining the peanut gallery: opinion extraction and semantic classification of product reviews. In *Proceedings of the 12th international conference on World Wide Web*, WWW '03, pages 519–528, New York, NY, USA. ACM.

Kerstin Denecke. 2008. Using sentiwordnet for multilingual sentiment analysis. In *Data Engineering Workshop, 2008. ICDEW 2008. IEEE 24th International Conference on*, pages 507–512. IEEE.

Hatem Ghorbel and David Jacot. 2011. Sentiment analysis of french movie reviews. *Advances in Distributed Agent-Based Retrieval Tools*, pages 97–108.

Aitor Gonzalez-Agirre, Egoitz Laparra, and German Rigau. 2012. Multilingual central repository version 3.0. In Nicoletta Calzolari (Conference Chair), Khalid Choukri, Thierry Declerck, Mehmet Uğur Doğan, Bente Maegaard, Joseph Mariani, Jan Odijk, and Stelios Piperidis, editors, *Proceedings of the Eight International Conference on Language Resources and Evaluation (LREC'12)*, Istanbul, Turkey, may. European Language Resources Association (ELRA).

Minqing Hu and Bing Liu. 2004. Mining and summarizing customer reviews. In *Proceedings of the tenth ACM SIGKDD international conference on Knowledge discovery and data mining*, KDD '04, pages 168–177, New York, NY, USA. ACM.

Eugenio Martínez-Cámara, M. Teresa Martín-Valdivia, and L. Alfonso Ureña López. 2011. Opinion classification techniques applied to a spanish corpus. In *Proceedings of the 16th international conference on Natural language processing and information systems*, NLDB'11, pages 169–176, Berlin, Heidelberg. Springer-Verlag.

M. Teresa Martín-Valdivia, Eugenio Martínez-Cámara, Jose M. Perea-Ortega, and L. Alfonso Ureña López. 2012. Sentiment polarity detection in spanish reviews combining supervised and unsupervised approaches. *Expert Systems with Applications*. In press.

George A. Miller. 1995. Wordnet: a lexical database for english. *Communications of the ACM*, 38(11):39–41.

Arturo Montejo-Ráez, Eugenio Martínez-Cámara, M. Teresa Martín-Valdivia, and L. Alfonso Ureña López. 2012. Random walk weighting over sentiwordnet for sentiment polarity detection on twitter. In *Proceedings of the 3rd Workshop in Computational Approaches to Subjectivity and Sentiment Analysis*, pages 3–10, Jeju, Korea, July. Association for Computational Linguistics.

Lawrence Page, Sergey Brin, Rajeev Motwani, and Terry Winograd. 1999. The pagerank citation ranking: Bringing order to the web. Technical Report 1999-66, Stanford InfoLab, November. Previous number = SIDL-WP-1999-0120.

Bo Pang and Lillian Lee. 2008. Opinion mining and sentiment analysis. *Found. Trends Inf. Retr.*, 2(1-2):1–135, January.

Bo Pang, Lillian Lee, and Shivakumar Vaithyanathan. 2002. Thumbs up?: Sentiment classification using machine learning techniques. In *Proceedings of the ACL-02 conference on Empirical methods in natural language processing - Volume 10*, EMNLP '02, pages 79–86, Stroudsburg, PA, USA. Association for Computational Linguistics.

Mohammed Rushdi-Saleh, M. Teresa Martín-Valdivia, L. Alfonso Ureña López, and José M. Perea-Ortega. 2011a. OCA: Opinion corpus for Arabic. *Journal of the American Society for Information Science and Technology*, 62(10):2045–2054, October.

Mohammed Rushdi-Saleh, Maria Teresa Martn-Valdivia, Luis Alfonso Urea-Lpez, and Jos M. Perea-Ortega. 2011b. Bilingual Experiments with an Arabic-English Corpus for Opinion Mining. In Galia Angelova, Kalina Bontcheva, Ruslan Mitkov, and Nicolas Nicolov, editors, *RANLP*, pages 740–745. RANLP 2011 Organising Committee.

Maite Taboada and Jack Grieve. 2004. Analyzing appraisal automatically. In *Proceedings of AAAI Spring Symposium on Exploring Attitude and Affect in Text (AAAI Technical Re# port SS# 04# 07), Stanford University, CA, pp. 158q161. AAAI Press*.

Maite Taboada. 2008. Sfu review corpus. `http://www.sfu.ca/~mtaboada/research/SFU_Review_Corpus.html`.

Peter D. Turney. 2002. Thumbs up or thumbs down?: semantic orientation applied to unsupervised classification of reviews. In *Proceedings of the 40th Annual Meeting on Association for Computational Linguistics*, ACL '02, pages 417–424, Stroudsburg, PA, USA. Association for Computational Linguistics.

RA-SR: Using a ranking algorithm to automatically building resources for subjectivity analysis over annotated corpora

Yoan Gutiérrez, Andy González
University of Matanzas, Cuba
yoan.gutierrez@umcc.cu,
andy.gonzalez@infonet.umcc.cu

Antonio Fernández Orquín, Andrés Montoyo, Rafael Muñoz
University of Alicante, Spain
antonybr@yahoo.com, {montoyo, rafael}@dlsi.ua.es

Abstract

In this paper we propose a method that uses corpora where phrases are annotated as Positive, Negative, Objective and Neutral, to achieve new sentiment resources involving words dictionaries with their associated polarity. Our method was created to build sentiment words inventories based on senti-semantic evidences obtained after exploring text with annotated sentiment polarity information. Through this process a graph-based algorithm is used to obtain auto-balanced values that characterize sentiment polarities well used on Sentiment Analysis tasks. To assessment effectiveness of the obtained resource, sentiment classification was made, achieving objective instances over 80%.

1 Introduction

In recent years, textual information has become one of the most important sources of knowledge to extract useful data. Texts can provide factual information, such as: descriptions, lists of characteristics, or even instructions to opinion-based information, which would include reviews, emotions or feelings. These facts have motivated dealing with the identification and extraction of opinions and sentiments in texts that require special attention. Among most widely used terms in Natural Language Processing, in concrete in Sentiment Analysis (SA) and Opinion Mining, is the subjectivity term proposed by (Wiebe, 1994). This author defines it as "linguistic expression of somebody's opinions, sentiments, emotions, evaluations, beliefs and speculations". Another important aspect opposed to subjectivity is the objectivity, which constitute a fact expression (Balahur, 2011). Other interesting terms also proposed by (Wiebe *et al.*, 2005) considers, private state, theses terms involve opinions, beliefs, thoughts, feelings, emotions, goals, evaluations and judgments.

Many researchers such as (Balahur *et al.*, 2010; Hatzivassiloglou *et al.*, 2000; Kim and Hovy, 2006; Wiebe *et al.*, 2005) and many others have been working in this way and related areas. To build systems able to lead SA challenges it is necessary to achieve sentiment resources previously developed. These resources could be annotated corpora, affective semantic structures, and sentiment dictionaries.

In this paper we propose a method that uses annotated corpora where phrases are annotated as Positive, Negative, Objective and Neutral, to achieve new resources for subjectivity analysis involving words dictionaries with their associated polarity.

The next section shows different sentiment and affective resources and their main characteristics. After that, our proposal is developed in section 3. Section 4, present a new sentiment resource obtained after evaluating RA-SR over many corpora. Section 5 described the evaluation and analysis of the obtained resource, and also an assessment of the obtained resource in Sentiment Classification task. Finally, conclusion and further works are presented in section 6.

2 Related work

It is known that the use of sentiment resources has proven to be a necessary step for training and evaluation for systems implementing sentiment analysis, including also fine-grained opinion mining (Balahur, 2011).

Different techniques have been used into product reviews to obtain lexicons of subjective words with their associated polarity. We can study the relevant research promoted by (Hu and Liu, 2004) which start with a set of seed adjectives ("good" and "bad") and reinforce the semantic knowledge applying a expanding the lexicon with synonymy and antonymy relations provided by WordNet (Miller *et al.*, 1990). As result of Hu and Liu researches an Opinion Lexicon is obtained with around 6800 positive and negative English words (Hu and Liu, 2004; Liu *et al.*, 2005).

A similar approach has been used in building WordNet-Affect (Strapparava and Valitutti, 2004). In this case the building method starting from a larger of seed affective words set. These words are classified according to the six basic categories of emotion (joy, sadness, fear, surprise, anger and disgust), are also expanded increase the lexicon using paths in WordNet.

Other widely used in SA has been SentiWordNet resource (Esuli and Sebastiani, 2006)). The main idea that encouraged its construction has been that "terms with similar glosses in WordNet tend to have similar polarity".

Another popular lexicon is MicroWNOp (Cerini *et al.*, 2007). It contains opinion words with their associated polarity. It has been built on the basis of a set of terms extracted from the General Inquirer[1] (Stone *et al.*, 1996).

The problem is that these resources do not consider the context in which the words appear. Some methods tried to overcome this critique and built sentiment lexicons using the local context of words.

We can mentioned to (Pang *et al.*, 2002) whom built a lexicon with associated polarity value, starting with a set of classified seed adjectives and using conjunctions ("and") disjunctions ("or", "but") to deduce orientation of new words in a corpus.

(Turney, 2002) classifies words according to their polarity based on the idea that terms with similar orientation tend to co-occur in documents.

On the contrary in (Balahur and Montoyo, 2008b), is computed the polarity of new words using "polarity anchors" (words whose polarity is known beforehand) and Normalized Google Distance (Cilibrasi and Vitányi, 2007) scores using as training examples opinion words extracted from "pros and cons reviews" from the same domain. This research achieved the lexical resource Emotion Triggers (Balahur and Montoyo, 2008a).

Another approach that uses the polarity of the local context for computing word polarity is the one presented by (Popescu and Etzioni, 2005), who use a weighting function of the words around the context to be classified.

All described resources have been obtained manually or semi-automatically. Therefore, we focus our target in archiving automatically new sentiment resources supported over some of aforementioned resources. In particular, we will offer contributions related with methods to build sentiment lexicons using the local context of words.

3 Our method

We propose a method named RA-SR (using Ranking Algorithms to build Sentiment Resources) to build sentiment words inventories based on senti-semantic evidences obtained after exploring text with annotated sentiment polarity information. Through this process a graph-based algorithm is used to obtain auto-balanced values that characterize sentiment polarities widely used on Sentiment Analysis tasks. This method consists of three main stages: **(I)** Building contextual words graphs; **(II)** Applying ranking algorithm; and **(III)** Adjusting sentiment polarity values.

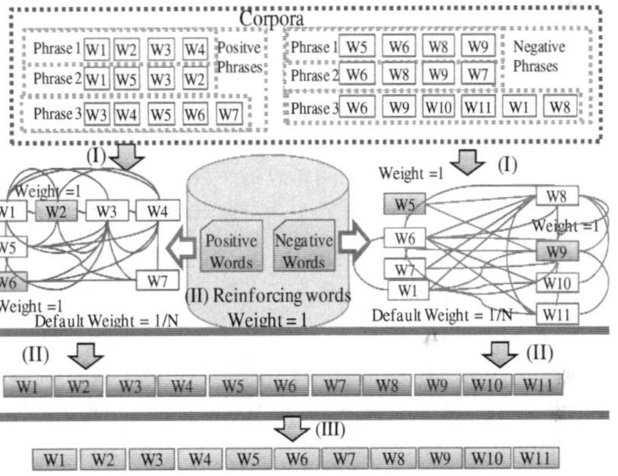

Figure 1. Resource walkthrough development process.

These stages are represented in the diagram of Figure 1, where the development process begins introducing two corpuses of annotated sentences with positive and negative sentences respectively. Initially, a preprocessing of the text is made applying Freeling pos-tagger (Atserias *et al.*, 2006) version 2.2 to convert all words to lemmas[2]. After that, all lemmas lists obtained are introduced in RA-SR, divided in two groups (i.e. positive and negative candidates, $Spos$ and $Sneg$).

3.1 Building contextual words graphs

Giving two sets of sentences ($Spos$ and $Sneg$) annotated as positive and negative respectively, where $Spos = [L_{pos1}, \ldots, L_{posM}]$ and $Sneg = [L_{neg1}, \ldots, L_{negM}]$ contains list L involving words lemmatized by Freeling 2.2 Pos-Tagger

[1] http://www.wjh.harvard.edu/~inquirer/

[2] Lemma denotes canonic form of the words.

(Atserias *et al.*, 2006), a process to build two lexical contextual graphs, $Gpos$ and $Gneg$ is applied. Those sentences are manually annotated as positive and negative respectively. These graphs involve lemmas from the positive and negative sentences respectively.

A contextual graph G is defined as an undirected graph $G = (V, E)$, where V denotes the set of vertices and E the set of edges. Given the list $L = [l_1 \dots l_N]$ a lemma graph is created establishing links among all lemmas of each sentence, where words involved allow to interconnect sentences l_i in G. As a result word/lemma networks $Gpos$ and $Gneg$ are obtained, where $L = V = [l_1 \dots l_N]$ and for every edge $(l_i, l_j) \in E$ being $l_i, l_j \in V$. Therefore, l_i and v_i are the same.

Then, having two graphs, we proceed to initialize weight to apply graph-based ranking techniques in order to auto-balance the particular importance of each v_i into $Gpos$ and $Gneg$.

3.2 Applying ranking algorithm

To apply a graph-based ranking process, it is necessary to assign weights to the vertices of the graph. Words involved into $Gpos$ and $Gneg$ take the default value $1/\mathrm{N}$ as their weight to define the weight of v vector, which is used in our proposed ranking algorithm. In the case where words are identified on the sentiment repositories (see Table 2) as positive or negative, in relation to their respective graph, a weight value of 1 (in a range $[0 \dots 1]$) is assigned. N represents the maximum quantity of words in the current graph. Thereafter, a graph-based ranking algorithm is applied in order to structurally raise the graph vertexes' voting power. Once the reinforcement values are applied, the proposed ranking algorithm is able to increase the significance of the words related to these empowered vertices.

The PageRank (Brin and Page, 1998) adaptation, which was popularized by (Agirre and Soroa, 2009) in Word Sense Disambiguation thematic, and the one that has obtained relevant results, was an inspiration to us in this work. The main idea behind this algorithm is that, for each edge between v_i and v_j in graph G, a vote is made from v_i to v_j. As a result, the relevance of v_j is increased.

On top of that, the vote strength from i to j depends on $v_i's$ relevance. The philosophy behind it is that, the more important the vertex is, the more strength the voter would have. Thus, PageRank is generated by applying a random walkthrough from the internal interconnection of G, where the final relevance of v_i represents the random walkthrough probability over G, and ending on v_i.

In our system, we apply the following equation and configuration:

$$\mathbf{Pr} = cM\mathbf{Pr} + (1-c)v \quad (1)$$

Where: M is a probabilistic transition matrix $N \times N$, being $M_{j,i} = \frac{1}{d_i}$ if a link from v_i to v_j exist, in other case zero is assigned; v is a vector $N \times 1$ with values previously described in this section; $\mathbf{Pr}$ is the probabilistic structural vector obtained after a random walkthrough to arrive to any vertex; c is a dumping factor with value 0.85, and like in (Agirre and Soroa, 2009) we used 30 iterations.

A detailed explanation about the PageRank algorithm can be found in (Agirre and Soroa, 2009).

After applying PageRank, in order to obtain standardized values for both graphs, we normalize the rank values by applying the following equation:

$$\mathbf{Pr}_i = \mathbf{Pr}_i / Max(\mathbf{Pr}) \quad (2)$$

Where $Max(\mathbf{Pr})$ obtains the maximum rank value of $\boldsymbol{Pr}$ vector.

3.3 Adjusting sentiment polarity values

After applying the PageRank algorithm on $Gpos$ and $Gneg$, and having normalized their ranks, we proceed to obtain a final list of lemmas (named Lf) while avoiding repeated elements. Lf is represented by Lf_i lemmas, which would have, at that time, two assigned values: Positive, and Negative, which correspond to a calculated rank obtained by the PageRank algorithm.

At that point, for each lemma from Lf, the following equations are applied in order to select the definitive subjectivity polarity for each one:

$$Pos = \begin{cases} Pos - Neg\,; & Pos > Neg \\ 0 & ; otherwise \end{cases} \quad (3)$$

$$Neg = \begin{cases} Neg - Pos\,; & Neg > Pos \\ 0 & ; otherwise \end{cases} \quad (4)$$

Where Pos is the Positive value and Neg the Negative value related to each lemma in Lf.

In order to standardize the Pos and Neg values again and making them more representative in a [0…1] scale, we proceed to apply a normalization process over the Pos and Neg values.

Following and based on the objective features commented by (Baccianella *et al.*, 2010), we assume their same premise to establish objective values of the lemmas. Equation (5) is used to this proceeding, where Obj represent the objective value.

$$Obj = 1 - |Pos - Neg| \quad (5)$$

4 Sentiment Resource obtained

At the same time we have obtained a Lf where each word is represented by Pos, Neg and Obj values, acquired automatically from annotated sentiment corpora. With our proposal we have been able to discover new sentiment words in concordance of contexts in which the words appear. Note that the new obtained resource involves all lemmas identified into the annotated corpora. Pos, Neg, and Obj are nominal values between range [0 ... 1].

5 Evaluation

In the construction of the sentiment resource we used the annotated sentences provided from corpora described on Table 1. Note that we only used the sentences annotated positively and negatively. The resources involved into this table were a selection made to prove the functionality of the words annotation proposal of subjectivity and objectivity.

The sentiment lexicons used were provided from WordNetAffect_Categories [3] and opinion-words[4] files and shown in detail in Table 2.

Corpus	Neg	Pos	Obj	Neu	Obj or Neu	Unknow	Total
computational-intelligence[5]	6982	6172	-	-	-	-	13154
tweeti-b-sub.dist_out.tsv[6]	176	368	110	34	-	-	688
b1_tweeti-objorneu-b.dist_out.tsv[6]	828	1972	788	1114	1045	-	5747
stno[7]	1286	660		384	-	10000	12330
Total	9272	9172	898	1532	1045	10000	31919

Table 1. Corpora used to apply RA-SR.

Sources	**Pos**	**Neg**	**Total**
WordNet-Affects_Categories (Strapparava and Valitutti, 2004)	629	907	1536
opinion-words (Hu and Liu, 2004; Liu *et al.*, 2005)	2006	4783	6789
Total	2635	5690	8325

Table 2. Sentiment Lexicons.

Some issues were taking into account through this process. For example, after obtaining a contextual graph G factotum words are present in mostly of the involved sentences (i.e. verb *"to be"*). This aspect is very dangerous after applying PageRank algorithm, because this algorithm because this algorithm strengthens the nodes possessing many linked elements. For that reason, the subtractions $Pos - Neg$ and $Neg - Pos$ are applied, where the most frequently words in all contexts obtains high values and being the subtraction a damping factor.

Following an example; when we take the verb *"to be"*, before applying equation (2), verb *"to be"* archives the highest values into each context graph ($Gpos$ and $Gneg$), 9.94 and 18.67 rank values respectively. These values, applying equation (2), are normalized obtaining both $Pos = 1$ and $Neg = 1$ in a range [0...1]. Finally, when the next steps are executed (Equations (3) and (4)) verb *"to be"* achieves $Pos = 0$, $Neg = 0$ and therefore $Obj = 1$. Through this example it seems as we subjectively discarded words that appear frequently in both contexts (Positive and Negative contexts).

Using the corpora from Table 1 we obtain 25792 sentimentally annotated lemmas with Pos, Neg and Obj features. Of them 12420 positive and 11999 negative lemmas were discovered, , and 1373 words already derived from existing lexical resources.

Another contribution has been the Pos, Neg and Obj scores assigned to words of lexical inventory, which were used to reinforce the contextual graphs in the building process. Those words in concordance to our scenario count 842 Positives and 383 Negatives.

5.1 Sentiment Resource Applied on Sentiment Analysis

To know if our method offers resources that improve the SA state of the art, we propose a **baseline** supported on the sentiment dictionaries, and other method (Ranking Sentiment Resource (**RSR**)) supported over our obtained resource. The **baseline** consists on analyzing sentences applying Equation (6) and Equation (7).

$$PosMeasure = \frac{PosCount}{WordCount} \quad (6)$$

$$NegMeasure = \frac{NegCount}{WordCount} \quad (7)$$

Where: $PosCount$ is the total of positive words (aligned with the sentiment dictionaries) in the sentence; $NegCount$ is the total of negative words (aligned with the sentiment dictionaries)

[3] http://wndomains.fbk.eu/wnaffect.html
[4] http://www.cs.uic.edu/~liub/FBS/sentiment-analysis.html
[5] A sentimental corpus obtained applying techniques developed by GPLSI department. See (http://gplsi.dlsi.ua.es/gplsi11/allresourcespanel)
[6] Train dataset of Semeval-2013 (Task 2. Sentiment Analysis in Twitter, subtask b.)
[7] Test dataset of NTCIR Multilingual Opinion Analysis Task (MOAT) http://research.nii.ac.jp/ntcir/ntcir-ws8/meeting/

in the sentence; $WordCount$ is the total of words in the sentence.

Using these measures over the analyzed sentences, for each sentence, we obtain two attributes, $PosMeasure$ and $NegMeasure$; and a third attribute (named Classification) corresponding to its classification.

On the other hand, we propose **RSR**. This SA method uses in a different way the Equation (6) and Equation (7), and introduces Equation (8).

$$ObjMeasure = \frac{ObjCount}{WordCount} \quad (8)$$

Being $PosCount$ the sum of Positive ranking values of the sentence words, aligned with the obtained resource (Lf); $NegCount$ the sum of Negative ranking values of the sentence words, aligned with the obtained resource (Lf); and $ObjCount$ the sum of Objective ranking values of the sentence words, aligned with the obtained resource (Lf).

In RSR method we proved with two approach, RSR ($1/d_i$) and RSR ($1-(1/d_i)$). The first approach is based on a resource developed using PageRank with $M_{j,i} = 1/d_i$ and the other approach is using $M_{j,i} = 1 - (1/d_i)$. Table 3 shows experimentation results.

The evaluation has been applied over a corpus provided by "Task 2. Sentiment Analysis in Twitter, subtask b", in particular tweeti-b-sub.dist_out.tsv file. This corpus contains 597 annotated phrases, of them Positives (314), Negatives (155), Objectives (98) or Neutrals (30). For our understanding this quantity of instances offers a representative perception of RA-SR contribution; however we will think to evaluate RA-SR over other corpora in further researches.

	C	I	R. Pos (%)	R. Neg (%)	R. Obj (%)	R. Neu (%)	Total P. (%)	Total R. (%)
Baseline	366	231	91.1	51.6	0.0	0.0	48.2	61.3
RSR($1/d_i$)	416	181	87.3	39.4	80.6	6.7%	67.8	69.7
RSR($1-(1/d_i$)	469	128	88.5	70.3	81.6	6.7%	76.8	78.6

Table 3. Logistic function (Cross-validation 10 folds) over tweeti-b-sub.dist_out.tsv[8] corpus (597 instances). Recall (R), Precision (P), Correct (C), Incorrect (I).

As we can see the baseline only is able to dealing with negative and positive instances. Is important to remark that our proposal starting up knowing only the words used in baseline and is able to growing sentiment information to other words related to them. We can see this fact on Table 3, RSR is able to classify objective instances over 80% of Recall and the baseline does not.

Other relevant element is the recall difference between RSR ($1/d_i$) and RSR $(1 - (1/d_i)$. Traditionally $(1/d_i)$ result value has been assigned to M in PageRank algorithm. We have demonstrated that in lexical contexts RSR ($1-(1/d_i)$) approach offers a better performance of PageRank algorithm, showing recall differences around 10 perceptual points.

6 Conclusion and further works

As a conclusion we can say that our proposal is able to automatically increase sentiment information, obtaining 25792 sentimentally annotated lemmas with Pos, Neg and Obj features. Of them 12420 positive and 11999 negative lemmas were discovered.

In other hand, The RSR is capable to classify objective instances over 80% and negatives over 70%. We cannot tackle efficiently neutral instances, perhaps it is due to the lack of neutral information in the sentiment resource we used. Also, it could be due to the low quantity of neutral instances in the evaluated corpus.

In further research we will evaluate RA-SR over different corpora, and we are also going to deal with the number of neutral instances.

The variant RSR$(1 - (1/d_i)$ performs better than RSR$(1/d_i)$ one. This demonstrates that in lexical contexts using PageRank with $M_{j,i} = 1 - (1/d_i)$ offers a better performance. Other further work consists in exploring Social Medias to expand our retrieved sentiment resource obtaining real time evidences that occur in Web 2.0.

Acknowledgments

This research work has been partially funded by the Spanish Government through the project TEXT-MESS 2.0 (TIN2009-13391-C04), "Análisis de Tendencias Mediante Técnicas de Opinión Semántica" (TIN2012-38536-C03-03) and "Técnicas de Deconstrucción en la Tecnologías del Lenguaje Humano" (TIN2012-31224); and by the Valencian Government through the project PROMETEO (PROMETEO/2009/199).

References

Agirre, E. and A. Soroa. Personalizing PageRank for Word Sense Disambiguation. Proceedings of the 12th conference of the European chapter of the

[8] Semeval-2013 (Task 2. Sentiment Analysis in Twitter, subtask b.)

Association for Computational Linguistics (EACL-2009), Athens, Greece, 2009. p.

Atserias, J.; B. Casas; E. Comelles; M. González; L. Padró and M. Padró. FreeLing 1.3: Syntactic and semantic services in an opensource NLP library. Proceedings of LREC'06, Genoa, Italy, 2006. p.

Baccianella, S.; A. Esuli and F. Sebastiani. SENTIWORDNET 3.0: An Enhanced Lexical Resource for Sentiment Analysis and Opinion Mining. 7th Language Resources and Evaluation Conference, Valletta, MALTA., 2010. 2200-2204 p.

Balahur, A. Methods and Resources for Sentiment Analysis in Multilingual Documents of Different Text Types. Department of Software and Computing Systems. Alacant, Univeristy of Alacant, 2011. 299. p.

Balahur, A.; E. Boldrini; A. Montoyo and P. Martinez-Barco. The OpAL System at NTCIR 8 MOAT. Proceedings of NTCIR-8 Workshop Meeting, Tokyo, Japan., 2010. 241-245 p.

Balahur, A. and A. Montoyo. Applying a culture dependent emotion trigger database for text valence and emotion classification. Procesamiento del Lenguaje Natural, 2008a. p.

Balahur, A. and A. Montoyo. Building a recommender system using community level social filtering. 5th International Workshop on Natural Language and Cognitive Science (NLPCS), 2008b. 32-41 p.

Brin, S. and L. Page The anatomy of a large-scale hypertextual Web search engine Computer Networks and ISDN Systems, 1998, 30(1-7): 107-117.

Cerini, S.; V. Compagnoni; A. Demontis; M. Formentelli and G. Gandini Language resources and linguistic theory: Typology, second language acquisition, English linguistics (Forthcoming), chapter Micro-WNOp: A gold standard for the evaluation of automatically compiled lexical resources for opinion mining., 2007.

Cilibrasi, R. L. and P. M. B. Vitányi The Google Similarity Distance IEEE TRANSACTIONS ON KNOWLEDGE AND DATA ENGINEERING, 2007, VOL. 19, NO 3.

Esuli, A. and F. Sebastiani. SentiWordNet: A Publicly Available Lexical Resource for Opinion Mining. Fifth international conference on Languaje Resources and Evaluation Genoa - ITaly., 2006. 417-422 p.

Hatzivassiloglou; Vasileios and J. Wiebe. Effects of Adjective Orientation and Gradability on Sentence Subjectivity. International Conference on Computational Linguistics (COLING-2000), 2000. p.

Hu, M. and B. Liu. Mining and Summarizing Customer Reviews. Proceedings of the ACM SIGKDD International Conference on Knowledge Discovery and Data Mining (KDD-2004), USA, 2004. p.

Kim, S.-M. and E. Hovy. Extracting Opinions, Opinion Holders, and Topics Expressed in Online News Media Text. In Proceedings of workshop on sentiment and subjectivity in text at proceedings of the 21st international conference on computational linguistics/the 44th annual meeting of the association for computational linguistics (COLING/ACL 2006), Sydney, Australia, 2006. 1-8 p.

Liu, B.; M. Hu and J. Cheng. Opinion Observer: Analyzing and Comparing Opinions on the Web. Proceedings of the 14th International World Wide Web conference (WWW-2005), Japan, 2005. p.

Miller, G. A.; R. Beckwith; C. Fellbaum; D. Gross and K. Miller Introduction to WordNet: An On-line Lexical Database International Journal of Lexicography, 3(4):235-244., 1990.

Pang, B.; L. Lee and S. Vaithyanathan. Thumbs up? Sentiment Classification using machine learning techniquies. EMNLP -02, the Conference on Empirical Methods in Natural Language Processing, USA, 2002. 79-86 p.

Popescu, A. M. and O. Etzioni. Extracting product features and opinions from reviews. Proccedings of HLT-EMNLP, Canada, 2005. p.

Stone, P.; D. C.Dumphy; M. S. Smith and D. M. Ogilvie The General Inquirer: A Computer Approach to Content Analysis The MIT Press, 1996.

Strapparava, C. and A. Valitutti. WordNet-Affect: an affective extension of WordNet. Proceedings of the 4th International Conference on Language Resources and Evaluation (LREC 2004), Lisbon, 2004. 1083-1086 p.

Turney, P. D. Thumbs up or thumbs down? Semantic orientation applied to unsupervised classification of reviews. Proceeding 40th Annual Meeting of the Association for Computational Linguistic. ACL 2002, USA, 2002. 417-424 p.

Wiebe, J. Tracking point of view in narrative Computational Linguistic, 1994, 20(2): 233-287.

Wiebe, J.; T. Wilson and C. Cardie. Annotating Expressions of Opinions and Emotions in Language. Kluwer Academic Publishers, Netherlands, 2005. p.

Sentiment analysis on Italian tweets

Valerio Basile
University of Groningen
v.basile@rug.nl

Malvina Nissim
University of Bologna
malvina.nissim@unibo.it

Abstract

We describe TWITA, the first corpus of Italian tweets, which is created via a completely automatic procedure, portable to any other language. We experiment with sentiment analysis on two datasets from TWITA: a generic collection and a topic-specific collection. The only resource we use is a polarity lexicon, which we obtain by automatically matching three existing resources thereby creating the first polarity database for Italian. We observe that albeit shallow, our simple system captures polarity distinctions matching reasonably well the classification done by human judges, with differences in performance across polarity values and on the two sets.

1 Introduction

Twitter is an online service which lets subscribers post short messages ("tweets") of up to 140 characters about anything, from good-morning messages to political stands.

Such micro texts are a precious mine for grasping opinions of groups of people, possibly about a specific topic or product. This is even more so, since tweets are associated to several kinds of meta-data, such as geographical coordinates of where the tweet was sent from, the id of the sender, the time of the day — information that can be combined with text analysis to yield an even more accurate picture of who says what, and where, and when. The last years have seen an enormous increase in research on developing opinion mining systems of various sorts applying Natural Language Processing techniques. Systems range from simple lookups in polarity or affection resources, i.e. databases where a polarity score (usually positive, negative, or neutral) is associated to terms, to more sophisticated models built through supervised, unsupervised, and distant learning involving various sets of features (Liu, 2012).

Tweets are produced in many languages, but most work on sentiment analysis is done for English (even independently of Twitter). This is also due to the availability of tools and resources. Developing systems able to perform sentiment analysis for tweets in a new language requires at least a corpus of tweets and a polarity lexicon, both of which, to the best of our knowledge, do not exist yet for Italian.

This paper offers three main contributions in this respect. First, we present the first of corpus of tweets for Italian, built in such a way that makes it possible to use the exact same strategy to build similar resources for other languages without any manual intervention (Section 2). Second, we derive a polarity lexicon for Italian, organised by senses, also using a fully automatic strategy which can replicated to obtain such a resource for other languages (Section 3.1). Third, we use the lexicon to automatically assign polarity to two subsets of the tweets in our corpus, and evaluate results against manually annotated data (Sections 3.2–3.4).

2 Corpus creation

We collected one year worth of tweets, from February 2012 to February 2013, using the Twitter filter API[1] and a language recognition strategy which

[1] https://dev.twitter.com/docs/api/1/post/statuses/filter

we describe below. The collection, named TWITA, consists of about 100 million tweets in Italian enriched with several kinds of meta-information, such as the time-stamp, geographic coordinates (whenever present), and the username of the twitter. Additionally, we used off-the-shelf language processing tools to tokenise all tweets and tag them with part-of-speech information.

2.1 Language detection

One rather straightforward way of creating a corpus of language-specific tweets is to retrieve tweets via the Twitter API which are matched with strongly language-representative words. Tjong Kim Sang and Bos (2012) compile their list of highly typical Dutch terms manually to retrieve Dutch-only tweets. While we also use a list of strongly representative Italian words, we obtain such list *automatically*. This has the advantage of making the procedure more objective and fully portable to any other language for which large reference corpora are available. Indeed, we relied on frequency information derived from ItWac, a large corpus of Italian (Baroni et al., 2009), and exploited Google n-grams to rule out cross-language homographs. For boosting precision, we also used the publicly available language recognition software *langid.py* (Lui and Baldwin, 2012). The details of the procedure are given below:

1. extract the 1.000 most frequent lemmas from ItWaC;
2. extract tweets matched by the selected representative words and detect the language using a freely available software;[2]
3. filter out the terms in the original list which have high frequency in a conflicting language. Frequency is obtained from Google N-grams;
4. use high frequency terms in the resulting cleaner list to search the Twitter API.

The 20 top terms which were then used to match Italian-only tweets are: *vita Roma forza alla quanto amore Milano Italia fare grazie della anche periodo bene scuola dopo tutto ancora tutti fatto*. In the extraction, we preserved metadata about user, time, and geographical coordinates whenever available.

Both precision and recall of this method are hard to assess. We cannot know how many tweets that are in fact Italian we're actually missing, but the amount of data we can in any case collect is so high that the issue is not so relevant.[3] Precision is more important, but manual checking would be too time-consuming. We inspected a subset of 1,000 tweets and registered a precision of 99.7% (three very short tweets were found to be in Spanish). Considering that roughly 2.5% of the tweets also include the geographical coordinates of the device used to send the message, we assessed an approximate precision indirectly. We plotted a one million tweets randomly chosen from our corpus and obtained the map shown in Figure 1 (the map is clipped to the Europe area for better identifiability). We can see that Italy is clearly outlined, indicating that precision, though not quantifiable, is likely to be satisfactory.

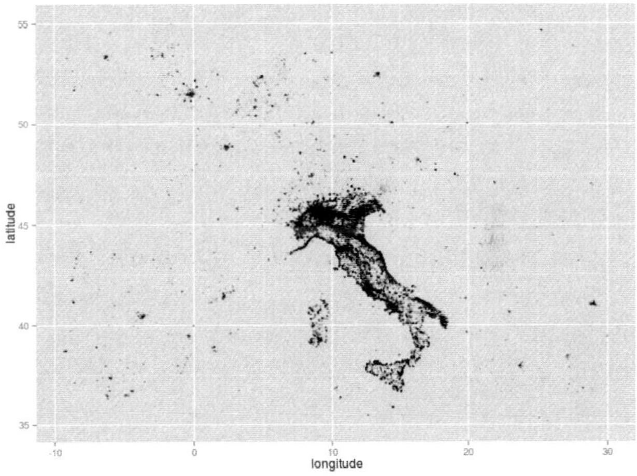

Figure 1: Map derived by plotting geo-coordinates of tweets obtained via our language-detection procedure.

2.2 Processing

The collected tweets have then been enriched with token-level, POS-tags, and lemma information. Meta-information was excluded from processing. So for POS-tagging and lemmatisation we substituted hashtags, mentions (strings of the form *@user-*

[2]Doing so, we identify other languages that share character sequences with Italian. The large majority of tweets in the first search were identified as Portuguese, followed by English, Spanish and then Italian.

[3]This is because we extract generic tweets. Should one want to extract topic-specific tweets, a more targeted list of characterising terms should be used.

name referring to a specific user) and URLs with a generic label. All the original information was re-inserted after processing. The tweets were tokenised with the UCTO rule-based tokeniser[4] and then POS-tagged using TreeTagger (Schmid, 1994) with the provided Italian parameter file. Finally, we used the morphological analyser morph-it! (Zanchetta and Baroni, 2005) for lemmatisation.

3 Sentiment Analysis

The aim of sentiment analysis (or opinion mining) is detecting someone's attitude, whether positive, neutral, or negative, on the basis of some utterance or text s/he has produced. While a first step would be determining whether a statement is objective or subjective, and then only in the latter case identify its polarity, it is often the case that only the second task is performed, thereby also collapsing objective statements and a neutral attitude.

In SemEval-2013's shared task on "Sentiment Analysis in Twitter"[5] (in English tweets), which is currently underway, systems must detect (i) polarity of a given word in a tweet, and (ii) polarity of the whole tweet, in terms of positive, negative, or neutral. This is also what we set to do for Italian. We actually focus on (ii) in the sense that we do not evaluate (i), but we use and combine each word's polarity to obtain the tweet's overall polarity.

Several avenues have been explored for polarity detection. The simplest route is detecting the presence of specific words which are known to express a positive, negative or neutral feeling. For example, O'Connor et al. (2010) use a lexicon-projection strategy yielding predictions which significantly correlate with polls regarding ratings of Obama. While it is clear that deeper linguistic analysis should be performed for better results (Pang and Lee, 2008), accurate processing is rather hard on texts such as tweets, which are short, rich in abbreviations and intra-genre expressions, and often syntactically ill-formed. Additionally, existing tools for the syntactic analysis of Italian, such as the DeSR parser (Attardi et al., 2009), might not be robust enough for processing such texts.

Exploiting information coming from a polarity lexicon, we developed a simple system which assigns to a given tweet one of three possible values: *positive*, *neutral* or *negative*. The only input to the system is the prior polarity coded in the lexicon per *word sense*. We experiment with several ways of combining all the polarities obtained for each word (sense) in a given tweet. Performance is evaluated against manually annotated tweets.

3.1 Polarity lexicon for Italian

Most polarity detection systems make use, in some way, of an affection lexicon, i.e. a language-specific resource which assigns a negative or positive prior polarity to terms. Such resources have been built by hand or derived automatically (Wilson et al., 2005; Wiebe and Mihalcea, 2006; Esuli and Sebastiani, 2006; Taboada et al., 2011, e.g.). To our knowledge, there isn't such a resource already available for Italian. Besides hand-crafting, there have been proposals for creating resources for new languages in a semi-automatic fashion, using manually annotated sets of seeds (Pitel and Grefenstette, 2008), or exploiting twitter emoticons directly (Pak and Paroubek, 2011). Rather than creating a new polarity lexicon from scratch, we exploit three existing resources, namely MultiWordNet (Pianta et al., 2002), SentiWordNet (Esuli and Sebastiani, 2006; Baccianella et al., 2010), and WordNet itself (Fellbaum, 1998) to obtain an annotated lexicon of senses for Italian. Basically, we port the SentiWordNet annotation to the Italian portion of MultiWordNet, and we do so in a completely automatic fashion.

Our starting point is SentiWordNet, a version of WordNet where the independent values *positive*, *negative*, and *objective* are associated to 117,660 synsets, each value in the zero-one interval. MultiWordNet is a resource which aligns Italian and English synsets and can thus be used to transfer polarity information associated to English synsets in SentiWordNet to Italian synsets. One obstacle is that while SentiWordNet refers to WordNet 3.0, MultiWordNet's alignment holds for WordNet 1.6, and synset reference indexes are not plainly carried over from one version to the next. We filled this gap using an automatically produced mapping between synsets of Wordnet versions 1.6 and 3.0 (Daud et al., 2000), making it possible to obtain SentiWordNet annotation for the Italian synsets of MultiWordNet. The

[4]http://ilk.uvt.nl/ucto/

[5]www.cs.york.ac.uk/semeval-2013/task2/.

coverage of our resource is however rather low compared to the English version, and this is due to the alignment procedure which must exploit an earlier version of the resource. The number of synsets is less than one third of that of SentiWordNet.

3.2 Polarity assignment

Given a tweet, our system assigns a polarity score to each of its tokens by matching them to the entries in SentiWordNet. Only matches of the correct POS are allowed. The polarity score of the complete tweet is given by the sum of the polarity scores of its tokens.

Polarity is associated to synsets, and the same term can occur in more than one synset. One option would be to perform word sense disambiguation and only pick the polarity score associated with the intended sense. However, the structure of tweets and the tools available for Italian do not make this option actually feasible, although we might investigate it in the future. As a working solution, we compute the positive and negative scores for a term occurring in a tweet as the means of the positive and negative scores of all synsets to which the lemma belongs to in our lexical resource. The resulting polarity score of a lemma is the difference between its positive and negative scores. Whenever a lemma is not found in the database, it is given a polarity score of 0.

One underlying assumption to this approach is that the different senses of a given word have similar sentiment scores. However, because this assumption might not be true in all cases, we introduce the concept of "polypathy", which is the characterising feature of a term exhibiting high variance of polarity scores across its synsets. The polypathy of a lemma is calculated as the standard deviation of the polarity scores of the possible senses. This information can be used to remove highly polypathic words from the computation of the polarity of a complete tweet, for instance by discarding the tokens with a polypathy higher than a certain threshold. In particular, for the experiments described in this paper, a threshold of 0.5 has been empirically determined. To give an idea, among the most polypathic words in SentiWordNet we found *weird* (.62), *stunning* (.61), *conflicting* (.56), *terrific* (.56).

Taboada et al. (2011) also use SentiWordNet for polarity detection, either taking the first sense of a term (the most frequent in WordNet) or taking the average across senses, as we also do — although we also add the polypathy-aware strategy. We cannot use the first-sense strategy because through the alignment procedure senses are not ranked according to frequency anymore.

3.3 Gold standard

For evaluating the system performance we created two gold standard sets, both annotated by three independent native-speakers, who were given very simple and basic instructions and performed the annotation via a web-based interface. The value to be assigned to each tweet is one out of *positive*, *neutral*, or *negative*. As mentioned, the neutral value includes both objective statements as well as subjective statements where the twitter's position is neutral or equally positive and negative at the same time (see also (Esuli and Sebastiani, 2007)).

All data selected for annotation comes from TWITA. The first dataset consists of 1,000 randomly selected tweets. The second dataset is topic-oriented, i.e. we randomly extracted 1,000 tweets from all those containing a given topic. Topic-oriented, or target-dependent (Jiang et al., 2011), classification involves detecting opinions about a specific target rather than detecting the more general opinion expressed in a given tweet. We identify a topic through a given hashtag, and in this experiment we chose the tag "Grillo", the leader of an Italian political movement. While in the first set the annotators were asked to assign a polarity value to the message of the tweet as a whole, in the second set the value was to be assigned to the author's opinion concerning the hashtag, in this case Beppe Grillo. This is a relevant distinction, since it can happen that the tweet is, say, very negative about someone else while being positive or neutral about Grillo at the same time. For example, the tweet in (1), expresses a negative opinion about Vendola, another Italian politician, but is remaining quite neutral towards Grillo, the target of the annotation exercise.

(1) #Vendola dà del #populista a #Grillo è una barzelletta o ancora non si è accorto che il #comunismo è basato sul populismo?

Thus, in the topic-specific set we operate a more subtle distinction when assigning polarity, something which should make the task simpler for a human annotator while harder for a shallow system.

As shown in Table 1, for both sets the annotators detected more than half of the tweets as neutral, or they were disagreeing – without absolute majority, a tweet is considered neutral; however these cases account for only 7.7% in the generic set and 6.9% in the topic-specific set.

Table 1: Distribution of the tags assigned by the absolute majority of the raters

set	**positive**	**negative**	**neutral**
generic	94	301	605
topic-specific	293	145	562

Inter-annotator agreement was measured via Fleiss' Kappa across three annotators. On the generic set, we found an agreement of $Kappa = 0.321$, while on the topic-specific set we found $Kappa = 0.397$. This confirms our expectation that annotating topic-specific tweets is actually an easier task. We might also consider using more sophisticated and fine-grained sentiment annotation schemes which have proved to be highly reliable in the annotation of English data (Su and Markert, 2008a).

3.4 Evaluation

We ran our system on both datasets described in Section 3.3, using all possible variations of two parameters, namely all combinations of part-of-speech tags and the application of the threshold scheme, as discussed in Section 3.2. We measure overall accuracy as well as precision, recall, and f-score per polarity value. In Tables 2 and 3, we report best scores, and indicate in brackets the associated POS combination. For instance, in Table 2, we can read that the recall of 0.701 for positive polarity is obtained when the system is run without polypathy threshold and using *n*ouns, *v*erbs, and *a*djectives (nva).

We can draw several observations from these results. First, a fully automatic approach that leverages existing lexical resources performs better than a wild guess. Performance is boosted when highly polypathic words are filtered out.

Second, while the system performs well at recognising especially neutral but also positive polarity, it is really bad at detecting negative polarity. Especially in the topic-specific set, the system assigns too many positive labels in place of negative ones, causing at the same time positive's precision and negative's recall to drop. We believe there are two explanations for this. The first one is the "positive-bias" of SentiWordNet, as observed by Taboada et al. (2011), which causes limited performance in the identification of negative polarity. The second one is that we do not use any syntactic clues, such as for detecting negated statements. Including some strategy for dealing with this should improve recognition of negative opinions, too.

Table 2: Best results on the generic set. In brackets POS combination: (n)oun, (v)erb, (a)djective, adve(r)b.

without polypathy threshold, best accuracy: 0.505 (a)			
	positive	**negative**	**neutral**
best precision	0.440 (r)	0.195 (v)	0.664 (nar)
best recall	0.701 (nva)	0.532 (var)	0.669 (a)
best F-score	0.485 (nvar)	0.262 (vr)	0.647 (a)

with polypathy threshold, best accuracy: 0.554 (r)			
	positive	**negative**	**neutral**
best precision	0.420 (r)	0.233 (v)	0.685 (nar)
best recall	0.714 (nvar)	0.457 (var)	0.785 (r)
best F-score	0.492 (nar)	0.296 (vr)	0.698 (r)

Table 3: Best results on the topic-specific set. In brackets POS combination: (n)oun, (v)erb, (a)djective, adve(r)b.

without polypathy threshold, best accuracy: 0.487 (r)			
	positive	**negative**	**neutral**
best precision	0.164 (a)	0.412 (a)	0.617 (nar)
best recall	0.593 (nva)	0.150 (nr)	0.724 (a)
best f-score	0.251 (nv)	0.213 (nr)	0.637 (a)

with polypathy threshold, best accuracy: 0.514 (r)			
	positive	**negative**	**neutral**
best precision	0.163 (nvar)	0.414 (a)	0.623 (nar)
best recall	0.593 (nvar)	0.106 (nar)	0.829 (r)
best f-score	0.256 (nvar)	0.166 (nar)	0.676 (r)

Third, the lower performance on the topic-specific dataset confirms the intuition that this task is harder, mainly because we operate a more subtle distinction when assigning a polarity label as we refer to one specific subject. Deeper linguistic analysis, such as dependency parsing, might help, as only certain words would result as related to the intended target while others wouldn't.

As far as parts of speech are concerned, there is a tendency for adverbs to be good indicators towards overall accuracy, and best scores are usually obtained exploiting adjectives and/or adverbs.

4 Related work

We have already discussed some related work concerning corpus creation, the development of an affection lexicon, and the use of such polarity-annotated resources for sentiment analysis (Section 3). As for results, because this is the first experiment on detecting polarity in Italian tweets, comparing performance is not straightforward. Most work on sentiment analysis in tweets is on English, and although there exist relatively complex systems based on statistical models, just using information from a polarity resource is rather common. Su and Markert (2008b) test SentiWordNet for assigning a subjectivity judgement to word senses on a gold standard corpus, observing an accuracy of 75.3%. Given that SentiWordNet is the automatic expansion over a set of manually annotated seeds, at word-level, this can be considered as an upper bound in sense subjectivity detection. Taboada et al. (2011) offer a survey of lexicon-based methods which are evaluated on adjectives only, by measuring overall accuracy against a manually annotated set of words. Using SentiWordNet in a lexicon-projection fashion yields an accuracy of 61.47% under best settings. These are however scores on single words rather than whole sentences or microtexts.

Considering that we assign polarity to tweets rather than single words, and that in the creation of our resource via automatic alignment we lose more than two thirds of the original synsets (see Section 3.1), our results are promising. They are also not that distant from results reported by Agarwal et al. (2011), whose best system, a combination of unigrams and the best set of features, achieves an accuracy of 60.50% on a three-way classification like ours, evaluated against a manually annotated set of English tweets. Best f-scores reported for positive, negative, and neutral are comprised between 59% and 62%. Similar results are obtained by Pak and Paroubek (2010), who train a classifier on automatically tagged data, and evaluate their model on about 200 English tweets. Best reported f-score on a three-way polarity assignment is just over 60%.

5 Conclusions and future work

We have presented the first corpus of Italian tweets obtained in a completely automatic fashion, the first polarity lexicon for Italian, and the first experiment on sentiment analysis on Italian tweets using these two resources. Both the corpus and the lexicon are as of now unique resources for Italian, and were produced in a way which is completely portable to other languages. In compliance with licensing terms of the sources we have used, our resources are made available for research purposes after reviewing.

Simply projecting the affection lexicon, using two different polarity scoring methods, we experimented with detecting a generic sentiment expressed in a microtext, and detecting the twitter's opinion on a specific topic. As expected, we found that topic-specific classification is harder for an automatic system as it must discern what is said about the topic itself and what is said more generally or about another entity mentioned in the text.

Indeed, this contribution can be seen as a first step towards polarity detection in Italian tweets. The information we obtain from SentiWordNet and the ways we combine it could obviously be used as feature in a learning setting. Other sources of information, to be used in combination with our polarity scores or integrated in a statistical model, are the so-called *noisy labels*, namely strings (such as emoticons or specific hashtags (Go et al., 2009; Davidov et al., 2010)) that can be taken as positive or negative polarity indicators as such. Speriosu et al. (2011) have shown that training a maximum entropy classier using noisy labels as class predictors in the training set yields an improvement of about three percentage points over a lexicon-based prediction.

Another important issue to deal with is figurative language. During manual annotation we have encountered many cases of irony or sarcasm, which is a phenomenon that must be obviously tackled. There have been attempts at identifying it automatically in the context of tweets (González-Ibáñez et al., 2011), and we plan to explore this issue in future work.

Finally, the co-presence of meta and linguistic information allows for a wide range of linguistic queries and statistical analyses on the whole of the corpus, also independently of sentiment information, of course. For example, correlations between parts-of-speech and polarity have been found (Pak and Paroubek, 2010), and one could expect also correlations with sentiment and time of the day, or month of the year, and so on.

Acknowledgments

We would like to thank Manuela, Marcella e Silvia for their help with annotation, and the reviewers for their useful comments. All errors remain our own.

References

Apoorv Agarwal, Boyi Xie, Ilia Vovsha, Owen Rambow, and Rebecca Passonneau. 2011. Sentiment analysis of twitter data. In *Proceedings of the Workshop on Languages in Social Media*, LSM '11, pages 30–38, Stroudsburg, PA, USA. Association for Computational Linguistics.

Giuseppe Attardi, Felice Dell'Orletta, Maria Simi, and Joseph Turian. 2009. Accurate dependency parsing with a stacked multilayer perceptron. In *Proceeding of Evalita 2009*, LNCS. Springer.

Stefano Baccianella, Andrea Esuli, and Fabrizio Sebastiani. 2010. Sentiwordnet 3.0: An enhanced lexical resource for sentiment analysis and opinion mining. In Nicoletta Calzolari et al., editor, *Proceedings of LREC 2010*.

Marco Baroni, Silvia Bernardini, Adriano Ferraresi, and Eros Zanchetta. 2009. The WaCky wide web: a collection of very large linguistically processed web-crawled corpora. *Language Resources and Evaluation*, 43(3):209–226.

Jordi Daud, Llus Padr, and German Rigau. 2000. Mapping wordnets using structural information. In *38th Annual Meeting of the Association for Computational Linguistics (ACL'2000).*, Hong Kong.

Dmitry Davidov, Oren Tsur, and Ari Rappoport. 2010. Enhanced sentiment learning using twitter hashtags and smileys. In *Proceedings of the 23rd International Conference on Computational Linguistics: Posters*, COLING '10, pages 241–249, Stroudsburg, PA, USA. Association for Computational Linguistics.

Andrea Esuli and Fabrizio Sebastiani. 2006. Sentiwordnet: A publicly available lexical resource for opinion mining. In *In Proceedings of the 5th Conference on Language Resources and Evaluation (LREC06*, pages 417–422.

Andrea Esuli and Fabrizio Sebastiani. 2007. Pageranking wordnet synsets: An application to opinion mining. In *Proceedings of the 45th Annual Meeting of the Association of Computational Linguistics*, pages 424–431, Prague, Czech Republic, June. Association for Computational Linguistics.

Christiane Fellbaum, editor. 1998. *WordNet. An Electronic Lexical Database*. The MIT Press.

Alec Go, Richa Bhayani, and Lei Huang. 2009. Twitter sentiment analysis using distant supervision. `http://cs.wmich.edu/~tllake/fileshare/TwitterDistantSupervision09.pdf`.

Roberto González-Ibáñez, Smaranda Muresan, and Nina Wacholder. 2011. Identifying sarcasm in twitter: A closer look. In *Proceedings of the 49th Annual Meeting of the Association for Computational Linguistics: Human Language Technologies*, pages 581–586, Portland, Oregon, USA, June. Association for Computational Linguistics.

Long Jiang, Mo Yu, Ming Zhou, Xiaohua Liu, and Tiejun Zhao. 2011. Target-dependent twitter sentiment classification. In *Proceedings of the 49th Annual Meeting of the Association for Computational Linguistics: Human Language Technologies*, pages 151–160, Portland, Oregon, USA, June. Association for Computational Linguistics.

Bing Liu. 2012. *Sentiment Analysis and Opinion Mining*. Synthesis Lectures on Human Language Technologies. Morgan & Claypool Publishers.

Marco Lui and Timothy Baldwin. 2012. langid.py: An off-the-shelf language identification tool. In *ACL (System Demonstrations)*, pages 25–30. The Association for Computer Linguistics.

Brendan O'Connor, Ramnath Balasubramanyan, Bryan R. Routledge, and Noah A. Smith. 2010. From tweets to polls: Linking text sentiment to public opinion time series. In William W. Cohen and Samuel Gosling, editors, *Proceedings of the Fourth International Conference on Weblogs and Social Media, ICWSM 2010, Washington, DC, USA, May 23-26*. The AAAI Press.

Alexander Pak and Patrick Paroubek. 2010. Twitter as a corpus for sentiment analysis and opinion mining. In Nicoletta Calzolari et al., editor, *Proceedings of the International Conference on Language Resources and Evaluation, LREC 2010, 17-23 May 2010, Valletta, Malta*. European Language Resources Association.

Alexander Pak and Patrick Paroubek. 2011. Twitter for sentiment analysis: When language resources are not available. *23rd International Workshop on Database and Expert Systems Applications*, 0:111–115.

Bo Pang and Lillian Lee. 2008. Opinion mining and sentiment analysis. *Found. Trends Inf. Retr.*, 2(1-2):1–135, January.

Emanuele Pianta, Luisa Bentivogli, and Christian Girardi. 2002. MultiWordNet: developing an aligned multilingual database. In *Proceedings of the First International Conference on Global WordNet*, pages 21–25.

Guillaume Pitel and Gregory Grefenstette. 2008. Semi-automatic building method for a multidimensional affect dictionary for a new language. In *Proceedings of LREC 2008*.

Helmut Schmid. 1994. Probabilistic part-of-speech tagging using decision trees.

Michael Speriosu, Nikita Sudan, Sid Upadhyay, and Jason Baldridge. 2011. Twitter polarity classification with label propagation over lexical links and the follower graph. In *Proceedings of the First workshop on Unsupervised Learning in NLP*, pages 53–63, Edinburgh, Scotland, July. Association for Computational Linguistics.

Fangzhong Su and Katja Markert. 2008a. Eliciting subjectivity and polarity judgements on word senses. In *Proceedings of COLING 2008 Workshop on Human Judgements in Computational Linguistics, Manchester, UK.*

Fangzhong Su and Katja Markert. 2008b. From words to senses: A case study of subjectivity recognition. In Donia Scott and Hans Uszkoreit, editors, *Proceedings of COLING 2008, Manchester, UK*, pages 825–832.

Maite Taboada, Julian Brooke, Milan Tofiloski, Kimberly Voll, and Manfred Stede. 2011. Lexicon-based methods for sentiment analysis. *Comput. Linguist.*, 37(2):267–307, June.

Erik Tjong Kim Sang and Johan Bos. 2012. Predicting the 2011 dutch senate election results with twitter. In *Proceedings of the Workshop on Semantic Analysis in Social Media*, pages 53–60, Avignon, France, April. Association for Computational Linguistics.

Janyce Wiebe and Rada Mihalcea. 2006. Word sense and subjectivity. In Nicoletta Calzolari, Claire Cardie, and Pierre Isabelle, editors, *ACL*. The Association for Computer Linguistics.

Theresa Wilson, Janyce Wiebe, and Paul Hoffmann. 2005. Recognizing contextual polarity in phrase-level sentiment analysis. In *Proceedings of the Human Language Technology and Empirical Methods in Natural Language Processing Conference, 6-8 October, Vancouver, British Columbia, Canada.*

Eros Zanchetta and Marco Baroni. 2005. Morph-it! a free corpus-based morphological resource for the italian language. In *Proceedings of Corpus Linguistics 2005.*

Sentence-Level Subjectivity Detection Using Neuro-Fuzzy Models

Samir Rustamov
Georgia Institute of Technology
225 North Avenue NW
Atlanta, GA 30332, USA
samir.rustamov@gmail.com

Mark A. Clements
Georgia Institute of Technology
225 North Avenue NW
Atlanta, GA 30332, USA
clements@ece.gatech.edu

Abstract

In this work, we attempt to detect sentence-level subjectivity by means of two supervised machine learning approaches: a Fuzzy Control System and Adaptive Neuro-Fuzzy Inference System. Even though these methods are popular in pattern recognition, they have not been thoroughly investigated for subjectivity analysis. We present a novel "Pruned ICF Weighting Coefficient," which improves the accuracy for subjectivity detection. Our feature extraction algorithm calculates a feature vector based on the statistical occurrences of words in a corpus without any lexical knowledge. For this reason, these machine learning models can be applied to any language; i.e., there is no lexical, grammatical, syntactical analysis used in the classification process.

1 Introduction

There has been a growing interest, in recent years, in identifying and extracting subjective information from Web documents that contain opinions. Opinions are usually subjective expressions that describe people's sentiments, appraisals, or feelings. Subjectivity detection seeks to identify whether the given text expresses opinions (subjective) or reports facts (objective) (Lin et al., 2011). Automatic subjectivity analysis methods have been used in a wide variety of text processing and natural language applications. In many natural language processing tasks, subjectivity detection has been used as a first phase of filtering to generate more informative data.

The goal of our research is to develop learning methods to create classifiers that can distinguish subjective from objective sentences. In this paper, we achieve sentence-level subjectivity classification using language independent feature weighting. As a test problem, we employed a subjectivity database from the "Rotten Tomatoes" movie reviews (see http://www.cs.cornell.edu/people/pabo/movie-review-data).

We present two supervised machine learning approaches in our development of sentence-level subjectivity detection: Fuzzy Control System (FCS), and Adaptive Neuro-Fuzzy Inference System (ANFIS). Even though these methods are popular in pattern recognition, they have not been thoroughly investigated for subjectivity analysis. We present a novel "Pruned ICF Weighting Coefficient," which improves the accuracy for subjectivity detection. Our feature extraction algorithm calculates a feature vector based on statistical occurrences of words in the corpus without any lexical knowledge. For this reason, the machine learning models can be applied to any language; i.e., there is no lexical, grammatical, syntactical analysis used in the classification process.

2 Related work

In recent years, several different supervised and unsupervised learning algorithms were investigated for defining subjective information in text or speech.

Riloff and Wiebe (2003) presented a bootstrapping method to learn subjectivity classifiers from a collection of non-annotated texts. Wiebe and Riloff (2005) used a similar method, but they also learned objective expressions apart from subjective expressions.

Pang and Lee (2004) proposed a MinCut based algorithm to classify each sentence as being subjective or objective. The goal of this research was to remove objective sentences from each review to improve document-level sentiment classification (82.8% improved to 86.4%).

Grefenstette et al. (2004) presented a Web mining method for identifying subjective adjectives.

Wilson et al. (2004) and Kim et al. (2005) presented methods of classifying the strength of opinion being expressed in individual clauses (or sentences).

Riloff et al. (2006) defined subsumption relationships among unigrams, n-grams, and lexicosyntactic patterns. They found that if a feature is subsumed by another, the subsumed feature is not needed. The subsumption hierarchy reduces a feature set and reduced feature sets can improve classification performance.

Raaijmakers et al (2008) investigated the use of prosodic features, word n-grams, character n-grams, and phoneme n-grams for subjectivity recognition and polarity classification of dialog acts in multiparty conversation. They found that for subjectivity recognition, a combination of prosodic, word-level, character-level, and phoneme-level information yields the best performance and for polarity classification, the best performance is achieved with a combination of words, characters and phonemes.

Murray and Carenini (2009) proposed to learn subjective patterns from both labeled and unlabeled data using n-gram word sequences with varying level of lexical instantiation. They showed that learning subjective trigrams with varying instantiation levels from both annotated and raw data can improve subjectivity detection and polarity labeling for meeting speech and email threads.

Martineau and Finin (2009) presented Delta TFIDF, an intuitive general purpose technique, to efficiently weight word scores before classification. They compared SVM Difference of TFIDFs and SVM Term Count Baseline results for subjectivity classification. As a result, they showed that SVM based on Delta TFIDF gives high accuracy and low variance.

Barbosa and Feng (2010) classified the subjectivity of tweets (postings on Twitter) based on two kind of features: meta-information about the words on tweets and characteristics of how tweets are written.

Yulan He (2010) proposed subjLDA for sentence-level subjectivity detection by modifying the latent Dirichlet allocation (LDA) model through adding an additional layer to model sentence-level subjectivity labels.

Benamara et al. (2011) proposed subjectivity classification at the segment level for discourse-based sentiment analysis. They classified each segment into four classes, S, OO, O and SN, where S segments are segments that contain explicitly lexicalized subjective and evaluative expressions, OO segments are positive or negative opinion implied in an objective segment, O segments contain neither a lexicalized subjective term nor an implied opinion, SN segments are subjective, though non-evaluative, segments that are used to introduce opinions.

Remus (2011) showed that by using readability formulae and their combinations as features in addition to already well-known subjectivity clues leads to significant accuracy improvements in sentence-level subjectivity classification.

Lin et al, (2011) presented a hierarchical Bayesian model based on latent Dirichlet allocation, called subjLDA, for sentence-level subjectivity detection, which automatically identifies whether a given sentence expresses opinion or states facts.

All the aforementioned work focused on English data and most of them used an English subjectivity dictionary. Recently, there has been some work on subjectivity classification of sentences in Japanese (Kanayama et al., 2006), Chinese (Zagibalov et al., 2008; Zhang et al., 2009), Romanian (Banea et al., 2008; Mihalcea et al., 2007), Urdu (Mukund and Srihari, 2010), Arabic (Abdul-Mageed et al., 2011) and others based on different machine learning algorithms using general and language specific features.

Mihalcea et al., (2007) and Banea et al., (2008) investigated methods to automatically generate resources for subjectivity analysis for a new target language by leveraging the resources and tools available for English. Another approach (Banea et al., 2010) used a multilingual space with meta classifiers to build high precision classifiers for subjectivity classification.

Recently, there has been some work focused on finding features that can be applied to any language. For example, Mogadala and Varma (2012) presented sentence-level subjectivity classification using language independent feature weighting and performed experiments on 5 different languages including English and a South Asian language (Hindi).

Rustamov et. al., (2013) applied hybrid Neuro-Fuzzy and HMMs to document level sentiment analysis of movie reviews.

In the current work, our main goal is to apply supervised methods based on language independent features for classification of subjective and objective sentences.

3 Feature Extraction

Most language independent feature extraction algorithms are based on the presence or occurrence statistics within the corpus. We describe such an algorithm which is intuitive, computationally efficient, and does not require either additional human annotation or lexical knowledge.

We use a subjectivity dataset 1v.0: 5000 subjective and 5000 objective processed sentences in movie reviews [Pang/Lee ACL 2004].

As our target does not use lexical knowledge, we consider every word as one code word. In our algorithm we do not combine verbs in different tenses, such as present and past ("decide" vs "decided") nor nouns as singular or plural ("fact" vs "facts"). Instead, we consider them as the different code words.

Below, we describe some of the parameters:

- N is the number of classes (in our problem N=2: i.e. subjective and objective classes);
- M is the number of different words (terms) in the corpus;
- R is the number of observed sequences in the training process;
- $O^r = \{o_1^r, o_2^r, \ldots o_{T_r}^r\}$ are the sentences in the training dataset, where T_r is the length of r-th sentence, $r = 1,2,..., R$;
- $\mu_{i,j}$ describes the association between i-th term (word) and the j-th class $(i = 1, \ldots M; j = 1,2, \ldots N)$;
- $c_{i,j}$ is the number of times i-th term occurred in the j-th class;
- $t_i = \sum_j c_{i,j}$ denotes the occurrence times of the i-th term in the corpus;
- frequency of the i-th term in the j-th class

$$\bar{c}_{i,j} = \frac{c_{i,j}}{t_i};$$

We present a new weighting coefficient, which affects the accuracy of the system, so that instead of the number of documents we take the number of classes in the well-known IDF (Inverse-Document Frequency) formula. Similar to IDF, we call it Pruned ICF (Inverse-Class Frequency)

$$ICF_i = \log_2\left(\frac{N}{dN_i}\right),$$

where i is a term, dN_i is the number of classes containing the term i, which $\bar{c}_{i,j} > q$, where

$$q = \frac{1}{\delta \cdot N}.$$

The value of δ is found empirically with $\delta = 1.4$ being best for the corpus investigated.

The membership degree of the terms ($\mu_{i,j}$) for appropriate classes can be estimated by experts or can be calculated by analytical formulas. Since a main goal is to avoid using human annotation or lexical knowledge, we calculated the membership degree of each term by an analytical formula as follows $(i = 1, \ldots M; j = 1,2, \ldots N)$:

$$\text{TF:} \quad \mu_{i,j} = \frac{\bar{c}_{i,j}}{\sum_{v=1}^{N} \bar{c}_{i,v}}; \qquad (1)$$

$$\text{TF} \cdot \text{ICF}: \quad \mu_{i,j} = \frac{\bar{c}_{i,j} \cdot ICF_j}{\sum_{v=1}^{N} \bar{c}_{i,v} \cdot ICF_v}; \qquad (2)$$

4 Subjectivity detection using Fuzzy Control System

We use a statistical approach for estimation of the membership function, instead of expert knowledge, at the first stage. Then we apply fuzzy operations and modify parameters by the back-propagation algorithm.

We now introduce our algorithm ($r = 1,2,..., R$).

1. The membership degree of terms ($\mu_{i,j}^r$) of the r-th sentence are calculated from formulas (1)-(2).

2. Maximum membership degree is found with respect to the classes for every term of the r-th sentence

$$\bar{\mu}_{i,j}^r = \mu_{i,j}^r,$$
$$j = \arg\max_{1 \le v \le N} \mu_{i,v}^r, \qquad (3)$$
$$i = 1, \ldots M.$$

3. Means of maxima are calculated for all classes:

$$\bar{\bar{\mu}}_j^r = \frac{\sum_{k \in Z_j^r} \bar{\mu}_{k,j}^r}{T_r},$$

$$Z_j^r = \left\{ i : \bar{\mu}_{i,j}^r = \max_{1 \le v \le N} \mu_{i,v}^r \right\} \qquad (4)$$

$$j = 1, \ldots, N.$$

We use the Center of Gravity Defuzzification (CoGD) method for the defuzzification operation.

Objective and subjective sentences selected according to classes are trained by a fuzzy control model. The objective function is defined as follows (Aida-zade et. al, 2012):

$$E(y) = \frac{1}{2} \sum_{r=1}^{R} \left(\frac{\sum_{j=1}^{N} \bar{\bar{\mu}}_j^r y_j}{\sum_{j=1}^{N} \bar{\bar{\mu}}_j^r} - d_r \right)^2 \to \min_{y \in R^N}, \qquad (5)$$

$y = (y_1, y_2, \ldots, y_N)$, $d_r \in \{1, 2, \ldots, N\}$ desired output.

The partial derivatives of this function are calculated in following form:

$$\frac{\partial E(y)}{\partial y_t} = \sum_{r=1}^{R} \frac{\bar{\bar{\mu}}_t^r}{\sum_{j=1}^{N} \bar{\bar{\mu}}_j^r} \left(\frac{\sum_{j=1}^{N} \bar{\bar{\mu}}_j^r y_j}{\sum_{j=1}^{N} \bar{\bar{\mu}}_j^r} - d_r \right), \ t = 1, 2, \ldots, N.$$

Function (5) is minimized by the conjugate gradient method with the defined optimal values of y^*.

Rounding of $\bar{\bar{y}}$ shows the index of the classes obtained in the result:

$$\bar{\bar{y}} = \frac{\sum_{j=1}^{N} \bar{\bar{\mu}}_j y_j^*}{\sum_{j=1}^{N} \bar{\bar{\mu}}_j}. \qquad (6)$$

Acceptance strategy (s):

$$s = \begin{cases} i_s \in I, & if \ \bar{\bar{y}} \in (i_s - \Delta_1, i_s + \Delta_1) \\ reject, & otherwise \end{cases},$$

where i_s is the index of the appropriate class, $I = \{1, 2, \ldots, N\}$. Here $\Delta_1 \in [0; 0.5]$ is the main quantity, which influences the reliability of the system.

It is straightforward to check which feature vector gives the best results for FCS. Table 1. shows average accuracy over 10 fold cross validation of FCS based on (1)-(2) features in the non-restricted case. Note that these results depend on the classification method these results might be different for different classifiers.

Features	Accuracy (%)
TF	89.87
$TF \cdot ICF$	91.3

Table 1. Results of FCS based on TF and $TF \cdot ICF$ features.

We also checked FCS based on Delta TFIDF features (Martineau and Finin, 2009). As DeltaIDF weighting coefficients of both classes are the same, application of DeltaIDF weighting does not change the accuracy of the FCS. As we see from Table 1., the accuracy of the method increases after application of Pruned ICF weighting.

We show results of subjectivity detection by FCS with different values of Δ_1 based on $TF \cdot ICF$ in Table 2. It can be seen that the rejection percentage is 0.01 for $\Delta_1 = 0.5$. In the testing process 0.01% of the sentences have such words, which after pruned ICF weighting, becomes 0 and the system rejects such sentences.

	Correct (%)	Rejection (%)	Error (%)
$\Delta_1 = 0.3$	76.41	20.86	2.73
$\Delta_1 = 0.4$	85.11	10.14	4.75
$\Delta_1 = 0.5$	91.3	0.01	8.69

Table 2. Average results of 10 folds cross validation accuracy of FCS based on $TF \cdot ICF$ feature with different value of Δ_1.

5 Subjectivity detection using Adaptive Neuro Fuzzy Inference System

Fig. 1 illustrates the general structure of Adaptive Neuro Fuzzy Inference System. In response to linguistic statements, the fuzzy interface block provides an input vector to a Multilayer Artificial Neural Network (MANN) (Fuller, 1995).

We used statistical estimation of membership degree of terms by (2) instead of linguistic statements at the first stage. Then we applied fuzzy operations (3) and (4).

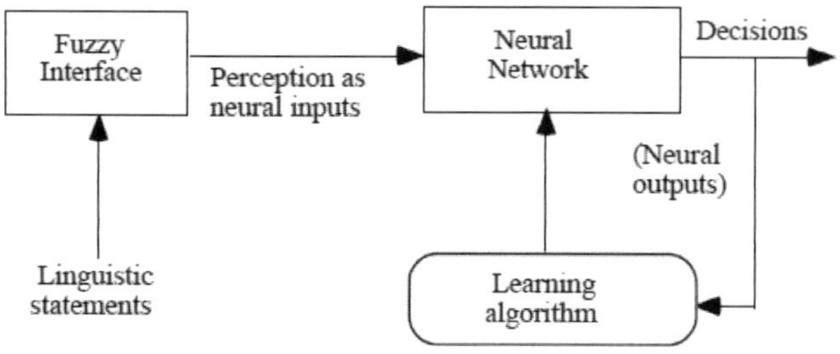

Fig. 1. The structure of ANFIS.

MANN was applied to the output of the fuzzyfication operation. The input vector of neural network is taken from the output vector of the fuzzyfication operation (fig. 2). Outputs of MANN are taken as indexes of classes appropriate to the sentences. MANN is trained by the back-propagation algorithm.

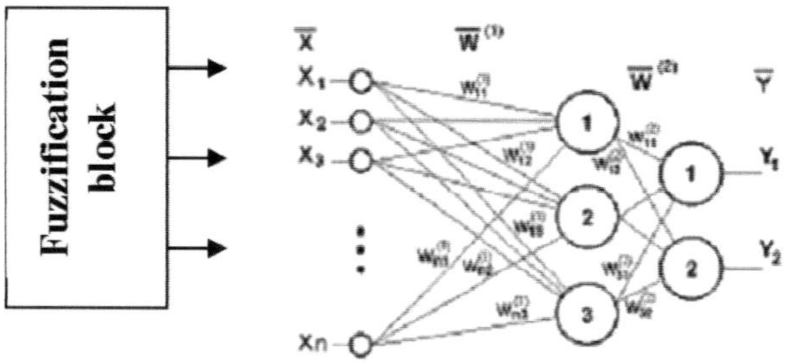

Fig. 2. The structure of MANN in ANFIS.

We set two boundary conditions for the acceptance decision:

1) $\bar{y}_k \geq \Delta_2$,

2) $\bar{y}_k - \tilde{y}_p \geq \Delta_3$,

where y is the output vector of MANN, $\bar{y}_k$ and $\tilde{y}_p$ are two successive maximum elements of the vector y, i.e.

$$\bar{y}_k = \max_{1 \leq i \leq N} y_i, \quad k = \arg \max_{1 \leq i \leq N} y_i,$$

$$\tilde{y}_p = \max_{1 \leq i \leq k-1; k+1 \leq i \leq N} y_i.$$

There is shown results of subjectivity detection in movie reviews by ANFIS with different values of Δ_2 and Δ_3 in Table 3.

	Correct (%)	Rejection (%)	Error (%)
$\Delta_2 = 0.8; \Delta_3 = 0.5$	78.66	18.84	2.5
$\Delta_2 = 0.5; \Delta_3 = 0.5$	85.77	8.62	5.61
No restriction	91.66	0.01	8.33

Table 3. Average results of 10 folds cross validation accuracy ANFIS based on $TF \cdot ICF$ for subjectivity detection in movie reviews.

The accuracy of the ANFIS (91.66%) is higher than that of FCS (91.3%) at the cost of additional variables being required in the middle layer of the neural network.

6 Conclusion

We have described two different classification system structures, FCS, ANFIS, and applied them to sentence-level subjectivity detection in a movie review data base. We have specifically shown how to train and test these methods for classification of sentences as being either objective or subjective. A goal of the research was to formulate methods that did not depend on linguistic knowledge and therefore would be applicable to any language. An important component of these methods is the feature extraction process. We focused on analysis of informative features that improve the accuracy of the systems with no language-specific constraints. As a result, a novel "Pruned ICF Weighting Function" was devised with a parameter specifically estimated for the subjectivity data set.

When comparing the current system with others, it is necessary to emphasize that the use of linguistic knowledge does improve accuracy. Since we do not use such knowledge, our results should only be compared with other methods having similar constraints, such as those which use features based on bags of words that are tested on the same data set. Examples include studies by Pang and Lee (2004) and Martineau and Finin (2009). Pang and Lee report 92% accuracy on sentence-level subjectivity classification using Naıve Bayes classifiers and 90% accuracy using SVMs on the same data set. Martineau and Finin (2009) reported 91.26% accuracy using SVM Difference of TFIDFs. The currently reported results: FCS (91.3%), ANFIS (91.7%) are similar. However, our presented methods have some advantages. Because the function (5) is minimized only with respect to $y = (y_1, y_2, \ldots, y_N)$ (in the defined problem N=2), FCS is the fastest algorithm among supervised machine learning methods. At the cost of additional variables added within the middle layer of the neural network, ANFIS is able to improve accuracy a small amount. It is anticipated that when IF-THEN rules and expert knowledge are inserted into ANFIS and FCS, accuracy will improve to a level commensurate with human judgment.

References

Aditya Mogadala. Vasudeva Varma. 2012. Language Independent Sentence-Level Subjectivity Analysis with Feature Selection. *Proceedings of the 26th Pacific Asia Conference on Language,Information and Computation,* pages 171–180.

Alina Andreevskaia and Sabine Bergler. 2006. Mining wordnet for fuzzy sentiment: Sentiment tag extraction from WordNet glosses. *In Proceedings of EACL 2006.*

Bing Liu. Sentiment Analysis and Opinion Mining. 2012. *Synthesis Lectures on Human Language Technologies.*

Bo Pang and Lillian Lee. 2004. A sentimental education: Sentiment analysis using subjectivity summarization based on minimum cuts. *In Proceedings of the 42nd Annual Meeting on Association for Computational Linguistics (ACL),* pp. 271-278.

Bo Pang and Lillian Lee. 2008. Opinion Mining and Sentiment Analysis. *Now Publishers Inc.*

Carmen Banea, Rada Mihalcea, and Janyce Wiebe. 2010. Multilingual subjectivity: are more languages better. *Proceedings of the 23rd International Conference on Computational Linguistics (Coling 2010),* pp. 28–36.

Carmen Banea, Rada Mihalcea, Janyce Wiebe and Samer Hassan. 2008. Multilingual subjectivity analysis using machine translation. *Proceedings of the Conference on Empirical Methods in Natural Language Processing,* pp. 127–135.

Chenghua Lin, Yulan He and Richard Everson. 2011. Sentence Subjectivity Detection with Weakly-Supervised Learning. *Proceedings of the 5th International Joint Conference on Natural Language Processing,* pp. 1153–1161.

Ellen Riloff and Janyce Wiebe. 2003. Learning Extraction Patterns for Subjective Expressions. *In: Proceedings of the Conference on Empirical Methods in Natural Language Processing*, pp. 105–112.

Ellen Riloff, Siddharth Patwardhan, and Janyce Wiebe. Feature subsumption for opinion analysis. 2006. *In Proceedings of the Conference on Empirical Methods in Natural Language Processing (EMNLP-2006).*

Farah Benamara, Baptiste Chardon, Yannick Mathieu, and Vladimir Popescu. 2011. Towards Context-Based Subjectivity Analysis. *In Proceedings of the 5th International Joint Conference on Natural Language Processing (IJCNLP-2011).*

Gabriel Murray and Giuseppe Carenini. 2009. Predicting subjectivity in multimodal conversations. *In Proceedings of the Conference on Empirical Methods in Natural Language Processing (EMNLP),* pages 1348–1357.

Gregory Grefenstette, Yan Qu, David A. Evans, and James G. Shanahan. 2006. Validating the Coverage of Lexical Resources for Affect Analysis and Automatically Classifying New Words along Semantic Axes. *In: Proceedings of AAAI Spring Symposium on Exploring Attitude and Affect in Text: Theories and Applications*, pp. 93–107.

Hiroshi Kanayama and Tetsuya Nasukawa. 2006. Fully automatic lexicon expansion for domain-oriented sentiment analysis. Proceedings of the 2006 Conference on Empirical Methods in Natural Language Processing, pages 355–363.

Janyce Wiebe and Ellen Riloff. 2005. Creating subjective and objective sentence classifiers from unannotated texts. *Computational Linguistics and Intelligent Text Processing, Springer*, pp. 486–497.

Justin Martineau, and Tim Finin. 2009. Delta TFIDF: An Improved Feature Space for Sentiment Analysis. *In Proceedings of the 3rd AAAI International Conference on Weblogs and Social Media.*

Kamil Aida-zade, Samir Rustamov, Elshan Mustafayev, and Nigar Aliyeva, 2012. Human-Computer Dialogue Understanding Hybrid System. *IEEE Xplore, International Symposium on Innovations in Intelligent Systems and Applications. Trabzon, Turkey,* pp. 1-5.

Luciano Barbosa and Junlan Feng. 2010. Robust sentiment detection on twitter from biased and noisy data. *In Proceedings of the International Conference on Computational Linguistics (CO LING-2010).*

Muhammad Abdul-Mageed, Mona T. Diab, and Mohammed Korayem. 2011. Subjectivity and sentiment analysis of modern standard Arabic, *In Proceedings of the 49th Annual Meeting of the Association for Computational Linguistics: short papers,* pages 587–591.

Rada Mihalcea, Carmen Banea and Janyce Wiebe. 2007. Learning multilingual subjective language via cross-lingual projections. *Proceedings of the 45th Annual Meeting of the Association of Computational Linguistics,* pages 976–983.

Robert Fuller. Neural Fuzzy Systems, 1995.

Robert Remus. 2011. Improving Sentence-level Subjectivity Classification through Readability Measurement. *NODALIDA-2011 Conference Proceedings*, pp. 168–174.

Samir Rustamov, Elshan Mustafayev, Mark Clements. 2013. Sentiment Analysis using Neuro-Fuzzy and Hidden Markov Models of Text. IEEE Southeastcon 2013, Jacksonvilla, Florida,USA.

Smruthi Mukund and Rohini K. Srihari. 2010. A vector space model for subjectivity classification in Urdu aided by co-training. In *Proceedings of Coling 2010:* Poster Volume, pages 860–868.

Soo-Min Kim and Eduard Hovy. 2005. Automatic Detection of Opinion Bearing Words and Sentences. *In: Companion Volume to the Proceedings of the International Joint Conference on Natural Language Processing*, pp. 61–66.

Stephan Raaijmakers, Khiet Truong, and Theresa Wilson. 2008. Multimodal subjectivity analysis of multiparty conversation. *In Proceedings of the Conference on Empirical Methods in Natural Language Processing (EMNLP)*, pages 466–474.

Taras Zagibalov and John Carroll. 2008. Unsupervised classification of sentiment and objectivity in Chinese text. *In Proceedings of International Joint Conference on Natural Language Processing (IJCNLP-2008)*, pp. 304–311.

Theresa Wilson, Janyce Wiebe, Rebecca Hwa. 2004. Just How Mad Are You? Finding Strong and Weak Opinion Clauses. *In: Proceedings of the National Conference on Artificial Intelligence*, pp. 761–769.

Yulan He. 2010. Bayesian Models for Sentence-Level Subjectivity Detection. *Technical Report KMI-10-02, June 2010.*

Ziqiong Zhang, Qiang Ye, Rob Law, and Yijun Li. 2009. Automatic Detection of Subjective Sentences Based on Chinese Subjective Patterns. Proceedings of 20th International Conference, MCDM-2009, pp. 29-36.

Sentiment Classification using Rough Set based Hybrid Feature Selection

Basant Agarwal
Department of Computer Engineering
Malaviya National Institute Technology
Jaipur, India
thebasant@gmail.com

Namita Mittal
Department of Computer Engineering
Malaviya National Institute Technology
Jaipur, India
nmittal@mnit.ac.in

Abstract

Sentiment analysis means to extract opinion of users from review documents. Sentiment classification using Machine Learning (ML) methods faces the problem of high dimensionality of feature vector. Therefore, a feature selection method is required to eliminate the irrelevant and noisy features from the feature vector for efficient working of ML algorithms. Rough Set Theory based feature selection method finds the optimal feature subset by eliminating the redundant features. In this paper, Rough Set Theory (RST) based feature selection method is applied for sentiment classification. A Hybrid feature selection method based on RST and Information Gain (IG) is proposed for sentiment classification. Proposed methods are evaluated on four standard datasets viz. Movie review, product (book, DVD and electronics) review dataset. Experimental results show that Hybrid feature selection method outperforms than other feature selection methods for sentiment classification.

1 Introduction

Sentiment analysis is to extract the users' opinion by analysing the text documents (Pang et al. 2008). Nowadays people are using web for writing their opinion on blogs, social networking websites, discussion forums etc. Hence, it is very much needed to analyse these web contents. Thus, it increases the demand of sentiment analysis research. Sentiment analysis has been very important for the users as well as for business with the drastic increase of online content. For users, it is important to know past experiences about some product or services for taking decision in purchasing products. Companies can use sentiment analysis in improving their products based on the users' feedback written about their products on blogs. E-commerce based companies know the online trends about the products. Example of sentiment analysis is - knowing which model of a camera is liked by most of the users.

Sentiment classification can be considered as a text classification problem. Bag-of-Words (BOW) representation is commonly used for sentiment classification using machine learning approaches. The words present in all the documents create the feature vector. Generally, this feature vector is huge in dimension that is used by machine learning methods for classification. This high dimensional feature vector deteriorates the performance of machine learning algorithm. Rough set theory has been used for reducing the feature vector size for text classification (Jensen et al. 2001; Jensen et al. 2009; Wakaki et al. 2004). However, it has not been investigated for sentiment analysis yet.

Contribution of this paper:-

1. Rough Set theory based feature selection method is applied for sentiment classification.
2. Hybrid Feature selection method is proposed based on Rough Set and Information Gain which performs better than other feature selection methods.
3. Proposed methods are experimented with four different standard datasets.

The paper is organized as follows: A brief discussion of the earlier research work is given in Section 2. Section 3 describes the feature selections method used for sentiment classification. Dataset, Experimental setup and results are discussed in Section 4. Finally, Section 5 describes conclusions.

2 Related Work

Machine Learning methods have been widely applied for sentiment analysis (Pang et al. 2008; Pang et al. 2002; Tan et al. 2008). Pang and Lee (2004) experimented with various features like unigrams, bi-grams and adjectives for sentiment classification of movie reviews using different machine learning algorithms namely Naïve Bayes (NB), Support Vector Machines (SVM), and Maximum-Entropy (ME). Feature selection methods improve the performance of sentiment classification by eliminating the noisy and irrelevant features from feature vector. Tan et al. (2008) investigated with various feature selection methods with different machine learning algorithm for sentiment classification. Their experimental results show that IG performs better as compared to other feature selection methods and SVM is best machine learning algorithms. Categorical Probability Proportion Difference (CPPD) feature selection method is proposed which computes the importance of a feature based on its class discriminating ability for sentiment classification (Agarwal et al. 2012). Various features are extracted from the text for sentiment classification. Further, Minimum Redundancy Maximum Relevancy (mRMR) and IG feature selection methods are used to select prominent features for better sentiment classification by machine learning algorithms (Agarwal et al. 2013).
Rough set based dimensionality reduction method is applied for data reduction to characterize bookmarks and it is compared with conventional entropy based reduction method (Jensen et al. 2009). Dimension reduction method based on fuzzy-rough sets and Ant Colony Optimization (ACO) method is proposed (Jensen et al. 2006), which is applied to the web categorisation problem. Experimental result show significant reduction in the data redundancy. Rough set theory is applied to select relevant features for web-page classification. Their experimental results show that the rough set based feature selection method with SVM gives better accuracy (Wakaki et al. 2004). Applicability of RS theory for various existing text classification techniques are discussed in detail with e-mail categorization as an example application (Chouchoulas et al. 2001).

3 Methodology Used

3.1 Rough Set Attribute Reduction (RSAR)

Rough Sets Theory (RST) (Jensen et al. 2007) is a mathematical tool to make attribute reduction by eliminating redundant condition attributes (features). The rough set is the approximation of a vague concept (set) by a pair of precise concepts, called lower and upper approximations. Rough Set Attribute Reduction (RSAR) (Jensen et al. 2007) is a filter based method by which redundant features are eliminated by keeping the amount of knowledge intact in the System. Basic intuition behind RSAR is that objects belonging to the same category (same attributes) are not distinguishable (Jensen et al. 2009).
RSAR algorithm finds the vague attributes which do not have important role in the classification. Therefore, it is needed to remove redundant features without changing the knowledge embedded in the information system. An important issue in data analysis is to discover dependencies between the attributes. QUICKREDUCT method (Jensen et al. 2007; Jensen et al. 2009) calculate a minimal reduct without exhaustively generating all possible subsets, it is used in our experiments for obtaining optimal feature subset. Main advantage of RSAR is that it does not require any additional parameter to operate like threshold is required in case of IG.

3.2 Information Gain (IG)

Information gain (IG) is one of the important feature selection techniques for sentiment classification. IG is used to select important features with respect to class attribute. It is measured by the reduction in the uncertainty in identifying the class attribute when the value of the feature is known. The top ranked (important) features are selected for reducing the feature vector size in turn better classification results.

3.3. Proposed Hybrid Approach to Feature Selection

The usefulness of an attribute is determined by both its relevancy and redundancy. An attribute is relevant if it is predictive to the class attribute, otherwise it is irrelevant. An attribute is considered to be redundant if it is correlated with other attributes. Hence, The Aim is to find the attributes that are highly correlated with the class attribute, but not with other attributes for a good attribute subset (Jensen et al. 2007).

Information Gain based feature selection methods determine the importance of a feature in the documents. But, it has disadvantage that threshold value is required initially which is not known generally. This method does not consider the redundancy among the attributes. In addition, it will return large number of features when massive amount of documents are to be considered. RSAR can reduce most of the irrelevant and noisy features. It reduces the redundancy among the features. It has advantage that it considers the dependency of combination of features on decision attribute in contrast to other conventional feature selection methods (Jensen et al. 2007). However, it has some disadvantages. Firstly, to get an optimal reduct is a NP-hard problem, some heuristic algorithms are used to get approximate reduction (Jensen et al. 2004; Jensen et al. 2009). Secondly, it is very time consuming. Therefore, an integrated method is developed which can reduce most of the redundant features and get the minimal feature set with reduced time complexity for sentiment classification.

Proposed Algorithm works in two steps. Firstly, Information Gain (IG) of each feature is computed and all the features are taken which has information gain value to be greater than 0. So that initially irrelevant and noisy features are removed from the feature vector, by this a lot computational efforts are reduced. Main assumption and motivation behind this step is that IG would eliminate the features which are likely to be noisy and irrelevant features. Further, Reduced feature set is sent to the RSAR feature selection method to get optimal feature subset. So, by combining both the methods a feature selection is proposed which is more efficient in terms of computational and time complexity.

4 Dataset Used and Experimental Setup

For the evaluation of the proposed method, one of the most popular publically available movie review dataset (Pang et al. 2004) is used. This standard dataset contains 2000 reviews comprising 1000 positive and 1000 negative reviews. Product review dataset consisting amazon products reviews is also used provided by Blitzer et al. (2007). We used product reviews of books, DVD and electronics for experiments. Each domain has 1000 positive and 1000 negative labelled reviews. Documents are initially pre-processed as follows:

(i) Negation handling is performed as Pang et al. (2002), "NOT_" is added to every words occurring after the negation word (no, not, isn't, can't, never, couldn't, didn't, wouldn't, don't) and first punctuation mark in the sentence.

(ii) Words occurring in less than 3 documents are removed from the feature set.

Binary weighting scheme has been identified as a better weighting scheme as compared to frequency based schemes for sentiment classification (Pang et al. 2002); therefore we also used binary weighting method for representing text. In addition, there is no need of using separate discretisation method in case of binary weighting scheme as required by RSAR feature selection algorithm. Noisy and irrelevant features are eliminated from the feature vector generated after pre-processing using various feature selection methods discussed before. Further, prominent feature vector is used by machine learning algorithms. Support Vector Machine (SVM) and Naïve Bayes (NB) classifiers are the mostly used for sentiment classification (Pang et al. 2002; Tan et al. 2008). Therefore, we report the classification results of SVM and NB classifier for classifying review documents into positive or negative sentiment polarity. For the evaluation of proposed methods 10 fold cross validation method is used. F-measure value is reported as a performance measure of various classifiers (Agarwal et al. 2013)

4.1 Experimental results and discussions

Initially, unigram features are extracted from the review documents. Feature set without using any feature selection method is taken as a baseline. Further, various feature selection algorithms are used for selecting optimal feature subset. IG is used for comparison with the proposed feature selection method as it has been considered as one of the best feature selection method for sentiment classification (Pang et al. 2008; Tan et al. 2008). Feature subsets obtained after applying RSAR, IG and proposed hybrid feature selection algorithm are called Rough features, IG features and Hybrid IG-Rough features respectively. Feature vector lengths for various features used for sentiment classification of different datasets are shown in Table 1. In the experiments, Firstly, RSAR algorithm is applied to get the best optimal feature subset. Further, according to the feature subset size obtained from RSAR method, threshold is set for IG based to get the feature vector, which is further used for classification. Experiments are conducted in this way so that results of Rough features and IG features can be compared.

	Movie	Book	DVD	Electronics
Unigram Features	9045	5391	5955	4270
Rough Features	263	310	350	371
IG Features	263	310	350	371
Hybrid IG-Rough Features	339	410	403	405

Table 1. Feature Length for Various Features Used With Four Datasets

Experimental results show that both feature selection methods (RSAR and IG) are able to improve the performance from baseline (as shown in Table 2). For example from Table 2, F-measure is increased from 84.2% to 85.9% (+2.1) and 85.6% (+1.6) for Rough features and IG features respectively with SVM classifier when movie review dataset is considered. Similarly, when electronics dataset is used, SVM classifier increased the performance from 76.5% to 82.9% (+8.3) and 81.1% (+6.01) for Rough and IG features. It is due to the fact that RSAR algorithm removes the redundancy and selects the prominent feature subset, and IG selects the top ranked features by its importance to the class attribute.

When hybrid features selection approach is used for movie review dataset, F- measure is increased from 84.2% to 87.7 (+4.15) for SVM classifier as given in Table 1. Hybrid IG-Rough features gives better classification results as compare to other features with very small feature vector length. It is due to the fact that IG in its first phase eliminates the irrelevant and noisy features and in second phase RSAR algorithm decreases the redundancy among features and extracts the optimal feature subset. By combining both the methods, a more robust feature selection method is developed for sentiment classification which is more efficient in selecting optimal feature set for massive dataset. Because when dataset size would be very large, RSAR algorithm will take much time and IG algorithm would be having problem of large feature size and pre-setting the threshold value.

		Unigram Features	rough Features	IG Features	Hybrid IG-Rough Features
Movie	SVM	84.2	85.9 (+2.1)	85.6 (+1.6)	87.7 (+4.15)
	NB	77.1	78.7 (+2.1)	78.6 (+2.0)	80.9 (+4.9)
Book	SVM	76.2	78.0 (+2.3)	77.0 (+1.0)	80.2 (+5.2)
	NB	74.4	74.9 (+0.1)	76.3 (+2.5)	79.1 (+6.3)
DVD	SVM	77.3	80.4 (+4.0)	79.1 (+2.3)	83.2 (+7.6)
	NB	74.2	76.5 (+3.1)	75.1 (+1.2)	78.1 (+5.2)
Electronics	SVM	76.5	82.9 (+8.3)	81.1 (+6.0)	83.5 (+9.1)
	NB	74.9	75.5 (+0.1)	75.2 (+.04)	78.1 (+4.2)

Table 2 F-measure (in %) for various features with four datasets

5 Conclusion

Rough set based dimension reduction method is applied for sentiment analysis. It is capable of reducing the redundancy among the attributes. Rough set based methods computes the best feature subset based on minimized redundancy in contrast to information gain which computes the importance of the attribute based on the entropy. Hybrid feature selection method is proposed which is based on RSAR and IG. Experimental results show that Hybrid feature selection method with very less number of features produces better results as compared to other feature selection methods. All the methods are experimented using four standard datasets. In future, more methods can be explored for making rough set based feature selection method computationally more efficient by incorporating evolutionary approaches in selecting feature subsets.

References

Alexios Chouchoulas, Qiang Shen, "Rough set-aided key- word reduction for text categorization", *Applied Artificial Intelligence,* Vol. 15, No. 9, pp. 843-873. 2001.

Basant Agarwal, Namita Mittal, "Categorical Probability Proportion Difference (CPPD): A Feature Selection Method for Sentiment Classification", *In Proceedings of the 2nd Workshop on Sentiment Analysis where AI meets Psychology (SAAIP), COLING 2012*, pp 17–26, 2012.

Basant Agarwal, Namita Mittal, "Optimal Feature Selection Methods for Sentiment Analysis", *In 14th International Conference on Intelligent Text Processing and Computational Linguistics (CICLing 2013),* Vol-7817,pp:13-24, 2013.

Bo Pang, Lillian Lee. "Opinion mining and sentiment analysis*", Foundations and Trends in Information Retrieval*, Vol. 2(1-2):pp. 1–135, 2008.

Bo Pang, Lillian Lee, Shivakumar Vaithyanathan, "Thumbs up? Sentiment classification using machine learning techniques", *In the Proceedings of the Conference on Empirical Methods in Natural Language Processing (EMNLP)*, pp. 79–86. 2002.

Bo Pang, Lillian Lee, "A sentimental education: sentiment analysis using subjectivity summarization based on minimum cuts", *In the Proceedings of the Association for Computational Linguistics (ACL)*, 2004, pp. 271–278. 2004.

John Blitzer, Mark Dredze, Fernando Pereira, "Biographies, Bollywood, Boom-boxes and Blenders: Domain Adaptation for Sentiment Classification", *In Proc. Assoc. Computational Linguistics. ACL Press*, pp 440-447, 2007.

Richard Jensen, Qiang Shen, "Fuzzy-Rough Sets Assisted Attribute Selection*", In IEEE Transactions on Fuzzy Systems*, Vol. 15, No. 1, February 2007.

Richard Jensen, Qiang Shen, "A Rough Set-Aided System for Sorting WWW Bookmarks". *In N. Zhong et al. (Eds.), Web Intelligence: Research and Development.* pp. 95-105, 2001.

Richard Jensen, Qiang Shen, "New Approaches to Fuzzy-Rough Feature Selection", *In the IEEE Transactions on Fuzzy Systems,* vol. 17, no. 4, pp. 824-838, 2009.

Richard Jensen, Qiang Shen, "Webpage Classification with ACO-enhanced Fuzzy-Rough Feature Selection", *In the Proceedings of the Fifth International Conference on Rough Sets and Current Trends in Computing (RSCTC 2006), LNAI* 4259, pp. 147-156. 2006

Richard Jensen, Qiang Shen "Fuzzy-Rough Attribute Reduction with Application to Web Categorization". *In the Transaction on Fuzzy Sets and Systems 141(3),* pp. 469-485. 2004.

Songbo Tan , Jin Zhang "An empirical study of sentiment analysis for chinese documents*", In Expert Systems with Applications* , pp:2622–2629 (2008).

Toshiko Wakaki, Hiroyuki Itakura, Masaki Tamura, "Rough Set-Aided Feature Selection for Automatic Web-Page Classification". *In Proceedings of the IEEE/WIC/ACM International Conference on Web Intelligence*, Pages 70-76, 2004

Sentiment Analysis in Social Media Texts

Alexandra Balahur
European Commission Joint Research Centre
Vie E. Fermi 2749
21027 Ispra (VA), Italy
alexandra.balahur@jrc.ec.europa.eu

Abstract

This paper presents a method for sentiment analysis specifically designed to work with Twitter data (tweets), taking into account their structure, length and specific language. The approach employed makes it easily extendible to other languages and makes it able to process tweets in near real time. The main contributions of this work are: a) the pre-processing of tweets to normalize the language and generalize the vocabulary employed to express sentiment; b) the use minimal linguistic processing, which makes the approach easily portable to other languages; c) the inclusion of higher order n-grams to spot modifications in the polarity of the sentiment expressed; d) the use of simple heuristics to select features to be employed; e) the application of supervised learning using a simple Support Vector Machines linear classifier on a set of realistic data. We show that using the training models generated with the method described we can improve the sentiment classification performance, irrespective of the domain and distribution of the test sets.

1 Introduction

Sentiment analysis is the Natural Language Processing (NLP) task dealing with the detection and classification of sentiments in texts. Usually, the classes considered are "positive", "negative" and "neutral", although in some cases finer-grained categories are added (e.g. "very positive" and "very negative") or only the "positive" and "negative" classes are taken into account. Another related task - emotion detection - concerns the classification of text into several classes of emotion, usually the basic ones, as described by Paul Ekman (Ekman, 1992). Although different in some ways, some of the research in the field has considered these tasks together, under the umbrella of sentiment analysis.

This task has received a lot of interest from the research community in the past years. The work done regarded the manner in which sentiment can be classified from texts pertaining to different genres and distinct languages, in the context of various applications, using knowledge-based, semi-supervised and supervised methods (Pang and Lee, 2008). The result of the analyses performed have shown that the different types of text require specialized methods for sentiment analysis, as, for example, sentiments are not conveyed in the same manner in newspaper articles and in blogs, reviews, forums or other types of user-generated contents (Balahur et al., 2010).

In the light of these findings, dealing with sentiment analysis in Twitter requires an analysis of the characteristics of such texts and the design of adapted methods.

Additionally, the sentiment analysis method employed has to consider the requirements of the final application in which it will be used. There is an important difference between deploying a system working for languages such as English, for which numerous linguistic resources and analysis tools exist and a system deployed for languages with few such tools or one that is aimed at processing data from a large set of languages. Finally, a sentiment analysis system working with large sets of data (such as the one found in Twitter) must be able to process texts fast. Therefore, using highly complex methods may delay producing useful results.

In the light of these considerations, this paper

presents a method for sentiment analysis that takes into account the special structure and linguistic content of tweets. The texts are pre-processed in order to normalize the language employed and remove noisy elements. Special usage of language (e.g. repeated punctuation signs, repeated letters) are marked as special features, as they contribute to the expressivity of the text in terms of sentiment. Further on, sentiment-bearing words, as they are found in three highly-accurate sentiment lexicons - General Inquirer (GI) (Stone et al., 1966), Linguistic Inquiry and Word Count (LIWC) (Tausczik and Pennebaker, 2010) and MicroWNOp (Cerini et al., 2007) - are replaced with unique labels, correspoding to their polarity. In the same manner, modifiers (negations, intensifiers and diminishers) are also replaced with unique labels representing their semantic class. Finally, we employ supervised learning with Support Vector Machines Sequential Minimal Optimization (SVM SMO) (Platt, 1998) using a simple, linear kernel (to avoid overfitting of data) and the unigrams and bigrams from the training set as features. We obtain the best results by using unique labels for the affective words and the modifiers, unigrams and bigrams as features and posing the condition that each feature considered in the supervised learning process be present in the training corpora at least twice.

The remainder of this article is structured as follows: Section 2 gives an overview of the related work. In Section 3, we present the motivations and describe the contributions of this work. In the following section, we describe in detail the process followed to pre-process the tweets and build the classification models. In Section 5, we present the results obtained using different datasets and combinations of features and discuss their causes and implications. Finally, Section 6 summarizes the main findings of this work and sketches the lines for future work.

2 Related Work

One of the first studies on the classification of polarity in tweets was (Go et al., 2009). The authors conducted a supervised classification study on tweets in English, using the emoticons (e.g. ":)", ":(", etc.) as markers of positive and negative tweets. (Read, 2005) employed this method to generate a corpus of positive tweets, with positive emoticons ":)", and negative tweets with negative emoticons ":(". Subsequently, they employ different supervised approaches (SVM, Naïve Bayes and Maximum Entropy) and various sets of features and conclude that the simple use of unigrams leads to good results, but it can be slightly improved by the combination of unigrams and bigrams.

In the same line of thinking, (Pak and Paroubek, 2010) also generated a corpus of tweets for sentiment analysis, by selecting positive and negative tweets based on the presence of specific emoticons. Subsequently, they compare different supervised approaches with n-gram features and obtain the best results using Naïve Bayes with unigrams and part-of-speech tags.

Another approach on sentiment analysis in tweet is that of (Zhang et al., 2011). Here, the authors employ a hybrid approach, combining supervised learning with the knowledge on sentiment-bearing words, which they extract from the DAL sentiment dictionary (Whissell, 1989). Their pre-processing stage includes the removal of retweets, translation of abbreviations into original terms and deleting of links, a tokenization process, and part-of-speech tagging. They employ various supervised learning algorithms to classify tweets into positive and negative, using n-gram features with SVM and syntactic features with Partial Tree Kernels, combined with the knowledge on the polarity of the words appearing in the tweets. The authors conclude that the most important features are those corresponding to sentiment-bearing words. Finally, (Jiang et al., 2011) classify sentiment expressed on previously-given "targets" in tweets. They add information on the context of the tweet to its text (e.g. the event that it is related to). Subsequently, they employ SVM and General Inquirer and perform a three-way classification (positive, negative, neutral).

3 Motivation and Contribution

As we have seen in the previous section, several important steps have already been taken into analyzing the manner in which sentiment can be automatically detected and classified from Twitter data. The research we described in previous section has already dealt with some of the issues that are posed by short, informal texts, such as the tweets. However, these small snippets of text have several liguistic peculiarities that can be employed to improve the sentiment classification performance. We describe these peculiarities below:

- Tweets are short, user-generated text that may contain no more than 140 characters (strongly related to the standard 160-character length of SMS [1]). Users are marked with the "@" sign and topics with the "#" (hashtag) sign.
- In general, the need to include a large quantity of information in small limit of characters leads to the fact that tweets sometimes have no grammatical structure, contain misspellings and abbreviations.
- Some of the tweets are simply posted from the websites of news providers (news agencies, newspapers) and therefore they contain only titles of news. However, subjective tweets, in which users comment on an event, are highly marked by sentiment-bearing expressions, either in the form of affective words, or by employins specific modalities - e.g. the use of capital letters or repeated punctuation signs to stress upon specific words. Most of the times, these words are sentiment-bearing ones.
- The language employed in subjective tweets includes a specific slang (also called "urban expressions" [2]) and emoticons (graphical expressions of emotions through the use of punctuation signs).
- Most of the times, the topic that is discusses in the tweets is clearly marked using hashtags. Thus, there is no need to employ very complex linguistic tools to determine it.
- In major events, the rate of tweets per minute commenting or retweeting information surpasses the rate of thousands per minute.
- Twitter is available in more than 30 languages. However, users tweet in more than 80 languages. The information it contains can be useful to obtain information and updates about, for example, crisis events [3], in real time. In order to benefit from this, however, a system processing these texts has to be easily adaptable to other languages and it has to work in near real time.

Bearing this in mind, the main contributions we bring in this paper are:

1. The pre-processing of tweets to normalize the language and generalize the vocabulary employed to express sentiment. At this stage, we take into account the linguistic peculiarities of tweets, regarding spelling, use of slang, punctuation, etc., and also replace the sentiment-bearing words from the training data with a unique label. In this way, the sentence "I love roses." will be equivalent to the sentence "I like roses.", because "like" and "love" are both positive words according to the GI dictionary. If example 1 is contained in the training data and example 2 is contained in the test data, replacing the sentiment-bearing word with a general label increases the chance to have example 2 classified correctly. In the same line of thought, we also replaced modifiers with unique corresponding labels.
2. The use of minimal linguistic processing, which makes the approach easily portable to other languages. We employ only tokenization and do not process texts any further. The reason behind this choice is that we would like the final system to work in a similar fashion for as many languages as possible and for some of them, little or no tools are available.
3. The inclusion of bigrams to spot modifications in the polarity of the sentiment expressed. As such, we can learn general patterns of sentiment expression (e.g. "negation positive", "intensifier negative", etc.).
4. The use of simple heuristics to select features to be employed. Although feature selection algorithms are easy to apply when employing a data mining environment, the final choice is influenced by the data at hand and it is difficult to

[1] http://en.wikipedia.org/wiki/Twitter

[2] http://www.urbandictionary.com/

[3] http://blog.twitter.com/2012/10/hurricane-sandy-resources-on-twitter.html

employ on new sets of data. After performing various tests, we chose to select the features to be employed in the classification model based on the condition that they should occur at least once in the training set.

5. The application of supervised learning using a simple Support Vector Machines linear classifier on a set of realistic data.

We show that using the training models generated with the method described we can improve the sentiment classification performance, irrespective of the domain and distribution of the test sets.

4 Sentiment Analysis in Tweets

Our sentiment analysis system is based on a hybrid approach, which employs supervised learning with a Support Vector Machines Sequential Minimal Optimization (Platt, 1998) linear kernel, on unigram and bigram features, but exploiting as features sentiment dictionaries, emoticon lists, slang lists and other social media-specific features. We do not employ any specific language analysis software. The aim is to be able to apply, in a straightforward manner, the same approach to as many languages as possible. The approach can be extended to other languages by using similar dictionaries that have been created in our team. They were built using the same dictionaries we employ in this work and their corrected translation to Spanish. The new sentiment dictionaries were created by simultaneously translating from these two languages to a third one and considering the intersection of the trainslations as correct terms. Currently, new such dictionaries have been created for 15 other languages.

The sentiment analysis process contains two stages: pre-processing and sentiment classification.

4.1 Tweet Pre-processing

The language employed in Social Media sites is different from the one found in mainstream media and the form of the words employed is sometimes not the one we may find in a dictionary. Further on, users of Social Media platforms employ a special "slang" (i.e. informal language, with special expressions, such as "lol", "omg"), emoticons, and often emphasize words by repeating some of their letters. Additionally, the language employed in Twitter has specific characteristics, such as the markup of tweets that were reposted by other users with "RT", the markup of topics using the "#" (hash sign) and of the users using the "@" sign.

All these aspects must be considered at the time of processing tweets. As such, before applying supervised learning to classify the sentiment of the tweets, we preprocess them, to normalize the language they contain. The pre-processing stage contains the following steps:

- Repeated punctuation sign normalization

  In the first step of the pre-processing, we detect repetitions of punctuation signs (".", "!" and "?"). Multiple consecutive punctuation signs are replaced with the labels "multistop", for the fullstops, "multiexclamation" in the case of exclamation sign and "multiquestion" for the question mark and spaces before and after.

- Emoticon replacement

  In the second step of the pre-processing, we employ the annotated list of emoticons from SentiStrength[4] and match the content of the tweets against this list. The emoticons found are replaced with their polarity ("positive" or "negative") and the "neutral" ones are deleted.

- Lower casing and tokenization.

  Subsequently, the tweets are lower cased and split into tokens, based on spaces and punctuation signs.

- Slang replacement

  The next step involves the normalization of the language employed. In order to be able to include the semantics of the expressions frequently used in Social Media, we employed the list of slang from a specialized site [5].

- Word normalization

  At this stage, the tokens are compared to entries in Rogets Thesaurus. If no match is found, repeated letters are sequentially reduced to two or one until a match is found in the dictionary (e.g.

[4] http://sentistrength.wlv.ac.uk/

[5] http://www.chatslang.com/terms/social_media

"perrrrrrrrrrrrrrrrrrfeeect" becomes "perrfeect", "perfeect", "perrfect" and subsequently "perfect"). The words used in this form are maked as "stressed".

- Affect word matching

  Further on, the tokens in the tweet are matched against three different sentiment lexicons: GI, LIWC and MicroWNOp, which were previously split into four different categories ("positive", "high positive", "negative" and "high negative"). Matched words are replaced with their sentiment label - i.e. "positive", "negative", "hpositive" and "hnegative". A version of the data without these replacements is also maintained, for comparison purposes.

- Modifier word matching

  Similar to the previous step, we employ a list of expressions that negate, intensify or diminish the intensity of the sentiment expressed to detect such words in the tweets. If such a word is matched, it is replaced with "negator", "intensifier" or "diminisher", respectively. As in the case of affective words, a version of the data without these replacements is also maintained, for comparison purposes.

- User and topic labeling

  Finally, the users mentioned in the tweet, which are marked with "@", are replaced with "PERSON" and the topics which the tweet refers to (marked with "#") are replaced with "TOPIC".

4.2 Sentiment Classification of Tweets

Once the tweets are pre-processed, they are passed on to the sentiment classification module. We employed supervised learning using SVM SMO with a linear kernel, based on boolean features - the presence or absence of n-grams (unigrams, bigrams and unigrams plus bigrams) determined from the training data (tweets that were previousely pre-processed as described above). Bigrams are used specifically to spot the influence of modifiers (negations, intensifiers, diminishers) on the polarity of the sentiment-bearing words. We tested the approach on different datasets and dataset splits, using the Weka data mining software [6]. The training models are built on a cluster of computers (4 cores, 5000MB of memory each). However, the need for such extensive resources is only present at the training stage. Once the feature set is determined and the models are built using Weka, new examples must only be represented based on the features extracted from the training set and the classification is a matter of miliseconds.

The different evaluations scenarios and results are presented in the following section.

5 Evaluation and Discussion

Although the different steps included to eliminate the noise in the data and the choice of features have been refined using our in-house gathered Twitter data, in order to evaluate our approach and make it comparable to other methods, we employ three different data sets, which are described in detail in the following subsections.

5.1 Data Sets

- SemEval 2013 Data

  The first one is the data provided for training for the upcoming SemEval 2013 Task 2 "Sentiment Analysis from Twitter" [7]. The initial training data has been provided in two stages: 1) sample datasets for the first task and the second task and 2) additional training data for the two tasks. We employ the joint sample datasets as test data (denoted as $t*$) and the data released subsequently as training data (denoted as $T*$). We employ the union of these two datasets to perform cross-validation experiments (the joint dataset is denoted as $T * +t*$. The characteristics of the dataset are described in Table 1. On the last column, we also include the baseline in terms of accuracy, which is computed as the number of examples of the majoritary class over the total number of examples:

- Set of tweets labeled with basic emotions.

  The set of emotion-annotated tweets by (Mohammad, 2012), which we will denote as $TweetEm$. It contains 21051 tweets annotated according to the Ekman categories of ba-

[6]http://www.cs.waikato.ac.nz/ml/weka/

[7]http://www.cs.york.ac.uk/semeval-2013/task2/

sic emotion - anger, disgust, fear, joy, sadness, surprise. We employ this dataset to test the results of our best-performing configurations on the test set. This set contains a total of 21051 tweets (anger - 1555, disgust - 761, fear - 2816, joy - 8240, sadness - 3830, surprise - 3849). As mentioned in the paper by (Mohammad, 2012), a system that would guess the classes, would perfom at aroung 49.9% accuracy.

- Set of short blog sentences labeled with basic emotions.

  The set of blog sentences employed by (Aman and Szpakowicz, 2007), which are annotated according to the same basic emotions identified by Paul Ekman, with the difference that the "joy" category is labeled as "happy". This test set contains also examples which contain no emotions. These sentences were removed. We will denote this dataset as $BlogEm$. This set contains 1290 sentences annotated with emotion (anger - 179, disgust - 172, fear - 115, joy - 536, sadness - 173, surprise - 115). We can consider as baseline the case in which all the examples are assigned to the majority class (joy), which would lead to an accuracy of 41.5%.

Data	#Tweet	#Pos.	#Neg.	#Neu.	Bl%
T*	19241	4779	2343	12119	62
t*	2597	700	393	1504	57
T*+t*	21838	5479	2736	13623	62

Table 1: Characteristics of the training (T*), testing (t*) and joint training and testing datasets.

5.2 Evaluation and Results

In order to test our sentiment analysis approach, we employed the datasets described above. In the case of the SemEval data, we performed an exhaustive evaluation of the possible combination of features to be employed. We tested the entire dataset of tweets (T*+t*) using 10-fold cross-validation. The first set of evaluations concerned the use of the preprocessed tweets in which the affective words and modifiers were have not been replaced. The combination of features tested were: unigrams (U), bigrams (B), unigrams and bigrams together ($U + B$) and unigrams and bigrams together, selecting only the features that appear at least twice in the data ($U + B + FS$). The second set of evaluations aimed at quantifying the difference in performance when the affective words and the modifiers were replaced with generic labels. We tested the best performing approaches from the first set of evaluations ($U + B$ and $U + B + FS$), by replacing the words that were found in the affect dictionaries and the modifiers with their generic labels. These evaluations are denoted as $U + B + D$ and $U + B + D + FS$. The results of these evaluations are shown in Table 2.

Features	10-f-CV T*+t*
U	71.82
B	66.30
$U + B$	82.01
$U + B + D$	81.15
$U + B + FS$	74.00
$U + B + D + FS$	85.07

Table 2: Results in terms of accuracy for 10-fold cross-validation using different combinations of features for the sentiment classification of tweets on the entire set of SemEval 2013 training data.

The same experiments are repeated by employing T* as training data and t* as test data. The aim of these experiments is to test how well the method can perform on new data. The results of these evaluations are shown in Table 3. In order to test if indeed the use of sentiment dictionaries, modifiers and the simple feature selection method improves on the best performing approach that does not employ these additional features, we tested both the approaches on the $TweetEm$ and $BlogEm$ datasets. In this case,

Features	Train(T*) & test(t*)
U	74.90
B	63.27
$U + B$	77.00
$U + B + D$	76.45
$U + B + FS$	75.69
$U + B + D + FS$	79.97

Table 3: Results in terms of accuracy for the different combination of features for the sentiment classification of tweets, using T* as training and t* as test set.

however, the classification is done among 6 different classes of emotions. Although the results are lower(as it can be seen in Table 4, they are comparable to those obtained by (Mohammad, 2012) (when using $U + B$) and show an improvement when using the affect dictionaries and simple feature selection. They also confirm the fact that the best performance on the data is obtained replacing the modifiers and the words found in affect dictionaries with generic labels, using unigrams and bigrams as and eliminating those n-grams that appear only once.

Features	**Tweet Em**	**Blog Em**
$U + B$	49.00	51.08
$U + B + D + FS$	51.08	53.70

Table 4: Results in terms of accuracy for the different combination of features for the emotion classification of tweets and short blog sentences.

The results obtained confirm that the use of unigram and bigram features (appearing at least twice) with generalized affective words and modifiers obtains the best results. Although there is a significant improvement in the accuracy of the classification, the most important difference in the classification performance is given by the fact that using this combination, the classifier is no longer biased by the class with the highest number of examples. We can notice this for the case of tweets, for which the confusion matrices are presented in Table 5 and Table 6. In the table header, the correspondence is: a = joy, b = fear, c = surprise, d = anger, e = disgust, f = sadness. In the first case, the use of unigrams and bigrams leads to the erroneous classification of examples to the majoritary class. When employing the features in which affective words and modifiers have been replaced with generic labels, the results are not only improved, but they classifier is less biased towards the majoritary class. In this case, the incorrect assignments are made to classes that are more similar in vocabulary (e.g. anger - disgust, anger - sadness). In the case of surprise, examples relate both to positive, as well as negative surprises. Therefore, there is a similarity in the vocabulary employed to both these classes.

	a	b	c	d	e	f
a	5879	178	865	246	349	723
b	657	1327	339	67	59	367
c	1243	248	1744	123	129	362
d	549	189	79	419	48	271
e	167	55	45	89	160	245
f	570	405	611	625	233	1386

Table 5: Confusion matrix for the emotion classification of the $TweetEm$ dataset employing the sentiment dictionaries.

	a	b	c	d	e	f
a	6895	252	395	57	20	622
b	1384	861	207	49	11	302
c	1970	147	1258	39	13	421
d	884	133	88	101	18	332
e	433	54	60	32	40	142
f	2097	192	287	72	23	1160

Table 6: Confusion matrix for the emotion classification of the $TweetEm$ dataset without employing the sentiment dictionaries.

5.3 Discussion

From the results obtained, we can conclude that, on the one hand, the best features to be employed in sentiment analysis in tweets are unigrams and bigrams together. Secondly, we can see that the use of generalizations, by employing unique labels to denote sentiment-bearing words and modifiers highly improves the performance of the sentiment classification. The usefulness of pre-processing steps is visible from the fact that among the bigrams that were extracted from the training data we can find the unique labels employed to mark the use of repeated punctuation signs, stressed words, affective words and modifiers and combinations among them. Interesting bigrams that were discovered using these generalizations are, e.g. "negative multiexclamation", "positive multiexclamation", "positive multistop" - which is more often found in negative tweets -,"negator positive", "diminisher positive", "mostly diminisher", "hnegative feeling", "hnegative day", "eat negative","intensifier hnegative". All these extracted features are very useful to detect and classify sentiment in tweets and most of them would be ignored if the vocabulary were different in the training and test data or if, for example, a stressed word would be written under different forms or a punctuation sign would be repeated a different number of times. We can see that the method employed obtains good results, above the ones reported so far with the state-of-the-art approaches. We have seen that the use of affect and modifier lexica generalization has an impact on both the quantitative performance of the classification, as well as on the quality of the results, making the classifier less biased towards the class with a significantly larger number of examples. In practice, datasets are not balanced, so it is imporant that a classifier is able to assign (even incorrectly) an example to a class that is semantically similar and not to a class with totally opposite affective orientation. In this sense, as we have seen in the detailed results obtained on the $TweetEm$ dataset, it is preferable that, e.g. the examples pertaining to the emotion classes of anger and sadness are mistakenly classified as the other. However, it is not acceptable to have such a high number of examples from these classes labeled as "joy". Finally, by inspecting some of the examples in the three datasets, we noticed that a constant reason for error remains the limited power of the method to correctly spot the scope of the negations and modifiers. As such, we plan to study the manner in which skip-bigrams (bigrams made up of non-consecutive tokens) can be added and whether or not they will contribute to (at least partially) solve this issue.

6 Conclusions and Future Work

In this article, we presented a method to classify the sentiment in tweets, by taking into account their peculiarities and adapting the features employed to their structure and content. Specifically, we employed a pre-processing stage to normalize the language and generalize the vocabulary employed to express sentiment. This regarded spelling, slang, punctuation, etc., and the use of sentiment dictionaries and modifier lists to generalize the patterns of sentiment expression extracted from the training data. We have shown that the use of such generalized features significantly improves the results of the sentiment classification,when compared to the best-performing approaches that do not use affect dictionaries. Additionally, we have shown that we can obtain good results even though we employ minimal linguistic processing. The advantage of this approach is that it makes the method easily applicable to other languages. Finally, we have shown that the use of a simple heuristic, concerning filtering out features that appear only once, improves the results. As such, the method is less dependent on the dataset on which the classification model is trained and the vocabulary it contains. Finally, we employed a simple SVM SMO linear classifier to test our approach on three different data sets. Using such an approach avoids overfitting the data and, as we have shown, leads to comparable performances on different datasets. In future work, we plan to evaluate the use of higher-order n-grams (3-grams) and skip-grams to extract more complex patterns of sentiment expressions and be able to identify more precisely the scope of the negation. Additionally, we plan to evaluate the influence of deeper linguistic processing on the results, by performing stemming, lemmatizing and POS-tagging. Further on, we would like to extend our approach on generalizing the semantic classes of words and employing unique labels to group them (e.g. label mouse, cat and dog as "animal"). Finally, we would like to study the performance of our approach in the context of tweets related to specific news, in which case these short texts can be contextualized by adding further content from other information sources.

References

Saima Aman and Stan Szpakowicz. 2007. Identifying expressions of emotion in text. In *Proceedings of the 10th international conference on Text, speech and dialogue*, TSD'07, pages 196–205, Berlin, Heidelberg. Springer-Verlag.

Alexandra Balahur, Ralf Steinberger, Mijail Kabadjov, Vanni Zavarella, Erik van der Goot, Matina Halkia, Bruno Pouliquen, and Jenya Belyaeva. 2010. Sentiment analysis in the news. In Nicoletta Calzolari (Conference Chair), Khalid Choukri, Bente Maegaard, Joseph Mariani, Jan Odijk, Stelios Piperidis, Mike Rosner, and Daniel Tapias, editors, *Proceedings of the Seventh International Conference on Language Resources and Evaluation (LREC'10)*, Valletta, Malta, may. European Language Resources Association (ELRA).

S. Cerini, V. Compagnoni, A. Demontis, M. Formentelli, and G. Gandini, 2007. *Language resources and lin-*

guistic theory: Typology, second language acquisition, English linguistics., chapter Micro-WNOp: A gold standard for the evaluation of automatically compiled lexical resources for opinion mining. Franco Angeli Editore, Milano, IT.

Paul Ekman. 1992. An argument for basic emotions. *Cognition & Emotion*, 6(3-4):169–200, May.

Alec Go, Richa Bhayani, and Lei Huang. 2009. Twitter sentiment classification using distant supervision. *Processing*, pages 1–6.

Long Jiang, Mo Yu, Ming Zhou, Xiaohua Liu, and Tiejun Zhao. 2011. Target-dependent twitter sentiment classification. In *Proceedings of the 49th Annual Meeting of the Association for Computational Linguistics: Human Language Technologies - Volume 1*, HLT '11, pages 151–160, Stroudsburg, PA, USA. Association for Computational Linguistics.

Saif Mohammad. 2012. #emotional tweets. In **SEM 2012: The First Joint Conference on Lexical and Computational Semantics – Volume 1: Proceedings of the main conference and the shared task, and Volume 2: Proceedings of the Sixth International Workshop on Semantic Evaluation (SemEval 2012)*, pages 246–255, Montréal, Canada, 7-8 June. Association for Computational Linguistics.

Alexander Pak and Patrick Paroubek. 2010. Twitter as a corpus for sentiment analysis and opinion mining. In Nicoletta Calzolari (Conference Chair), Khalid Choukri, Bente Maegaard, Joseph Mariani, Jan Odijk, Stelios Piperidis, Mike Rosner, and Daniel Tapias, editors, *Proceedings of the Seventh conference on International Language Resources and Evaluation (LREC'10)*, Valletta, Malta; ELRA, may. European Language Resources Association. 19-21.

Bo Pang and Lillian Lee. 2008. Opinion mining and sentiment analysis. *Found. Trends Inf. Retr.*, 2(1-2):1–135, January.

John C. Platt. 1998. Sequential minimal optimization: A fast algorithm for training support vector machines. Technical report, Advances in Kernel Methods - Support Vector Learning.

Jonathon Read. 2005. Using emoticons to reduce dependency in machine learning techniques for sentiment classification. In *Proceedings of the ACL Student Research Workshop*, ACLstudent '05, pages 43–48, Stroudsburg, PA, USA. Association for Computational Linguistics.

Philip J. Stone, Dexter C. Dunphy, Marshall S. Smith, and Daniel M. Ogilvie. 1966. *The General Inquirer: A Computer Approach to Content Analysis.* MIT Press.

Yla R. Tausczik and James W. Pennebaker. 2010. The Psychological Meaning of Words: LIWC and Computerized Text Analysis Methods. *Journal of Language and Social Psychology*, 29(1):24–54, March.

Cynthia Whissell. 1989. The Dictionary of Affect in Language. In Robert Plutchik and Henry Kellerman, editors, *Emotion: theory, research and experience*, volume 4, The measurement of emotions. Academic Press, London.

Ley Zhang, Riddhiman Ghosh, Mohamed Dekhil, Meichun Hsu, and Bing Liu. 2011. Combining lexicon-based and learning-based methods for twitter sentiment analysis. Technical Report HPL-2011-89, HP, 21/06/2011.

Author Index